Advertising 2.0

Advertising 2.0

SOCIAL MEDIA MARKETING IN A WEB 2.0 WORLD

Tracy L. Tuten

PRAEGER

Westport, Connecticut
London

Library of Congress Cataloging-in-Publication Data

Tuten, Tracy L., 1967–
  Advertising 2.0 : social media marketing in a web 2.0 world / Tracy L. Tuten.
    p. cm.
  Includes bibliographical references and index.
  ISBN 978–0–313–35296–6 (alk. paper)
1. Internet advertising. 2. Internet marketing. 3. Branding (Marketing) 4. Online social
networks. I. Title.
HF6146.I58T88 2008
659.14′4—dc22   2008016491

British Library Cataloguing in Publication Data is available.

Library of Congress Catalog Card Number: 2008016491
ISBN: 978–0–313–35296–6

First published in 2008

Praeger Publishers, 88 Post Road West, Westport, CT 06881
An imprint of Greenwood Publishing Group, Inc.
www.praeger.com

Printed in the United States of America

The paper used in this book complies with the
Permanent Paper Standard issued by the National
Information Standards Organization (Z39.48–1984).

10 9 8 7 6 5 4 3 2

For Daddy,
who reminds me there is no place like home, and
For Uncle Dave,
who inspires me still with his passion for storytelling and teaching

Table of Contents

Acknowledgments

Social media exists in the context of communities—communities built of people who develop and nurture relationships by creating, cocreating, sharing, commenting, and engaging in content. One could say that this book grew out of just such a community inasmuch as it has benefited from the contributions of others. My community includes people playing in many roles: sponsor, believer, assistant, coach, cheerleader, and friend. I thank Jeff Olson (and the rest of the Praeger family) for believing in this project and for his encouragement and advice as it developed. I am indebted to those whose work is cited herein. There are many working to develop the field of online advertising, particularly the emerging social-media advertising platforms. I am truly honored by the praise and enthusiasm offered for the book by Bob Witeck of Witeck-Combs Communications, Kristen Cavallo of The Martin Agency, Nina Lentini of *Marketing Daily News,* and Ellen Kolsto of GSD&M's Idea City. I extend my sincere thanks to Thomas Gresham, Rebecca Ortiz, Caitlin Judd, James Brown, Scott Sherman, Tom Donohue, and Joseph Charles, all of whom assisted me in various ways from planning promotional strategies to tracking down the latest developments and introducing me to the arena of alternate reality games, to offering smiles when it was in short supply. I am especially grateful for my "social network"—my family, especially Terry and Susan Tuten, Jackie and Russell Wynne, and Joyce and David Milligan, and those close as family, Presha, Rachel, and David—for their cheerleading along the way.

I ▪ ▪ ▪

Advertising Online
Engaging Consumers with Web 2.0

The advertising landscape has changed dramatically in recent years, and nowhere is this more visible than online. When the Web was linked with Netscape, the first commercial Internet browser, its adoption as a communication channel was fast and furious (at least as adoption of new forms of media goes), and now about thirteen years later, the result is approximately 70% penetration in the United States. The penetration worldwide looks bleak in comparison at 17%, according to the statistics provided at Internet World Stats, but the figure belies intense penetration in some countries and regions with sparse reach in more developing areas.[1] Further, if one considers the Triad, the major trading areas of the globe, encompassing the European Union, Japan, and North America, the figures are quite consistent with the United States' 70% penetration level.

While the Internet's consumer reach does not yet compete with that of television (which has hovered at about 98% for decades) as a truly general population medium, its coverage well blankets all but the oldest of generational segments and reaches even the elderly in affluent markets. The advertising industry has long sought to go where consumers go. Indeed, the industry has followed consumers online, even developing new forms of advertising to relate to consumers in their virtual reality. In fact, the very philosophy of advertising has changed, not wholly but in large part, as a result of the opportunities created online. Let's look at this shift.

■ Changes in the Roles and Meaning of Advertising

Advertising is a staple of the promotional mixes used by brands to reach members of their target audiences (both for business-to-consumer products and for business-to-business products). Organizations rely upon strategically developed marketing mixes to ensure a strong value proposition for customers, meaning that the organization can offer a product the customer wants, at a price the customer perceives as reasonable, delivered at the right place and the right time. The promotional arm of the marketing mix is tasked with ensuring customers understand the brand's value proposition, recall the brand at the point-of-purchase, prefer the brand to competing brands (due to a perceived advantage, likability, image congruence, or a host of other persuasive factors), and know why they should buy the brand, where they can buy it, and what they can expect to pay. To accomplish these tasks, components of a brand's promotion mix, of which advertising may be a part, communicate brand messages to the prospects in the target audience. This is, of course, a simplistic description of marketing and the role of promotion, but it serves to set the stage for the changed environment in which advertising now operates.

Advertising is commonly defined as paid, one-way promotional communication in any mass media. The American Marketing Association defines advertising as "the placement of announcements and persuasive messages in time or space purchased in any of the mass media by business firms, nonprofit organizations, government agencies, and individuals who seek to inform and/or persuade members of a particular target market or audience about their products, services, organizations, or ideas."[2] Advertising remains a primary component of a brand's promotional mix, used to inform and/or persuade target audiences about products. However, advertising, when conceived for an online environment and given contextual differences in its capabilities, functions, and the medium's nuances, requires a new paradigm.

The first flaw in the current advertising model is tied to the "mass media" component of the definition. The traditional forms of media, those that qualify under the umbrella of mass media, include television, magazines, newspaper, outdoor, and radio. The Internet is composed of an infinite number of niche sites and a relatively small number of sites such as Google and Yahoo! with truly mass reach. Advertising online might mean one-to-one advertising through permission-based, targeted e-mail messages, or it might mean mass coverage using a display ad on a behemoth search engine like Google. When defining advertising for online media, the size of the audience should not be used as a defining factor of advertising.

Even the varying forms of advertising change in a virtual environment. While mass media focuses on print and broadcast media, online advertising includes, among others, direct response tactics like permission e-mail and interactive, on-page rich media; targeted tactics like key-word or behaviorally targeted search engine advertising; and brand-building tactics that build upon social-media marketing.

Second, the current definition of advertising states that advertising must be paid communications. Certainly, that is the model by which advertising has operated since its conception. But now some of the most valuable advertising may be unpaid, or indirectly paid as in the case of CGM (consumer-generated media), some aspects of social-network advertising, and the viral spread of brand messages.

Third, advertising has traditionally been viewed as one-way communication, delivered from the marketer using ads through some media vehicle to a receiver, the target audience. Thinking of advertising as one-way communication limits what is possible, particularly online. In a world with Web 2.0, advertising encounters the "perfect storm." Web 2.0, loosely defined as developments in technology employed online that enable interactive capabilities in an environment characterized by user control, freedom, and dialogue, brings a new degree of interactivity and consumer involvement to advertising applications. It truly enables two-way (or multi-way) communication between brands and consumers.

Online, advertising becomes more about conversations, connections, and shared control and less about passive consumption of packaged content. Advertising via traditional media relied on a model of interrupting and disrupting consumer lives. Consumers accepted these interruptions, served in the form of advertising, because they accepted that it was a necessary price to pay for what was otherwise free content broadcast on television and radio, and printed in magazines. In that world, established content publishers controlled the distribution of content targeted at consumers. The interruption-disruption model is dying in the world of Web 2.0, where consumers control their media content. In fact, they may create the content! According to Deloitte & Touche's "The State of the Media Democracy" report, 40% of Internet users create some form of content whether it be editing videos, posting photos, or writing blogs, and 51% acknowledge reading and watching the content of other users online.[3] With younger consumers, the consumption of user-generated content is even higher with 71% reporting watching and/or reading user-generated content online. User-generated content, known by several phrases, including CGM, user-created content, and conversational media, basically refers to any content produced by end users and made public (typically online). The OECD (Organization for Economic Cooperation and Development), in its report entitled "Participative Web: User-Created Content," defines user-generated content as content that (1) is made publicly available online, (2) reflects some creative effort on the part of the user, and (3) is created outside professional practice.[4] User-generated content encompasses many forms, ranging from videos, photos, blogs (personal commentary published online) and vlogs (blogs with video content), blog responses, podcasts, posts on message boards, product reviews on opinion sites, contributions to wikis, news stories, and consumer-generated advertising.

Consumers have embraced media democracy, and the industry has responded by creating and encouraging consumers to create and cocreate content. Consequently, a host of new phrases have entered the industry lexicon. Phrases like "crowdsourcing," "digital dialogue," "citizen marketing," and "brand democratization" reflect this new paradigm. Crowdsourcing, the use of the general public to accomplish professional work, cuts across the media and advertising industry with journalists relying upon video captured by witnesses to events and marketers turning to consumers to create advertising spots. All the other phrases capture the essence of shared control over the development and distribution of content. Importantly, the democratization of media (and advertising) could not have occurred without Web 2.0 as a platform.

As marketers adjust to these changes, they have recognized that it isn't sufficient to simply accept that consumers can and will create and share content online. For brands to benefit from this phenomenon, they must invite consumer participation and encourage consumers to engage with their brand. Brand engagement, accepted now as the holy grail of advertising, is defined by the Advertising Research Foundation as "turning on a prospect to a brand idea enhanced by the surrounding context."[5] Engagement occurs as a "subtle, subconscious process in which consumers begin to combine the ad's messages with their own associations, symbols, and metaphors to make the brand more personally relevant."[6] How does engagement differ from brand democratization? Engagement is the outcome of democratization. Brand democratization is the *invitation* to consumers to participate in creating and then experiencing a brand's meaning. Ultimately, though, all of these concepts share the same foundation.

One brand serves as the exemplar of the brand-engagement movement: Converse. Converse's Brand Democracy campaign (yes, they so embraced the concept of citizen marketing that the very name of the campaign reflected its intent), created by Butler, Shine, Stern, and Partners, centered around the notion that the shoe is an American icon, possessed by the public. John Butler put it succinctly, saying, "People own this brand, not Converse."[7] Seeking to position the Converse brand as original, it sought out people with original views and asked them to create films that said something about the brand in twenty-four seconds of footage. The best work was featured on television, and other selections were posted in the Converse Web gallery.

As Converse boldly illustrates, brands should develop, maintain, extend, and intensify relationships with consumers. Yes, yes, of course, the "relationship marketing concept" has been around for decades now. The difference is that then marketers wanted to tell consumers what the brand stood for and what the rules of the relationship would be. By any definition of the term *relationship,* it wasn't one. A relationship presupposes an emotional connection. It assumes communication between the involved parties. Importantly, the nature of a relationship is interdependent; its characteristics, expectations, and outcomes are jointly created by the parties involved. This interdependence and cocreation is at the heart of every buzz word used in advertising right now.

Today's online advertising landscape is a product of the power of Web 2.0 combined with a genuine desire among brand innovators to converse with consumers. Bruner, in a report entitled "The Decade in Online Advertising, 1994–2004," captured the Internet's power in the lives of consumers.[8] He writes, "Unlike those other media, the Internet is literally a hands-on experience, where consumers, with their hands on mouse and keyboards, can read, research, watch, listen, write, send, meet, organize, post, program, purchase, and much more, all through various simple devices across a vast network of millions of collaborators and destinations."

Consequently, advertising is far more expansive that it once was. The old paradigm is too limiting for what is now possible because of the technological advances and social trends of the Internet.

■ Investments in Online Advertising

Online advertising got its start in the early 1990s. As companies embraced the potential for electronic commerce, the dot-com boom occurred, soon followed by a decline, the dot-com bust. Recent years were characterized by new advances in technology, growth in Internet penetration, domestic and abroad, changes in consumer media consumption, and challenges associated with advertising via other media. These factors converged to make for a rich landscape for advertisers as evidenced by the shift in advertising expenditures across media types. Mass media still account for the bulk of ad spending. TNS Media Intelligence, a company that tracks competitive ad spending, reports that television receives 44.1% of all advertising expenditures, magazines 21.1%, newspapers 17.2%, radio 7.0%, and outdoor 2.6%.[9] The Internet accounts for 8.0% of all spending. This might seem like a small amount given the chatter about online advertising. But, it is easily explained when one considers the shift in spending across media categories over time. Internet advertising has grown each year, while allocations to other media categories have consistently declined. Indeed, online advertising achieves the highest growth rate of any media and pulls spending from television, magazines, and newspapers into the online category. For instance, total online ad spending grew by 30% in 2005 reaching $12.5 billion, and continued to increase in 2006, reaching $16.9 billion. It hit $21.4 billion in 2007 and is predicted to reach $27.5 billion in 2008 and $42 billion by 2011.[10] This trend is not likely to end any time soon. Advertisers generally follow consumer media consumption patterns in allocating ad dollars. The Internet accounts for 20% of consumer media consumption. Given the current allocation of 8% of ad spending, continued growth in online advertising is practically a certainty.[11]

eMarketer, a leading provider of online market research, claims confidence in projections of continued growth, citing several reasons for its optimism:[12]

- Even if the economy slows down, continued growth in the online audience and the need for advertising to follow that audience will drive an ongoing shift away from other media, most notably newspapers and radio;
- The opportunities for better targeting and more accurate tracking offered by online advertising relative to other media makes spending on the Internet even more appealing in a soft economy;
- As online video advertising becomes more widely used, large brand marketers who have up to now only dipped their toes online will devote increasingly greater budget shares to the Internet.

Online advertising is diverse with numerous possible formats. These include paid search ads, display ads, classifieds, rich media, referrals or lead generation, promotional e-mail with embedded ads, and sponsorships. Paid search ads, sometimes thought of as pay-per-click ads, are the juggernaut of online advertising, commanding 40% of all ad expenditures. They refer to ads delivered on Web sites in response to specific search words or phrases entered by visitors to the search site. The search terms serve as a proxy for the consumer's interests. When the consumer enters the search term, it triggers relevant text ads with links to retail Web sites, which appear alongside the organic search results on the search engine. Organic search results are the listings generated by a search—not paid advertising. There are three categories of paid search: (1) paid listings, (2) contextual search listings, and (3) paid inclusion. Paid listings refer to text links that appear near organic search results, for which the ranking of a listing is determined by the amount paid for the key word. Contextual search is based upon the concept of contextual targeting. This means that the text ads appear on the site based on the content, and not from user searches of key words. For example, a visitor to the Web site Edmunds.com might see paid search ads from Ford because of the contextual content. Paid inclusion does not directly refer to text ads but, instead, guarantees that a link is indexed by the search engine. It aids in the ranking of search listings, betting on more clicks when listings are near the top. Google is the industry leader in search, parlaying its expertise in the "long tail effect," the ability online to reach small, niche markets efficiently, into the highly effective delivery of ads to relevant consumers.

Display ads, sometimes referred to as banner ads, are boxes presented on Web sites, which contain text and graphical images. They are similar to traditional print ads, though published online, with the enhanced capability of incorporating a response device with the ability on the part of interested consumers to clickthrough to the subsequent Web site. The IAB (Interactive Advertising Bureau) dictates three categories of display ads including (1) rectangles and pop-ups, (2) banners and buttons, and (3) skyscrapers. Within each category, several standardized ad unit sizes exist. These are detailed further on the IAB Web site.[13] Primarily, the terms refer to the shape of the display ad. For example, skyscrapers are tall, thin rectangles. However, pop-ups also encompass interstitials. Interstitials are the most intrusive of online ads and, frequently, the source of irritation among Internet users. Like traditional advertising, they rely heavily on the interruption-disruption model by forcing exposure. The use of this specific type of online ad is on the decline, having become less effective due to the use of pop-up blockers. Display ads command a relatively large portion of online ad spending, at 21.5%, but some criticize them suggesting that consumers suffer from "banner blindness." Enid Burns explains that banner blindness refers to the lack of attention consumers pay to display ads online; they are instead focused on site content and do not cognitively process the display ads.[14] The most effective ads are simple ones with text that highlights why the ad is relevant to the consumer.

Classified ads make up 17.0% of online ad spending. These are brief ads with small type that are typically presented by product category. They mirror the traditional form of classifieds published in newspapers and often appear on online newspaper Web sites. Popular community sites, like Craig's List, are available as well (though they feature free classified postings).

Rich media accounts for less than 10% of online ad spending but is among the fastest-growing format. As technology and broadband capacities have expanded, advertisers have been able to launch online ads that approximate the qualities of television commercials, including audio, streaming video, and animation. They also enable audience interaction with the ad. These video ads can be delivered in a variety of ways from placement on a Web site (akin to the placement of display ads) to pre- or post-roll delivery affixed to some content.

The category of lead generation, also known as referrals, accounts for 8.3% of online ad spending. This refers to fees that advertisers pay to advertising networks that refer qualified purchasers to the advertiser. These are charged using a cost per lead model. Many online sweepstakes are designed as lead generation devices.

Sponsorship accounts for just 2.0% of online ad spending. It includes a range of devices including (1) microsites or spotlights, custom Web sites branded with a particular campaign, (2) advergames, branded video games, (3) content or section sponsorships, for which an advertiser sponsors specific content on a third-party site, and (4) branded contests. Tide successfully used the microsite tactic as part of its 2008 Super Bowl ad. The television commercial directs viewers to visit Tide's www.mytalkingstain.com, a microsite, which then demonstrates the merits of Tide's Tide To Go Instant Stain Remover. The use of sponsorships may be on an upswing with many brands seeking to direct traffic to sites related to a specific campaign. Using a microsite benefits the brand by enhancing measurability for the campaign's effectiveness while preventing the campaign from interfering with retail traffic on the brand's primary site. Mentos used its microsite, www.mentosintern.com, to inspire viral buzz about the candy. During the campaign's run, visitors to the microsite could view and interact with an intern, even submitting work assignments. Perhaps the most famous microsite, though, is Burger King's Subservient Chicken. Created by Crispin Porter + Bogusky, the subservient chicken, an actor dressed in a chicken costume, performed a range of actions based on commands, such as dance, dust the furniture, and play air guitar, submitted by visitors to the site.

E-mail marketing, once popularized by its ability to send direct mail via a cheaper channel, represents a small portion of online ad spending. Table 1.1 illustrates the relative spending in each category of online advertising based on 2008 estimates from eMarketer.[15]

A relatively new development is the use of social-media marketing. eMarketer estimates that social-media marketing will account for about 10%, or $2.9 billion, in online advertising spending. Social-media marketing is a broad category of advertising spending, including advertising using social networks, virtual worlds, user-generated product reviews, blogger endorsements, RSS feeds of content and social news sites, podcasts, games, and consumer-generated advertising. A recent study from Manning Selvage & Lee, a public relations agency, found that 16% of marketers had used social networks for advertising, 18.3% had pursued blogger endorsements, 13.6% had used consumer-generated advertising, and 49.8% had drawn on online consumer feedback and reviews. Increasingly, social-media marketing is considered a necessary component of an interactive marketing communications campaign. While search advertising might make up a large portion of media spending for an online campaign, social media is seen as a valuable complement to a host of advertising tactics.

Importantly, while some online advertising options are response driven, meaning the goal is to drive traffic to brand Web sites where consumers can get product information and purchase products, others, like social media, are desired for their ability to build brand equity. Brand equity is basically the financial value of the brand. It derives from consumer preferences for the brand and is a function of the brand's level

Table 1.1   Online Ad Spending by Category

Format	Spending (%) (2008 estimates)
Paid search	40.0
Display ads	21.5
Classifieds	17.0
Rich media	9.5
Referrals/lead generation	8.3
Sponsorships	2.0
E-mail	1.8

of awareness among the target audience and the strength, favorability, and uniqueness of the brand's image.

Growth in advertising spending over the next five years is expected in both response-driven tactics (due to their inherent accountability) and brand-building efforts. The industry will focus spending on search engine advertising, behaviorally targeted advertising, social-media marketing, video/rich media advertising, and video game advertising.[16] Search is expected to grow in part because of the following: (1) the adoption of embedded search toolbars in Web browsers; (2) the increase in local search; and (3) advances in video search. Toolbar search queries grew more than 70% in the past year and represent 16% of all search queries in the United States.[17]

■ Reasons for Growth in Online Ad Spending

Why are marketers increasing appropriations dedicated to online advertising? It is not difficult to explain the shifting of ad dollars to the Internet medium. Several factors influence growth: (1) measurement and accountability, (2) consumer reach, and (3) technology-driven engagement opportunities.

Measurement and Accountability

The ability to measure response has certainly encouraged ad spending online. The early history of online advertising offered limited metrics, like page views and clickthrough rates for banner ads. Today we continue to use those metrics but also benefit from the ability to track consumer behavior online. We can monitor the length of time a visitor spends at a site, the specific pages that he or she views, where on the screen the mouse moves, the number of times a streaming video is played, how frequently a visitor comes to a site, purchase conversion, and more. Metrics now include measures such as cost per conversion, average frequency of ad exposures, interaction rate with rich media, brand impact lift, delayed site visits, share of voice, and cross-media econometric modeling, among others. Tracking technology provides enormous databases of customer behavior online, thereby enabling testing and refinement of every aspect of an online ad.

The possibility of accounting for advertising effectiveness is clearly a factor driving growth in online advertising. It is certainly a reason for the belief that online advertising is primarily a direct-response medium (though, fortunately the paradigm shift in the industry is pushing brand building to the forefront). It is no wonder, then, that search engine advertising with its pay-for-performance model represents the largest chunk of online ad spending.

Despite the complex processes involved in SEO (search engine optimization; a key reason we feature search in this book), search engine advertising is, in principle, quite straightforward. Advertisers bid on key words. The bids ensure that the ads appear on search results pages when consumers use those key words, and the relative placement of the value of one bid versus other bids on those same key words determines the rank positions of their ads. Best of all, advertisers pay the bid amount only when someone clicks on the ad. Even without the performance component, search engine advertising is a powerful influence on purchase behavior. A study commissioned by DoubleClick showed that about 50% of people who make a purchase online conducted a search for information sometime prior to the actual purchase visit.[18]

Consumer Reach

As consumers have allocated an increasing amount of their time to online activities, advertisers have followed! This explains growth in: (1) total online ad spending, (2) specific forms of online advertising (e.g., advergaming and search), and (3) specific online vehicles (e.g., social-networking sites).

What are the characteristics of Internet users? Demographically, who can we reach with online advertising? The most recent Pew Internet & American Life Project Tracking Survey provides a demographic snapshot of Internet users.[19] The percentages in Table 1.2 reflect the percentage of the population in each group who use the Internet. Clearly, Internet penetration is strong in the most pursued target markets, including all but the most elderly age categories, middle-income and affluent consumers, and those with moderate to high levels of education. The growth in Internet penetration among minority ethnic markets will make online advertising, which targets those markets, more viable in the very near future.

What are these consumers doing online? In Table 1.3, we highlight a few of the activities identified in the Pew Internet & American Life Project's Tracking Study, emphasizing those activities that relate to developments in online advertising.

Looking at this list of Internet activities, it is easy to see how user behavior drives online advertising. Internet users spend much of their time online e-mailing, and advertisers send permission e-mails and embed display ads in some e-mail sites. Searches using search engines like Google

Table 1.2   Demographic Characteristics of Internet Users

Category	Percentage of Internet users
Total adults	70
Women	69
Men	71
Age	
18–29	83
30–49	82
50–64	70
65+	33
Race/ethnicity	
White, non-Hispanic	72
Black, non-Hispanic	58
English-speaking Hispanic	69
Household income (per year)	
Less than $30,000	49
$30,000–$49,999	75
$50,000–$74,999	90
$75,000+	93
Educational attainment	
Less than high school	36
High school	59
Some college	84
College+	91

and Yahoo! are primary activities, and search engine advertising follows that behavior. Searching classified ads online is a popular activity, and local search and local display ads reflect this trend. Web users are increasingly playing online games, downloading podcasts (digital audio and video files used to broadcast content for play on mobile devices and computers) and widgets (small applications that interact with users), and visiting social-networking sites. At the same time, the advertising industry is rich with innovative, brand engagement devices like ARGs (alternate reality games), podvertising (branded, downloadable digital audio and video content), and social-network advertising. There is an online advertising device

Table 1.3   Online Activities

Activity	Participation reported (%)
Send or read e-mail	91
Use a search engine	91
Research a product before purchase	78
Search the Web for fun	62
Watch a video clip or listen to an audio clip	56
Download games, videos, or pictures	42
Send instant messages	39
Read a blog	39
Play games online	35
Search classifieds online	30
Rate a product online	28
Create content	19
Use social-networking site*	16
Download a podcast	12

* Results of the Pew study differ from those cited in recent reports of social-networking activity, which suggest that social networking is used by 45% of Internet users.

appropriate for practically every online consumer activity. In fact, Geoff Ramsey, CEO of eMarketer, insightfully notes that the Internet is becoming the central hub of most marketing campaigns.[20]

Likewise, advertising is placed on channels and in vehicles that are populated by online consumers. Data from Hitwise identifies the popular types of Web sites visited.[21] The top ten types of Internet properties are shown in Table 1.4.

Technology-Driven Engagement Opportunities

The opportunities created by technological advances affect the way in which advertising is created, targeted, and delivered as well as the manner in which consumers interact with those opportunities. In terms of the creative realm of advertising, it is far more than art direction and copywriting in online advertising. *Brandweek* predicts that advertising agencies will employ "engagement planners" in creative and strategy departments in the very near future. Engagement planning better reflects

Table 1.4   Web Site Categories as a Percentage of All Site Visits

Web site category	Percentage of all Web site visits
Adult	11.6
E-mail	9.9
Entertainment	8.6
Search engines	7.8
Business/finance	7.8
Shopping	7.6
Social networking	6.0
News	3.5
Education	2.8
Travel	1.8

Note: Percentages do not add up to 100 because only the top ten categories are shown.

the creative and strategic development of advertising, involving multimedia ARGs, contests for and distribution of consumer-generated advertising, and the execution of brand personalities in social networking. The ability to track consumers online and merge this valuable behavioral data with vast databases on demographics and off-line behaviors makes targeting, online, a veritable gold mine. Delivery, perhaps, represents the point at which efficiency is maximized. Google's success has largely come from its ability to access many smaller sites and connect those sites to advertisers through its AdSense program and its AdWords search program. It, in fact, meets the directive issued in Chris Anderson's book, *The Long Tail,* in that it enables advertisers to systematically reach beyond the most visited sites to access consumers who are literally "in the long tail" of millions of small, niche sites.[22]

As for consumer interaction, social-media marketing embodies the very notion of democratization and engagement. The many forms of social-media advertising (e.g., consumer-generated advertising; opinion-giving through message boards, review sites, and blogs; social networking; and social news, virtual worlds, ARGs, and video games) provide the opportunities for consumers to ingest aspects of a brand's persona, assess what the brand means to them, interact with that brand or even cocreate the brand's meaning, and distribute it to other consumers online. Looking back over the last few years of major Internet developments, technological advances, trends, and new site formats set the stage for the prevalence and desirability of social-media marketing. The history illustrates the birth of Web 2.0, albeit an extended development over time, and the accompanying entry of opportunities for consumers to freely engage in and control a multitude of activities and forms of expression online. Figure 1.1 provides a visual depiction of the key developments in the history of online advertising, particularly those that gave rise to brand democratization, brand engagement, and social-media marketing. For these reasons, this book focuses on online advertising opportunities, specifically in the realm of social media.

▪ Consumer Challenges on the Road to Engagement Online

Clearly, the industry desires to go beyond the goal of simple ad exposure to a model by which brands engage consumers. And while Web 2.0 and online consumer behavior provide the necessary foundation, there are challenges to be addressed. The first challenge is the media context affecting consumers online. The second is the consumers' perceptions of online advertising.

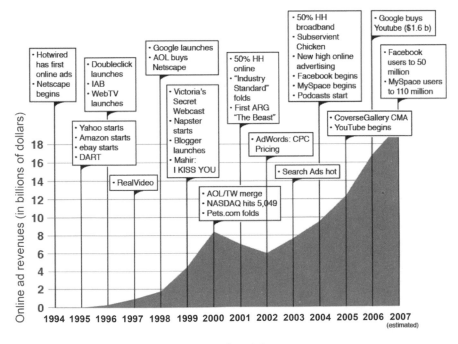

Figure 1.1   A brief history of online advertising.

Media Context

What is the context of media usage? It is one of media fragmentation (both macro and micro fragmentation), multitasking media usage, and media usage beleaguered with clutter. Media fragmentation is the breaking up of large audiences into smaller audience fragments due to the increase of media choices available. Every medium has experienced fragmentation within its own field, with hundreds of television channels, satellite radio, and magazines available for every interest group imaginable. Richard Fielding and Judy Bahary provide a comparison of the change in the media landscape, which perfectly highlights the challenge of media fragmentation (see Table 1.5).[23] Online media buying must successfully reaggregate fragmented audiences to provide advertisers with the ability to precisely target ads to hypersegmented audiences without sacrificing large reach. This is the essence of the "long tail effect," and it is increasingly achievable with the use of search engine advertising and media placement via advertising networks.

In addition to media fragmentation, multitasking media usage also affects the environment of online advertising. BIGresearch's Simultaneous Media Usage Study found that 70.7% of Internet users report consuming other forms of media while they are online.[24] This was similar to the figure for television; 67.9% watch television while using other media. What other media are consumed when users are online? The study found that 37.7% also watch television, 21.0% listen to the radio, and the remaining multitaskers are reading magazines or newspapers.[25]

Table 1.5   Consumer Media Options, Pre-Web and Now

Media option	1980s	Mid-2000s
Number of commercial TV stations	700	1,345
Average number of TV sets per home	1.8	2.6
Average number of channels available per TV household	11	103
Network prime-time market share (%)	75	36
Cable penetration (%)	40	92
VCR penetration (%)	1	87
Number of radio stations	8,748	13,838
Home computer penetration (%)	5	66
Number of consumer magazines	1,500	5,340
Number of place-based media options	–	Infinite

Advertising clutter exists in all forms of media, but perceptions of ad clutter online are second only to television clutter. Mindshare Online Research found that 62.6% of consumers felt the Internet was too cluttered with advertising.[26] Television had the highest perceived clutter with 81.0% stating it was too cluttered. What does the cluttered landscape mean for online advertisers? With the growth in online ad spending, it is not likely that sites will decrease advertising inventory. At the same time, advertisers can influence perceptions of value and relevance, which should act to decrease perceptions of clutter.

Consumer Perceptions of Online Advertising

Research suggests that advertising online is viewed positively by a lower percentage of consumers than any other advertising medium. The Magazine Publishers of America, in its report entitled "Engagement: Understanding Consumers' Relationships with Media," notes that only 30% indicated a positive attitude to Internet advertising, while 52% felt positively about television advertising and 61% reported a positive attitude toward magazine advertising. Only 21% felt that advertising aids their enjoyment of the Internet, while 32% said advertising on television is enjoyable and 48% said advertising in magazines provided enjoyment. Why might online users feel this way? The same report explained the following: (1) 49.2% of Internet users felt that ads appear at inconvenient moments, and (2) 47.4% felt that the same ads are repeated too often.[27] Other common reasons offered included a lack of credibility in the ads and similarity of advertising. What's important in this research is that consumer perceptions of online advertising primarily reflect Web 1.0 advertising, which emphasized display ads with heavy rotations on the same heavily trafficked sites. In the Web 2.0 world, we have the opportunity to develop advertising that is engaging, entertaining, informative, fun, credible, different—advertising that consumers invite into their lives.

■ What Online Advertising Can Accomplish for Marketers

Advertising online can accomplish all of the objectives commonly tasked to advertising in any media. Brand-building objectives like increasing brand equity, developing brand awareness, improving attitudes toward a brand, increasing brand likability, differentiating the brand from competitors, minimizing brand self-image incongruence and sales-related objectives like generating trial, improving repeat buying rates, providing pre-purchase information, building customer databases, driving retail site (on- and off-line) traffic, and providing a path to an online sales function can all be accomplished through online advertising. It further works to expand a brand's reach in some demographic markets (like the youth market) and reduce overall advertising costs by optimizing the efficiency of the brand's media plan. That is what online advertising does for brands.

What can it do for consumers? Rick Bruner, director of DoubleClick's research division, identifies a list of advertising functions that benefit consumers.[28] He dreams of a world of invertising (which he defines as using advertising in such a way that consumers invite advertising into their lives); invertising would:

- Help people make purchase decisions when they are seeking advice;
- Provide regular product and category information when requested by consumers;
- Underwrite the cost of premium content for consumers;
- Offer advertising that does not just passively await but encourages user engagement by being something consumers seek out; and
- Delight consumers with content that is entertaining, funny, inspiring, intriguing, challenging, and beguiling.

■ Getting Started

The remaining chapters of the book will take you on a journey through the social-centric realm of social-media marketing. Beginning with a deeper look at the phenomenon of social media, we'll cover social-network advertising, branding in virtual worlds, branding with ARGs, game advertising, user-generated product reviews, social news marketing, and consumer-generated advertising. In addition, because the Internet is ripe with opportunities to study consumer behavior, and nowhere is this truer than within social communities, conducting online research is featured. Lastly, no book on advertising would be complete without a discussion of the measurement of advertising effectiveness.

2 ▪ ▪ ▪

Socialcentricity and the Emergence of Social-Media Marketing

Arguably the most-talked-about trend in the realm of online advertising and branding in recent months is the growth and popularity of social communities and the potential to leverage these communities with social-media marketing techniques. The term "social community" encompasses a broad range of online venues, including forums, online social networks, brand-sponsored virtual worlds, open virtual worlds, social video and photo communities, and social news and bookmarking Web sites. Social-media marketing is a form of online advertising that uses the cultural context of social communities, including social networks (e.g., YouTube, MySpace, and Facebook), virtual worlds (e.g., Second Life, There, and Kaneva), social news sites (e.g., Digg and del.icio.us), and social opinion-sharing sites (e.g., Epinions), to meet branding and communication objectives.

Why use social-media marketing? Social-media marketing offers these primary benefits: It can encourage interaction between consumers and brands. It can enhance perceptions of the "brand as person," thereby strengthening a brand's personality, differentiating a brand from its competitors, and setting the stage for a perceived relationship. It can extend the exposure time for a brand's message by encouraging sticky interactions that last far beyond a thirty-second spot and repeat visits to the brand's site. It enhances opportunities for word-of-mouse communication to other friends and influentials about the brand. Assuming the brand's persona is likable and credible, it can facilitate message internalization (the process by which a consumer adopts a brand belief as his or her own) and strengthen the brand's equity. When well designed, a response device can be embedded in the conversation, enabling conversion from message exposure to purchase. Sound promising? It is. Not only does social-media marketing offer many notable benefits, but it does so at price tags far less than a single spot televised on the Super Bowl, and sometimes even less than a spot on a hit television program like *Lost*. Later in this chapter, we'll highlight the objectives appropriate for social-media marketing. For now, though, let's explore the context a bit. What is social media?

■ Social Media

Social media refers to online communities that are participatory, conversational, and fluid. These communities enable members to produce, publish, control, critique, rank, and interact with online content. The term can encompass any online community that promotes the individual while also emphasizing an individual's relationship to the community, the rights of all members to collaborate and be heard within a protective space, which welcomes the opinions and contributions of participants. As noted above, the phrase social media is an umbrella phrase for social-networking sites, virtual worlds, social news and bookmarking sites, wikis, and forums and opinion sites.

To some extent, all of these community formats are social networks because all feature the interaction and maintenance of relationships by a collection of participants. However, we will loosely categorize these social-community venues as either virtual worlds (recognizing that virtual worlds do encompass a social network) or social networks.

Social communities (virtual worlds and networks) have evolved, at least in part, to provide "contact comfort" in a society in which many of us spend increasing amounts of time with machines. Contact comfort captures the motive for developing and maintaining relationships online, particularly using social communities as well as with other communication technologies like instant messaging and text messaging. Through social communities, our need for contact comfort (think of this as a need for affiliation) can be addressed, while we also satisfy our need for entertainment (such as gaming and shopping) and resource acquisition (sharing of information). These social communities have commonalities and distinctions among them, but they all offer opportunities for brand promotion and engagement for those brands that learn to leverage the unique attributes of the community type in question. We'll begin with an overview of social communities. After discussing their commonalities and sources of differentiation, we'll set the stage for assessing and planning for the branding opportunities possible with social communities.

▪ Attributes and Distinctions of Social Communities

What do these types of social communities have in common? The key attribute is the social element itself. Every community category identified above is based upon the participation and interaction of the members. Social communities are social! They thrive when the members participate, discuss, share, and interact with others as well as recruit new members to the community. The more active the participation by a critical mass of members, the more healthy the community (note, though, that every community will include lurkers, people who explore the site passively). Each category (e.g., social video community) and specific vehicles (e.g., YouTube) focus on a theme. Examples include sharing, promoting, and commenting on video clips (e.g., YouTube), discussing political issues and candidates (e.g., Decision Virginia), critiquing entertainment programming and celebrities (e.g., Hey! Nielsen), and saving, categorizing, and sharing bookmarks (e.g., del.icio.us). Even within a category such as virtual worlds, content is thematic. For instance, Second Life offers the opportunity for fantasy role playing, while World of Warcraft, a massively multiplayer online role-playing game (known by the acronym MMORPG), emphasizes gaming. While the mission of each community expresses its theme, content is in large measure created by the members themselves. Thus, we can say that much of the content is consumer generated.

Social communities are predicated on the creation, cocreation, and sharing of user-generated content by participants, but community members do vary in how they participate. Forrester Research's Social Technographics report by Charlene Li categorizes participants into one of six groups according to the nature of activities in which they are involved.[1] The categories of social participation encompass activities ranging from the generation of original content to simply consuming content and go by the names (1) creators, (2) critics, (3) collectors, (4) joiners, (5) spectators, and (6) inactives. According to the report, creators (13% of users) are active developers of content, who may publish Web sites, maintain a blog, upload videos to sites like YouTube, and participate in consumer-generated advertising contests. Critics (19% of users) are those who comment on blogs and respond to video posts and contribute to product ratings and other reviews. Collectors (15% of users) consume user-generated content actively by using RSS feeds and tagging sites. They may rely on communities like del.icio.us and Digg to organize, search, and retrieve content. Joiners (19% of users) are participants in one or more social networks. Spectators (33% of users) consume media on a more passive level, simply reading blogs, watching user-generated videos, and listening to podcasts. Inactives (52%) are those Internet users who are not involved in social media.

The spread of content in the community is achieved via networks, enabling information to spread virally. Some of these social-centric communities, though, rely upon established networks of friends and colleagues (e.g., MySpace, Facebook, and LinkedIn), while others provide for communication networks to develop without the need to establish formalized links or nodes connecting members. All forms offer some degree of self-expression through the use of profiles, including pictures, preferences, and comments. In summary, social communities, whether virtual worlds, social networks, game communities, or news sites, are participatory, interconnected, thematic, functional, symbolic of self, and experiential, featuring member-generated content.

What of the distinctions between virtual worlds and social networks? There are several distinctions, some of which will likely grow increasingly fuzzy as social networks adopt advances of online technology. The differentiating characteristics of virtual worlds and social networks include the spatial dimensions (two-dimensional [2D] or three-dimensional [3D]) of the site, the degree of immersion possible, one's representation and control of identity in the space, the sense of "presence" with others in the same time and place, and complexity. In addition, it is useful to consider the community's primary mission (entertainment, skill- or career-building programs, information management, communication contact) and the type of sponsor or source of funding for the community.

Virtual worlds are 3D spaces and encourage visitors to immerse themselves in the virtual environment. During the session, the quality of the interface, the colors, sounds, and visual textures enhance the sense of being *in* the space. Participants can move and communicate via visual representations of their identity (which may be an extension of self, an idealized self, or a fantasy self) called avatars. These avatars can take on many forms, including variations of human or animal form and even representations of nonliving items (like a spoon or chair). Because of the semblance of a physical presence and the capabilities associated with that presence, participants can take part in virtual activities mimicking those possible in a real environment. For instance, virtual worlds have been used to offer skill-building simulations such as doctor-patient interactions or entertainment activities such as gaming, dancing, or attending a concert. The sense of community and pull to immerse one's self in the virtual world is tied to the ability to interact with others in the same place, at the same time. Virtual worlds provide for synchronous communication enhanced with the context of place. Virtual worlds can be complex environments with a steep learning curve for those who wish to participate. The level of complexity varies from community to community with some known for their relative ease of use (e.g., There).

Virtual worlds may also be classified as open or closed. Open worlds are managed and hosted by an organization that offers opportunities for brands to engage in the community. There and Second Life are two prominent examples of open virtual worlds. Closed worlds, in contrast, are branded by a specific commercial entity, which can then control the exclusivity and types of branding found in world. The Coca-Cola Company was one of the early entrants in the virtual-worlds arena, offering MyCoke.com, a branded virtual world, years ago. MyCoke.com still exists (and reportedly boasts about the same number of registered users as Second Life)[2] but has since developed a partnership for a virtual space within There. This space is known as CC Metro. Wells Fargo, an early corporate entrant in Second Life, now hosts its own branded virtual world, known as Stagecoach Island. Perhaps, one of the most successful closed worlds is MTV's Virtual Laguna Beach, which has truly captured the essence of brand engagement in a virtual environment. We'll be taking a close look at these virtual worlds and what their experiences can teach us in later chapters.

Webkinz, Club Penguin, and Barbie iDesign are examples of closed, branded spaces that target children. Importantly, these closed worlds, offered, promoted, and managed by major corporations targeting children, vary from open worlds like Second Life and closed worlds like Stagecoach Island on another point—membership rights are gained through the purchase of a hard good rather than simple registration or fees.

In contrast, social networks are primarily 2D spaces with no sense of physical movement of self in the space. One is unlikely to feel immersed in a social-network site. One's senses are not sufficiently stimulated through context in the environment using color, movement, sound, or simulated touch to promote immersion. The feeling of sharing space in place and time with others can be enhanced with the use of "online now" notifiers for those in one's network, but without the virtual impression of tangibility this experience is largely missing from social-networking communities.

Despite this, social networks have grown in popularity due to their ability to provide a platform for information sharing, communication, and relationship development and maintenance. For example, YouTube provides for sharing and promotion of videos and related opinions; Flickr enables photo sharing and reviewing; MySpace and Facebook support relationship building and maintenance; Facebook, in particular, serves to provide "contact comfort" for its users; LinkedIn provides a form of self-promotion and career networking; Dogster offers tips and information on caring for one's canine companion with the added benefit of being able to talk with others who are just as crazy about their dogs. These examples reflect the two types of social networks: (1) egocentric and (2) object-centric. An egocentric social network places the individual at the core of the network experience, while the object-centric network places a non-ego element at the center of the network. Orkut, Facebook, and LinkedIn are egocentric examples, while examples of object-centric networks include Flickr (object: photograph) and Digg (object: news item).

Social networks feature a relatively flat learning curve. Though there are advanced features for most sites, it is fairly simple to join and interact in the site. Consequently, the rate of adoption for social networking has been faster than that for participating in virtual worlds.

Identity construction is also substantially different for social networks than for virtual worlds. For both, identities can be based on the real, the enhanced or idealized self, or a fantasy version of one's self. But the construction of identity is based on vastly different components. In virtual worlds, one's self is depicted visually in the form of the avatar. The avatar is highly customizable and uses the inferences associated with visual clues to relay identity details. For instance, my avatar looks a lot like me (albeit with a more fashionable hair style and better selection of shoes). She mostly wears a business suit. Other avatars who interact with my avatar will know from the visual cues that I have chosen to present a professional persona "in world." They know the ethnicity and gender I have chosen to display. They can see whether I have chosen to stick with traditional social norms about dress and image management or decided to push the boundaries (or explode the boundaries) for what would be considered acceptable in the real world. Further, they can see how I behave in world and use my behavior as a source of information about who I am. (Am I attending a meeting at GSD&M's Idea City virtual office, dancing at a jazz club, touring the Metropolitan Museum of Art, or playing in a sandbox?)

But in a social network, one's identity cues are built using a profile. A primary identity building block in one's social-network profile is the picture one uses as their default representation on the site. This is the image that others in the network will see as they explore and communicate with members. Profiles might contain other pictures. They often contain demographic information like marital status, age, gender, political affiliations, educational levels achieved, and geographic locale. Psychographic information, including attitudes, interests, and opinions on a variety of topics from favorite hobbies to movies, books, and musical artists, is frequently revealed in social-network profiles. Increasingly, profiles include behavioral information like recent online shopping activities, communications with others in the network, and most anything a user chooses to share. Importantly, identity in social networks is in part constructed as a collaborative process. One's identity includes one's networked friends, comments from friends (like those posted on The Wall on Facebook), one's comments to others, and the groups and affiliations noted on the profile. Social-network identity is just that—it is one's identity in the context of the network itself. While virtual worlds may be supported by sales of goods and services, fees for virtual land and property rentals, sales of tangible goods, and advertising revenue, ad revenue is the primary source of financial support for social networks.

■ Social-Community Campaigns: Promotional Possibilities

Social-media marketing is rich with potential branding opportunities. Social media is touted for its engagement potential, but brands with many objectives can find social-media marketing appropriate. What objectives can be met with social-media marketing? Consider this list:

- Build brand awareness
- Maximize cross- and within-media integration
- Research consumer behavior
- Develop ideas for new marketing strategies
- Drive traffic to corporate Web sites
- Increase site stickiness, extending the brand message's exposure time

- Garner publicity from news coverage of social-media tactics
- Improve search engine rankings (due to organic links)
- Build awareness of the brand
- Enhance the brand's reputation and image
- Encourage message internalization
- Increase product sales
- Accomplish marketing goals with efficiency
- Engage consumers in a brand experience

Indeed, social-media marketing can serve as a tool for building brand awareness, researching consumer opinions and crowdsourcing, identifying opinion leaders (known in social media as influentials), driving traffic to brand Web sites, spreading specific messages virally, developing customer databases, instilling credibility and trust in a brand, and enhancing a brand's image, among others. Crowdsourcing is a great example of the unique benefits that can accrue to brands that think creatively about the social-media landscape. Crowdsourcing refers to mining a group of customers for product development ideas. For example, IBM invited 300,000 people to participate in a product development brainstorming session in Second Life. Starwood Hotels developed a hotel prototype (called Aloft) in Second Life and garnered feedback, reactions, and ideas from avatar guests.

But it is its potential for brand engagement that makes it a core topic here. Joe Plummer, the Advertising Research Foundation's Chief Research Officer, offered this definition of engagement: "Engagement is turning on a prospect to a brand idea enhanced by the surrounding context."[3] Given the context of community, Plummer's view of engagement serves to define a critical characteristic of social-media marketing. Certainly, social-media marketing has developed at least in part because of an industry recognition of the value of customer-brand engagement. If we seek to engage consumers with our brand, what is it really that we are trying to accomplish? Engagement tactics (whether launched using social media or any other media) should provide action-oriented experiences that enable consumers to interact with the brand. Engagement tactics should be aligned with the brand's promise. Above all, engagement seeks to develop and maintain brand-consumer relationships. When is engagement a success? When consumers perceive a meaningful, memorable, favorable, and ongoing relationship with the brand in question. Social media is an ideal brand engagement platform because its heart is made of relationships.

The menu of social-media marketing tactics includes traditional display and broadcast advertising (e.g., bill boards in a virtual world and video clip of an advertisement posted on a social network) offered within the online environment, sponsored groups (e.g., the Virtual Thirst MySpace group), sponsored events (e.g., U2's Second Life concert), branded spaces (e.g., the CC Metro space in There), and identity building (through the brand's identity profile, persona, and visual and aural cues). Importantly, multilayer brand experiences are a critical success factor.

Should your brand plan a social-media campaign? Answers to these questions can help guide your decision:

- Does the culture of social media fit your brand's positioning or fit with how your brand wishes to be perceived?
- Do you know where online your customers and prospects are? There are many social-media communities. Certainly, there is duplication in the membership from one to the next, but a brand must be able to locate its target audience in the social-media landscape.
- Are the relevant communities open and welcoming to brand participation? What opportunities exist within each community for brand promotion?
- Do you have the resources of time and money to commit to the campaign?
- Do you have a hook, a conversation starter, a point of engagement—something that will inspire interaction with your brand?
- Are you willing to take risks?

Did you answer yes to these questions? Excellent! In the next section, we'll review the steps in planning a campaign before ending this chapter with a list of social-media best practices.

▪ Campaign Planning: The Process

The list below contains the ten steps in the social-media marketing campaign planning process:

Step 1: Identify the overarching objective for the campaign and establish whether social media is appropriate for this purpose;

Step 2: Conduct a situation analysis, which highlights the brand's strengths, weaknesses, opportunities, and threats in the social-media environment and beyond;

Step 3: Specify the target audience and the characteristics of the audience;

Step 4: Elaborate on the individual goals the brand wishes to achieve over the course of the campaign, taking care to state these goals such that they are specific, measurable, realistic, and time-lined;

Step 5: Allocate a budget for the campaign, ensuring that sufficient resources are allocated to accomplish the goals set out in step 4;

Step 6: Choose a social-media marketing strategy, including the mix of social media to be used and the plot or story line that will be the basis for content;

Step 7: Specify tactics, including the specific social-media vehicles within each channel (e.g., if social networking is selected, which sites will be featured), the brand's positioning for each site, and the tie-ins throughout the campaign;

Step 8: Identify methods for activating the social-media campaign via other media (i.e., how can the brand's presence in a community be promoted outside that community?);

Step 9: Execute the campaign strategy and tactics, according to the social-media plan taking care to make adjustments based on community responsiveness and momentum; and

Step 10: Measure and evaluate the campaign's effectiveness to enable ongoing campaign revisions and insight for future social-media campaigns.

▦ Lessons in Social-Media Marketing

Ready to enter the social-media space? Take the time to learn from those who have gone before. The following seven lessons are success factors in social-media marketing: (1) set appropriate objectives, (2) embrace engagement, (3) make it relevant, (4) staff it, (5) integrate multiple social-media outlets, (6) build on the socialcentricity inherent in the communities, and (7) invest the time.

Set Appropriate Objectives

If the brand can benefit from social-media marketing, the next step in the process is to set objectives for the campaign. Setting objectives is a critical step in any communications and marketing planning process, but the objectives set must be appropriate for the arena. In traditional advertising circles, reach and frequency goals represent the bedrock of media objectives. Social media are not easily measured in terms of reach and frequency. There are no standardized definitions for gross rating points in the world of social media. Even when exposure occurs and can be counted, reach figures are typically low, compared to broadcast.[4]

Joseph Jaffe, a marketing consultant who advises clients on virtual opportunities, had this to say about objectives for social-media marketing, "This is not about reach anymore. This is about connecting. It's about establishing meaningful, impactful conversations."[5] His belief is reiterated in a comment made by Mike Donnelly, the Director of Global Interactive Marketing for Coke. Donnelly emphasized that the objective for Coke's Virtual Thirst social-media marketing campaign was not to sell more cans of Coke. Donnelly's goal was to "create a great brand experience."[6]

Of course, objectives will vary depending upon the brand and the brand's situation. Some brands may wish to improve brand awareness, others may wish to instill likability, and yet another may seek to find new direct-response devices. For Coke, awareness is not an appropriate goal. Reminder advertising is accomplished with Coke's broadcast and print media buy. For Coke, the objective for its social-media campaign was to provide an opportunity for customers to have a shared experience with the brand. Secondary objectives probably included the desire to experiment with social media and garner first-mover advantages in the social-media market.

Embrace Engagement

MTV's Virtual Laguna Beach is a star example of designing opportunities for customers to engage and interact with a brand. In fact, VLB won an Emmy from the National Academy of Television Arts & Sciences for Outstanding Achievement in Advanced Media Technology for Creation of Nontraditional Programs or Platforms due to its success in shifting fans of its programming from passive viewers to active participants in the virtual world.[7] What did MTV do with its Virtual Laguna Beach? Working with Makena Technologies (the noted developer for the virtual worlds There and Kaneva.com), MTV Networks created several 3D experiences, including Virtual Hills, Virtual Pimp My Ride, Virtual Real World, Virtual Newport Harbor, and Virtual Skatepark. Participants can shop, club-hop, attend events, visit with cast members and more, all virtually. Many of the activities offered in world mirror those of the story characters, enabling fans to live the dream.

Make It Relevant

Social-media marketing is not passive. It relies on the social elements of the communities in which it resides. It thrives when the community decides it should thrive. That means figuring out what the community wants; what will resonate with the community is the key. This principle is based on the same rule of thumb as for event sponsorship marketing. Charmin's placement of luxurious, clean, portable toilets at major concert and sporting events is a brilliant example of making a brand relevant to a social community (even a temporary community like that of sporting event attendees). Charmin recognized that event attendees enjoyed many aspects of the event but were universally frustrated by a shortage of bathroom facilities as well as the less-than-desirable conditions of those facilities. The brand received a negative and addressed it by making itself relevant to the audience in a memorable and meaningful way. Can a brand create memorable and meaningful relevance in a virtual world or on a social network? Absolutely—if the brand understands the culture of the community and the needs and wants of the audience, and thinks beyond brand placement within the social-media platform.

Consider Dell Computers' entry into Second Life. It built a facility (a typical step for brands entering a virtual world) but it also designed experiences in the facility with relevance to customers and prospects. Visitors to Dell's Second Life facility can tour the factory (interesting and educational given its reflection of real computing manufacturing facilities), explore the insides of a computer with a tutorial on computer functions, and order virtual computers as well as real-life computers (this is another best practice—link the social-media strategy to a direct-response device). All of these aspects promote a sense of relevance and make the Dell site more than a simple but flashy build in world. But Dell also added a benefit of relevance to Second Lifers. Second Life is notoriously challenging for newbies (those with little time spent and minimal expertise operating in world). To address this issue, Dell created its own orientation facility to offer lessons on using and advancing in Second Life. Avatars might not need computers, but many do want Second Life tutoring. Dell made its brand relevant by meeting this need.

Staff It

The initial imperative when it comes to social-media marketing is to simply get there—to have a presence in the community of interest. Focusing on presence can result in brand assets that are underutilized and underperforming in terms of the objectives set for the campaign. Companies focus on profiles and advertisements in social networks and "builds," like the Sun Pavilion in Second Life, in virtual worlds. These companies take an "if you build it, they will come" *Field of Dreams* approach, without addressing ways to build and maintain traffic and interest. Joel Greenberg of the Electric Sheep Company, an agency specializing in developing Second Life corporate presences, wrote in his blog, "Any web developer will tell you it's easier to get funding for a website than it is for moderator, hosts, or other human beings to keep a web community vibrant."[8]

A superior presence may attract an initial visit from consumers who stumble upon the profile, in-world build, or a Web site, or who have heard about the brand's work from some other source, but this is not sufficient to drive and sustain traffic. Consumers need a reason to stay once there and a reason to return. Developing interactivity, emphasizing relevance, monitoring the asset for needed maintenance, responding to visitor feedback, and providing new content will keep the asset fresh and inspire a curiosity to return among the core audience. Importantly, these components of successful social-media marketing require an ongoing commitment of human resources.

Don't Limit Your Campaign to One Social-Media Outlet

Embrace the lessons learned from integrated marketing communications and rely upon multiple social-media channels. For example, Coke's Virtual Thirst campaign was not based solely on its Virtual Thirst site in Second Life. It also utilized a MySpace profile (www.myspace.com/virtualthirst), a Flickr page, a video clip on YouTube, tags in del.icio.us, and information on Coke's own MyCoke.com site.[9] A front-page ranking on Digg can be as valuable for a driving traffic to a brand's content as an endorsement from Oprah is for generating book sales of a new release.

Remember the Socialcentricity Inherent to Social-Media Outlets

No matter the range of social-media outlets, whether social news and bookmarking sites, virtual worlds, social networks, or blogs and wikis, the community exists for the sake of community—not for the sake of branding. Did Webkinz or Neopets—virtual worlds with clear brand sponsorships—come to mind when reading that last statement? Regardless of the financial backer of a site, consumers are not joining the community because of their relationship with the brand. They join the community to be a part of something. They join to make friends, share stories, have fun, and to take part in the relational activities that make life interesting and enjoyable. They join for social support. They join to get to know others and to let others know them. For a brand to succeed in a social community, the brand must also be part of the community.

Guidelines from experts in all areas of social-media marketing emphasize the need to build relationships in order to use this approach. Even something as simple as requesting influential members on Digg to submit a content piece from the brand's Web site can be perceived as negative and overbearing if there is not a previous relationship in place. Forum posts that feature brand feedback are analyzed by fellow posters for the "member since" date to determine whether the information is credible and offered by a real member of the community or a trespasser with commercial objectives. In Second Life, big brands have been "griefed," a term that refers to resident vandal attacks, when launching in-world campaigns that are perceived by residents as disrespectful or irreverent to the Second Life community. For instance, a Nissan's build was attacked by helicopters protesting the rise of big business in world. The brand must want relationships, want to socialize with communities of consumers, and, perhaps most importantly, be willing to play by the rules set within the community.

Invest the Necessary Time

Social media works in a manner different from traditional advertising. While a television campaign can utilize a heavy buy early in its media plan to incite near-immediate awareness and build momentum, social media is just the opposite. Paul Gillin notes that it can take months for a social-media campaign to build awareness.[10] However, if designed for engagement, the campaign can continue to run indefinitely, with minor investments required to maintain it. Consequently, while the results may take longer to see, the overall effectiveness and efficiency of the social-media model can be well worth the patience and resources required.

These seven guidelines apply to the four targets for social-media marketing featured here: social networking, virtual worlds, and social news and bookmarking, and opinion-sharing communities. In the following chapters, we'll take a closer look at each of these social-media branding opportunities.

3 ▪ ▪ ▪

Friendvertising
Advertising and Brand Building with Social Networks

Social media encompass communication possible throughout all of the forms of social communities online. Social-media communities include forums, virtual worlds, social news organizations, social opinion-sharing sites, and social networks. Social networks are built around site platforms that enable members to develop identity profiles, interact with other members, and participate in various site activities. Social networks are 2D environments with identity representation limited to one's profile rather than by visually detailed avatars common to virtual worlds. Although interactions with others can seemingly approximate synchronous real-time communication, the messaging structure is static rather than dynamic. Networks can be thought of as utility-based tools. They are an elegant but fun way to organize content, socialize, and promote one's self-identity.

Despite this, social networks have grown in popularity from their ability to provide a platform for information sharing, communication, and relationship development and maintenance. In a world where individuals may have reduced physical contact and heightened time spent interacting with electronic devices, social networks have evolved to provide an online platform for personal, intimate, informal neighborhood and office chatter. They offer a sense of "contact comfort" in a society where many of us spend less time with actual people than we do with machines. Contact comfort helps to meet individual needs for affiliation and socialization. Social networks meet our need for contact comfort while also providing entertainment and information sharing.

Social networks are above all else communication hubs. While they all offer the core product of networking capabilities, networks do find ways to differentiate themselves. MySpace and Facebook support relationship building and maintenance. YouTube offers a venue for sharing and promoting videos and related opinions. Flickr enables photo sharing and reviewing. LinkedIn provides a form of self-promotion and career networking. There are niche sites as well focused on any number of hobbies and personal interests. Catster, for example, offers tips and information on caring for one's feline companion with the added benefit of being able to talk with others who define themselves in part by the pets they love. Several social networks will be described in this chapter.

Social networks, like other online communities, are participatory, conversational, and fluid. Members produce, publish, control, critique, rank, and interact with online content. On Facebook, for instance, the second most popular social network, members can build a profile that includes information about their education, habits, favorite movies and books, and other personality indicators. They can send and receive messages to members, "friend" people, and join groups and networks. Profiles can be complemented with pictures, news feeds on member activities (e.g., Tracy just went shopping), and a variety of widgets. Widgets are small applications made up of code embedded on a Web site. Facebook widgets enable members to virtually hug, wink, smile, and engage in a host of other behaviors. Most sites offer similar features, with messaging, profiling, and friending being the core functions of any network site. The interaction with others enhances the need to return to the site and continue the process of generating new content. The result is an online community of friends who may spend hours in the network each day.

Mashable, a social-networking news Web site, claims more than 350 social-networking sites exist. It wasn't terribly long ago that social networking was thought of primarily as a teenage pastime with general Internet population statistics suggesting only about 15% of Internet users visited social-networking sites.[1] Since those early days of online communities, social networking has taken off as a cultural phenomenon among youth with 70% of teens reporting use of online networking sites.[2] These days adults, too, are social-networking online. Social-networking sites are among the fastest growing and most commonly visited sites online. According to Nielsen/NetRatings, the top ten most-visited social-networking sites reach 45% of active Internet users.[3] Despite the diversity of sites targeting Internet users based on a host of hobbies, interests, and demographic characteristics, two sites, MySpace and Facebook, reach more than any of the others. It is reported by comScore that MySpace reached more than 40% and Facebook near 20% of Internet users in the United States. The raw figures amount to hundreds of millions of unique visitors at these sites.[4]

There is no doubt that much of this growth can be attributed to the attractive features social networks offer members. At the same time, the flat learning curve for new adopters surely plays a role. Most networking sites have advanced options for members, but the basics of joining, completing a profile, and sending and receiving messages are simple enough to be mastered in moments. The ease of use has resulted in a steep rate of adoption for social-networking sites.

Given the audience size and the length of exposure time consumers spend in the network, it is no wonder that advertisers have embraced social networks for social-media marketing more than any other community environment. eMarketer estimates that marketers spent $920 million on social-network advertising in 2007, including online display advertising, in-network community sites, and brand profile pages.[5] What's more, the research firm predicts spending on social-network advertising to reach nearly $3 billion in less than five years. This figure may sound more impressive than it actually is given that social-network advertising is still under 5% of the total expenditures on online advertising. Additionally, the vast majority of spending is directed at the two juggernauts of social networks, MySpace and Facebook. More than 70% of ad expenditures directed to social networks in the United States is placed in these two networks. Though social networks are strong in international markets, social-network advertising is for now a phenomenon focused on consumers in the United States; U.S. spending accounts for 75% of all advertising in this venue.

■ Social-Networking Sites and Categories

Social-networking sites can be classified into four primary categories. General social-networking sites, like MySpace, have social networking among friends as the primary focus. There are also several social-network sites that are affiliated with major portals (like Yahoo! 360). Because of their portal affiliation, they are typically separated from

Table 3.1   Examples of Social-Networking Sites by Category

General	Portal affiliation	Vertical
MySpace	MSN Spaces	Dogster
Facebook	Yahoo! 360	Gather
Friendster	Orkut	Xanga

general sites for classification purposes. Lastly, there are vertical social networks. Vertical social networks differentiate themselves by emphasizing some common hobby, interest, or characteristic that draws members to the site. These vertical networks do not attract the same traffic typical of general sites, but one might argue that the members are more involved because of the common interest that initially brought them to the site. Within this realm of vertical networks, sites exist for pet lovers (e.g., Catster), photography (e.g., Flickr), soccer fans (e.g., Joga), gays and lesbians (e.g., Glee), and more. Examples of each type of social-networking site are provided in Table 3.1.

Some social-networking sites are generating advertising revenue on a larger scale than others; eMarketer predicts that MySpace will capture a full 60% of the market for ad spending. Other major players for advertisers include smaller general sites like Facebook, Bebo, and Piczo, which are expected to earn about 23% of ad spending in the social-networking realm. Portal-affiliated sites will garner about 11% of ad spending and vertical sites about 5%.[6] It probably comes as no surprise that MySpace earns the lion's share of ad spending, at more than $510 million for 2007 alone!

The landscape of social-networking sites changes daily as new entrants seek to enter a growing market. The number of sites with reasonably large name recognition is fairly small, but the Mashable lists entries for 350 social-networking sites! A few examples are highlighted below.

MySpace.com: A Place for Friends

MySpace is a general social-networking site with more than 100 million registered profiles and unique visitors exceeding 64 million per month.[7] It is the mass market of social networking, akin to the Super Bowl for television advertising. In fact, the most recent Super Bowl broadcast partnered with MySpace to deliver additional advertising impressions for Super Bowl commercials by offering a MySpace community site dedicated to the ads. MySpace was initially intended for an audience of teens and young adults, but an analysis of MySpace user demographics from comScore corrects that perception. MySpace's age demographic is distributed over a range of ages with its largest category being the 35–54 age group (making up 40% of MySpace's user base).[8] A strength of MySpace is its broad appeal, developing at least in part from its vast array of features, including individual profiles, music, video, instant messaging capabilities, blogs, groups and communities, and a host of others. Given that social-networking sites exist (at least from the user perspective) to create and maintain personal relationships, using the largest network increases the likelihood of an existing friend base. Niche networks, in contrast, must rely on invitations from users to build membership and expand network. MySpace is the most successful network in leveraging what is known as the *network effect*. The network effect explains that a network gains value as more people join the network.

MySpace recently announced one of the most advanced developments in social-network advertising. It now offers an advertising solution for businesses that claims to microtarget ads to members. Because the ads are highly targeted based on the data in user profiles, the ads should have more relevance to and meaning for the target audience, resulting in a higher rate of response. This system promises to improve online advertising, especially for local advertisers, but its accuracy depends upon the accuracy of the data in user profiles and the quality of the data-mining function used to extract the segments for targeting. In addition to targeted display ads, brands can create brand profiles and communities.

Facebook

Facebook is the second largest social network. Though largely dwarfed by MySpace's size and traffic, it boasts highly involved members, many of whom report spending hours each day on the site and constantly checking for new Facebook messages on their mobile phones. When Facebook launched in February of 2004, it focused on high school and college students, relying on existing tangible networks to build the virtual network base. It has been enormously successful with the college audience. According to the GenX27 Youth Research Initiative, a higher percentage of college students use and prefer Facebook over MySpace. According to Student Monitor's Lifestyle & Media Study, Facebook is one of the top five "in" things to do on college campuses, second to iPods, named by 73% of students and tying with beer, which was named by 71% of students.[9] Early estimates suggest that about 85% of all college students use Facebook, with 60% of them logging in daily, spending about a half hour per day on the site. Since that time, it has opened the site to non-students, expanded to several other countries, and earned more than

27 million members.[10] An article featuring Facebook in *Fast Company* magazine reports that Facebook boasts 47,000 networks, 30 billion page views per month, and more photos than any other photo-sharing site, and is the sixth most trafficked Web site.[11]

Facebook has offered advertisers more strategic value than perhaps any other social network. It has accomplished this with a mix of strategic vehicles, including targeted display ads and sponsored stories, known as Social Ads and Sponsored Stories, branded profiles known as Facebook Pages, a developer incentive program to encourage content development called Facebook Developers, and a social news feed of brand-related user behavior called Beacon.

Facebook Social Ads are targeted at specific users based on member profiles and behavior in the network. For instance, Facebook Social Ads can be delivered to users whose friends have recently engaged with the brand's Facebook profile or visited the brand's Web site. Even the location of delivery for social ads can be targeted with ads appearing next to news feeds of friends (a Facebook feature that allows friends to update others on their recent activities) who mention the brand. By delivering ad impressions that are related to news feeds, Facebook encourages discussion and word-of-mouth communication about a brand.

Facebook Pages are brand equivalents to user profiles. It is the location on the site where brands develop their brand personas. They can be enhanced with applications from the business itself and from developer widget applications.

The free developers feature enables programmers to create widgets, mash-ups, tools, and projects for Facebook users. These small applications are popular with consumers and are useful to brands that utilize them to maintain a presence on user profiles. For example, FaceBank is a widget that enables Facebook users to track expenses (and share information about expenses with friends). Another popular application is Lickuacious, which lets users rank friends according to the popularity of their wall posts. The Wall is Facebook's comments feature.

Facebook Beacon offers brands a way to virally distribute information about user brand-related activity. News feeds notify friends of a user's engagement with a brand's profile and Web site along with specific product search history and purchases. The news feed stories act as a form of word-of-mouth promotion. Further, they are targeted in that the feeds are then seen by friends who are also likely to be interested in the brand. Beacon offers a potentially powerful way to utilize the influence tactic of social proof, the influence a group of others have over a consumer's decision. This feature should provide more value for advertisers who will benefit from the additional exposure and the easy transference of opinion-leader information to others in the network. However, it has been criticized by privacy advocates and some brands publicly expressed a discomfort with the degree of user information it reveals.

YouTube, Broadcast Yourself

YouTube is most often mentioned during discussions of user-generated content, viral video, and social-media space, and less so during discussions of social networking. It does, however, meet the basic criteria of social networking in that it enables the development and maintenance of networks on the site. It is a major player but far smaller than MySpace with approximately 47 million unique users.[12] YouTube is nearly gender neutral with 53.3% male members. The largest age segment represented is 35- to 64-year-olds, which make up 48% of the membership. Users 18–24 years make up 14% of its user base and teens age 12–17 form 11.5% of its users. It does not reach diverse ethnic groups; 92% of YouTube users are white.[13] Though YouTube has diversity across age groups, it is heavily used by teens and young adults. It is the second most popular Web site for young males, following Facebook, and the third most popular for young females, following Facebook and MySpace. Favorite videos can be stored with a user's profile, links can be e-mailed to YouTube members and nonmembers, and users can "subscribe" to the channels they like best.

Just as MySpace "owns" the general social-networking market, YouTube owns the video component of social networking. Other sites, including Google Video and MySpace, support streaming video and user-contributions of video, but YouTube is the top-of-mind brand for video. As advertisers identify vehicles for distributing commercial video online (whether it be commercials shown across media platforms or film "shorts" promoting the brand), sites like YouTube should be part of the mix. Advertisers can post to YouTube or let posts occur organically by enabling brand fans to capture video and post to the site. Smirnoff's "Tea Partay" video was posted on a Smirnoff Web site, but visitors were so enamored with the video that they put it on YouTube. Once on YouTube, the video was viewed more than 1.3 million times.[14] When compared to the cost of purchasing enough advertising time to generate that level of exposure, it is clear that the value YouTube offers in terms of media coverage is impressive.

Posting videos and encouraging fans to post on the site is perhaps the most obvious use of this social network for advertising, but two other options are notable. First, YouTube offers Community links, which can be branded like brand profiles on MySpace and Facebook. Second, the

Community area of YouTube features a list of contests sponsored by brands seeking consumer-generated advertising. The videos posted on the contest sites serve as promotional pieces for the brand and the site becomes a promotional vehicle and hosting service for the brands. Dunkin' Donuts, Puma, TurboTax, Chrysler, and Swiffer Sweeper, among others, host consumer-generated advertising contests here.

Dogster, For the Love of Dogs

Dogster, a vertical social-networking community, is one focused on developing a high degree of personal involvement with its members. It plays upon the commitment dog owners have to their "fur children" and provides an outlet for these pet parents to show off their dogs. Dogster has a sister site, Catster, for people with cats. Dogster's media kit emphasizes its affluent market of highly educated, moderately high-income women (81% of Dogster members are female) with a disposition to shop online. The online shopping behavior is emphasized for advertisers who recognize that sales conversions online are more likely if the people reached with the advertising are also willing to complete online purchases.

Dogster's membership size makes it clear why such a large portion of ad spending goes to bigger sites like MySpace. Dogster's membership includes just 300,000 registered users and 40 million page views. Importantly, though, advertising on Dogster (if the membership fits with a brand's target market) could be more effective despite the smaller reach because of the involvement the members have in the topical area (in this case, dogs). This is particularly true of brands that relate directly (and so have high relevance) to the site's theme. For instance, MilkBone is a major advertiser on Dogster.

Gather

Gather is another example of a niche site, one for the intellectual adult. It is less tightly tied to a topic in that hundreds of topics from literature, art, entertainment, and cooking are discussed on the site, but it clearly targets an educated, affluent audience. Catherine Holahan notes that Gather targets older users, more likely to listen to National Public Radio than hip hop.[15] As such, it is still a highly vertical network site. Tom Gerace, Gather's founder and CEO, said this about Gather's network personality: "The breadth, diversity, and timeliness of the shared perspectives create an environment that reflects a great dinner party, but can occur with anyone, at any time from any place. This conversation is truly the heart and soul of Gather.com."

Similar to the features of other social networks, Gather members can send and receive messages, participate in group spaces about a host of issues from living with cancer to dealing with blended families, and post videos and photos. An interesting aspect of the Gather site is its encouragement of user-generated content. All social networks rely on user-generated content, but Gather emphasizes that posting content is publishing. Members are invited to publish articles, videos, and photos. The result is an engaged audience with demographic characteristics that are largely absent from other social networks.

Brands can advertise on Gather with display ads, cost-per-click (the advertiser pays only if a viewer clicks on the ad) sponsored text ads, branded communities, and sponsorships of Gather content areas. Branded communities feature visual consistency with a brand's other promotional materials. The communities can be customized to continue the look and feel of the brand's own Web site. The sponsorship opportunity represents a form of contextual targeting. Contextually targeted online advertising matches the product type being promoted to the topical content on a Web site. Gather's sponsorships accomplish contextual targeting by enabling, for instance, a book publisher to sponsor its literature content area or a political candidate to sponsor the political content section.

Xanga

Xanga targets an audience of teenagers and young adults. With nearly 5 million members (called Xangans), it has grown beyond other social-networking sites targeting the same audience. Xanga emphasizes conversation over profiles in that a member's blog is his or her home on Xanga. Like Gather, Xanga offers behavioral and demographic targeting for advertisers based on stated interests and demographics. Using behavioral targeting to determine exposure to advertising on the site significantly enhances clickthrough rates. For instance, Xanga's media kit describes a case study for Mogs video game. Advertising on the site without targeting had a clickthrough rate of .85%, but advertising targeted at teens who had expressed an interest in gaming increased the clickthrough rate to 1.50%. Interestingly, a feature Xanga uses to differentiate itself for advertisers considering social-networking sites as a vehicle for advertising is the accuracy of the members' profiles. Profile accuracy is important for behavioral and demographic targeting to function effectively, yet members of sites may use the site to build an alter ego or ideal self rather than portray a more realistic self-portrait. Xanga's data card provides the basic information advertisers would need to know before selecting Xanga as one of a brand's communication vehicles. For instance, the site's data card reveals that Xanga is most popular with Caucasian teens and young adults who visit approximately three times per month for an average of three hours. The gender distribution among Xangans is roughly equal. The data card emphasizes Xanga's ability to deliver targeted ads based on demographic, geographic, and psychographic patterns.

These are just a few of the hundreds of social-networking sites available, but they effectively illustrate key considerations such as number of visitors (reach), member demographics and targeting, frequency of site visits and length of time spent on-site (site stickiness), and duplication with other sites. In addition, they serve as examples for the range of advertising options possible within the realm of social networking.

■ Thoughts on Friendvertising

The sheer size of the audience may seem like reason enough for brands to plan and execute a friending campaign. Perhaps it is, but there are numerous other advantages to social-network advertising. There are also plenty of reasons to be cautious when considering social-network advertising.

Although online social networks were launched years ago with early entrants like Tripod, Globe, and Friendster, advertisers have only recently begun to embrace their potential as a reach and engagement device. Social networking, like all forms of social media, differs from traditional advertising media in that it neither reaches large masses of people (like broadcast television) nor offers sufficiently segmented targeting opportunities. Advertisers were left wanting bigger audiences and access to specific demographic and behavioral markets. At least that was the situation until recently.

With advances in behavioral targeting, social-network advertising can not only target but also microtarget audiences. Social-network advertising enables brands to reach both mass markets (through major sites like MySpace) and niche markets (because of the many vertical sites like Dogster) while targeting specific segments using the segmentation tools offered by sites (based on user behaviors and demographic data). Behavioral targeting, in the context of online advertising, means delivering relevant display ads based on a user's behavior online. Ad network tracking programs trace the pattern of Web site and Web page visits to segment users based on their online behavior. That information is then used to serve highly relevant ads to a segment of users who are likely to be interested in the product. For example, a Facebook user who has just viewed the price of flights to Mardi Gras on Expedia might be shown a display ad for Orbitz. Results from a comparison of display ads delivered using behavioral targeting and those delivered based on contextual targeting showed that the clickthrough rate for behaviorally targeted ads is 108% higher than that for contextual ads.[16]

Not all sites can aid advertisers with behavioral targeting, but this will increasingly be available as social-network sites commit to earning revenues through advertising. For example, Gather offers behavioral targeting for advertisers based on key words, online behavior, and demographics of its members. The targeting technology benefits advertisers by encouraging higher clickthrough and conversion rates.

The most advanced developments in targeting come from MySpace and Facebook. MySpace's "SelfServe" platform, part of the company's "HyperTargeting" initiative introduced this summer, enables advertisers to purchase, create, and analyze the performance of ads throughout the MySpace social network. The program seeks to offer an easy, affordable, and efficient online advertising option to small businesses by making it simple to upload custom ads and select target audiences for delivery of ad impressions. The program segments the MySpace member base by geographic, demographic, and user interest factors. Because the ads are highly targeted based on the data in user profiles, the ads should have more relevance and meaning to the target audience, resulting in a higher rate of response to the ads. This system promises to improve online advertising, especially for local advertisers, but its accuracy is dependent upon the accuracy of the data in user profiles and the quality of the data-mining function used to extract the segments for targeting. In an article in the *New York Times,* Brad Stone questions whether MySpace trusts its own technology, pointing out that the company is using "relevance testers" to manually check member profiles against the categories the system assigns.[17]

Facebook's Social Ads promise targeting, too, along with the ability to build buzz for the brand. Like the MySpace SelfServe program, social ads are targeted based on member profiles and behavior in the network. The display ads can be used in conjunction with other Facebook features to promote word-of-mouth discussion about the brand among friends.

Targeted advertising is desirable given the enhanced effectiveness in generating consumer response, but Facebook's advertising options highlight the core reason brands can benefit from friendvertising. Social-network advertising inspires the viral spread of brand information by influential brand enthusiasts. The *Never Ending Friending* report claims that 40% of social-network users attribute their social network to their discovery of a brand they really like.[18] The report explains that advertising gains value on social networks by building a momentum effect. The momentum effect occurs when brands build on the basic value of their display advertising and brand profile by encouraging friends to share the brand's message. While display advertising and profiles will exist on the network site, friendvertising means that brands are not limited to paid advertising impressions in earning consumer exposure to the brand's message. Friends within the social network carry the message virally by discussing the brand, embedding branded symbols and widgets on profile pages, and reporting on brand-related activities. If a brand is well liked, relevant, and buzz worthy, the media value originating from nonpaid, word-of-mouth referrals for the brand can be enormous. This is the essence of the momentum effect.

Why does this work? Friends are awarded a special form of influence—social proof. Social proof works by encouraging consumers to make decisions that mimic those of people in their social network. If friends are favorable toward a brand or making brand purchases, the influenced others are likely to as well. Thus, social networks offer opportunities for word-of-mouse communication to other friends and influentials about the brand. Pete Snyder, CEO of New Media Strategies, notes that the rate of online reviews of products, including books, music, and movies, is three to five times higher on Facebook than on other electronic commerce sites with review functions.[19] Reviewers may doubt that their opinion will be recognized on a social opinion or retail site but are confident that their friends on a social network will find the opinion interesting and relevant.

Brands can flourish from the viral communication of brand messages and the accompanying social power with any social network. The viral impact of social networking cannot be underestimated. A person who forwards an e-mail marketing message to a few friends can make a small impact in the marketplace with this 1+1+1 model of distribution. However, if that same user posts a link to a video ad using a social network, the distribution grows exponentially.

Take, for instance, the brand Lichido, a type of liqueur. The brand's profile on MySpace includes about 3,000 "friends." Many of those friends also have thousands of friends, too. (Not all MySpace profiles boast such strong friend lists, but Lichido is a popular brand. Its friend list includes Beyonce, Jamie Foxx, and Michael Jordan, among others!) If even 1% of Lichido's friends share the link with their friends, the result could be exposure to more than 300,000 "friends"! MySpace provides a bulletin board function to make announcements to friends. Lichido uses the bulletin board to announce special events, news about the brand, and even seasonal drink recipes. Friends can then share these recipes with others.

This is just one of several ways that the network in social networking can aid advertisers. Think of the network as part of a conversational marketing program. The goal is to deliver a brand message to a target audience and encourage members of that audience to include that message in conversations with their friends.

The success of several widget applications on Facebook is another example of the effectiveness of organic, viral growth possible on social networks. As members use the widgets and alert people in their network, steady organic growth occurs, ultimately hitting a tipping point. Once that happens, the popularity of the widget explodes. The same thing can occur for branded profiles and branded widgets. Embedding branded widgets in a social network can extend the exposure time for a brand's message by encouraging sticky interactions that last far beyond a thirty-second spot and repeat visits to the brand's site. When well designed, a response device can be embedded in the conversation, enabling conversion from message exposure to purchase. Google launched OpenSocial recently, a platform that allows widget developers to make their widgets portable from one social network to another. The enhanced transferability will encourage users to maintain profiles across multiple sites.

Friendvertising relies on encouraging conversations among connected users in a network. Does it matter which friends start the conversation? It might. There are two schools of thought on how public interest builds. Malcolm Gladwell, author of *The Tipping Point*, posits that three factors work to "tip" a trend, in other words, to ignite interest in an idea, behavior, or product: (1) the law of the few, (2) stickiness, and (3) the power of context.[20] The law of the few refers to the three types of people who help to spread viral messages. Mavens are people who are knowledgeable about many things. Connectors are people who know many people and communicate with them. Salesmen are people who influence others with their natural persuasive power. By targeting mavens, connectors, and salesmen, brands enhance the likelihood that their messages will spread throughout a social network. How can we identify these types of people? Mavens and salespeople are not easily identified by profiles, but connectors are those with the most friends. Their networks are large and active. Ideas, or in this case brand messages, will be more viral if they inspire action on the part of the recipient. This is what Gladwell refers to as stickiness. Direct marketers have long known that creative content pulls best when bundled with a call to action. To the extent that brands can build such a call to action into their social-networking promotions, the campaign will be more effective. Lastly, Gladwell explains that messages can hit the reach of an epidemic only if they also have the power of context. Context means that mavens, connectors, and sales-people have enough enthusiasm for, knowledge about, and control over the message to build communities around it. Interestingly, this is exactly what brands seek to do when they develop branded communities in social networks.

This theory resonates with many who find it a good explanation of trends, but others suggest that messages spread from many rather than a few. Marian Salzman, chief strategy officer at Euro RSCG Worldwide and author of *Buzz: Harness the Power of Influence and Create Demand,* says that the key to moving brand messages through social networks is to cultivate "bees," hyperdevoted customers who live to spread the word about the brand.[21] Brands should build beehives by devoting extra attention to brand enthusiasts who are likely to serve as bees, offering product samples to these enthusiasts, encouraging them to share branded materials like widgets with friends, and providing them with compelling information—stories, brand gossip even—that they will want to share with others.

Duncan Watts, author of *Six Degrees,* warns that building buzz on social networks, or with the public at large, is not so clear-cut.[22] He advises brands to build the "six degrees effect" into their advertising. The six degrees effect is based on the notion of six degrees of separation, which refers to the idea that, if a person is one step away from each person he or she knows and two steps away from each person who is known by one of the people he or she knows, then everyone is an average of six "steps" away from every other person. In other words, it's a small world after all. MySpace highlights the six degrees of separation by revealing when one visits another person's profile, whether that person is in his or her extended network. In other words, the person is not a friend, but is a friend of a friend. Watts believes friends can spread brand messages and that some people have more influence than others. At the same time, it is difficult to systematically and strategically inspire the spread of a message. Instead, he advises marketers to aim broad. One never knows who is going to ulti-mately be the influential one who spreads the brand's message. Consequently, advertising must be aimed at the broadest group possible.

Obviously, brands want to make the most of the social network itself. It would be shortsighted for brands to view social networks as they would any other type of Web site, simply looking for audience size. Still, social networks do offer reach and extended periods of time for a brand message to be processed. Social networks have an advantage over many sites in that members tend to visit often, staying for an extended visit each time. Brands benefit from this time component. These sites have high "site stickiness" (meaning people tend to stay active on the site for a longer period of time), which results in more exposure of the brand message to the target market.

Social-networking sites offer brands many opportunities for engagement. When brand profiles are created, the brands can exist as "people" on the sites. Friends can interact with the brands, share information, photos, and videos, and participate in two-way communication—a real dialogue. The brand as person enhances the ability of a brand to use conversation marketing. Building a brand persona strengthens brand personality, differentiates brands from competitors, and sets the stage for a perceived relationship. Assuming the brand's persona is likable and credible, it can facilitate message internalization (the process by which a consumer adopts a brand belief as his or her own).

Why would a person "friend" a brand? There are lots of incentives for friending brands, as explained in the *Never Ending Friending* report.[23] These include incentive-driven motives like getting invitations to upcoming events, receiving information on sales and special offers and relationship-oriented motives such as a desire to support the company because it offers high-quality products, to associate with the brand and its image, and to respond to a friend's recommendation about the brand. The value proposition is already in place. The key to branding with friends, though, is to treat them like friends.

Ultimately, branding on social-networking sites promotes brand awareness, brand recall, and, if done well, builds on brand loyalty and brand equity. Social networks offer opportunities for brand promotion and engagement for those brands that learn to leverage the unique attributes of the network in question.

However, social networking is not without its flaws. Advertising, even when developed and distributed in superlative online venues, still suffers from the limitations facing all forms of advertising. Clutter is a tremendous distraction for people as they are faced with advertising in and on every imaginable media. Online readers are bombarded with sometimes numerous ads on a single page. With the many display ads, profile components, and widgets visible on social-network pages, clutter is an issue. There is also limited inventory for advertising space on the sites.

Social networks offer the greatest benefits to brands when the brands play to a network's culture, developing brand personas and engaging friends in dialogue. However, the workhorse of social-network advertising is still the display ad. Unfortunately, display ads are not nearly as effective on social-networking sites as they are on other types of Web sites.[24] Clickthrough rates are much lower.

Part of the power of online techniques is that they encourage the target market to seek out the brand—to find the brand's Web site, join a brand's friend list, and so on. But to shift to this state whereby consumers "pull" the brand to them, we first have to gain attention and interest, and encourage some form of consumer response. This is not an easy proposition.

There is media fragmentation online, and this is particularly true of the social-networking arena. Just think how many social-networking sites exist right now! Companies like Ning are making it possible for any company (or anyone) to create its own niche social-networking site. The fragmentation is worse when one considers the other Web sites competing for visitors, including search engines, e-mail service providers, entertainment sites, news sites, and more. But wait—we cannot forget that people use not only the Internet, as a communication medium, but also other media forms, including television, radio, magazines, and newspapers, and vehicles, including personal digital assistants, mobile phones, and MP3 players.

Because people have numerous hobbies and interests and social-networking sites have responded by providing sites tied to such pursuits, duplication in the audiences must be considered before selecting sites to advertise on. Many people who are active social-networkers network on multiple sites. For instance, 1up.com, a social network for gamers, knows its members are also active on other social-networking sites: 50% of its members are on MySpace, 18% on Facebook, and 9% on Xanga.[25] Xanga's media kit specifically addresses the question of duplication by providing the overlap it shares with other social-networking sites popular with teens. For Xanga, the primary competition is MTV.com.

One advantage for brands in developing social-network assets is the credibility attributed to these brands and to online word-of-mouth communication. If the brand is not perceived as credible, though, the network strategy can backfire. A Jupiter Research report "Viral Marketing: Beyond Social Media" revealed that 69% of consumers do not trust the information they get about brands from social-networking sites.[26] The finding suggests that consumers are responding to cloaking and other covert online activities by treating brand information from social networks with caution.

Social-networking sites may suffer from member attrition. This affects brands by masking the real prevalence of a site in the daily, weekly, and monthly activities of its users. Some sites are promoting their retention rates among members to minimize the concern for advertisers. MySpace, for instance, has the highest retention rate of all major sites at 67%. Facebook follows closely behind with 52%, and Xanga has 48%.[27] Attrition will likely be a greater problem for sites that do not benefit from regular infusions of user-generated content, which act to keep a site fresh.

▓ Vehicles for Friendvertising

To craft an effective friendvertising campaign, there are three general approaches possible: (1) advertising using display ads on social networks; (2) embedding the brand in the social network with brand profile pages, branded widgets, and promotions; and (3) building an exclusive branded social network. The simplest level of social-network advertising is to place display ads on various pages within the site. Some social-networking sites like Gather and Xanga offer search optimization options that can enable precise targeting of specific members based on their online behavior and demographics. Video can also be streamed on most sites to enable commercials or "shorts" (short films, longer than a typical commercial) to run. If video is offered as a site feature (either feature entertainment or informational or user-generated video), brands can opt to "pre-roll" or "post-roll," meaning that commercials can be shown prior to the viewing of the video or just afterwards. Brands may also integrate the advertising in the site with sponsorships, e-newsletter features, branded instant messaging, branded groups (forums and communities), and more. We discuss the most common and innovative of these options below.

Display Advertising

Social-networking sites will offer many options for advertisers who wish to use display ads. Space is sold using the IAB's standard online advertising units (see www.iab.net for all standard size options), including various sizes of rectangles, banners, and skyscrapers.

Just like the cost of placing ads in other media, the rates charged for advertising online is based on CPM (cost per thousand exposures). The CPM rate is a function of demand for the site's advertising inventory and the value of its audience. Audience value is difficult to define but includes the following considerations important to advertisers: sheer volume, segmentation characteristics, visit patterns (frequency of visits, how recent they were, and time spent per visit), and involvement in the site. For social-networking sites, CPM varies from as little as $5 to more than $40, depending upon the type and size of the ad and whether behavioral or demographic targeting is used.

Brand Membership (Profiles)

Among the highest-value activities are the development of brand profiles. Brand profiles give the brand a persona in the social-networking space. It is a natural expansion of the trend for brands to create personalities for themselves, both through the use of creative language, including style, imagery, tone, creative appeals, and music, and brand ambassadors, who literally provide a human persona for the brand.[28] GEICO offers one example of brand personality. GEICO's agency, The Martin Agency, built a personality of youth and irreverence for the GEICO brand, using humorous creative appeals, music, and characters like the infamous gecko. The gecko promotes his personality, and the GEICO brand, with its MySpace profile, www.myspace.com/geicogecko. This profile illustrates how the brand's personality can be distinguished in the information provided. The gecko emphasizes that he loves to help people save on car insurance (notice the consistency with other aspects of the GEICO campaign!) and his occupation is "animal advertiser." GEICO is off to a good start with its use of profile development in the social-network space, but it can do more. Compared to other brands, it has a small friend list (just fewer than 500 friends). This suggests that while GEICO recognizes the value of building brand awareness using social networking, it has not been seeking out friends or nurturing its existing relationships. In addition, there are several profile "squatters" using GEICO assets. If people visit the profiles registered to GEICO, gekko, or GEICOgecko, they will reach pages registered to individual people. The actual brand's profile is only found at GEICOgecko.

Jeep utilized its profile on MySpace in a systematic and integrated way to achieve its marketing objectives. Jeep uses the social-networking site to develop relationships with its target audience and to share information about its promotions and events. When it used a national concert tour played through the Jeep Compass' stereo speakers to highlight the advantage of the Compass stereo system, the MySpace site kept friends abreast of new concert dates and ticket information, drove traffic to the concerts, and built buzz with the sharing of photos and videos from the events. For the concert purpose, Jeep logged more than 1.3 million clicks on the MySpace profile and more than 12,000 friends.[29] Considering the expense involved (MySpace profiles are free), the reach and frequency of message exposure is phenomenal. Jeep continues to use its profile to promote other Jeep initiatives like its Action Sports Street Sessions.

Brand Communities

Brands can also develop "communities" on some social-networking sites. Sean Combs, aka P. Diddy, has used the brand community approach by setting up his own "channel" on YouTube. He uses it to post videos (webisodes), blog about his day, and show highlights from his concert tour.

Diddy's tour and his social-media sites are co-branded with Burger King, illustrating that even brands can leverage networks.[30] Diddy also recognizes that many social-networking sites attract some of the same users. While Diddy hosts the YouTube community, his well-developed profile on MySpace serves to direct friends (and he's got a lot of friends—nearly 800,000) to his YouTube channel and to other media properties.

Brands can also set up their own spaces entirely. MyCoke, Joga (by Nike), and OurChart are examples. OurChart is particularly interesting because the brand it promotes is Showtime's program, "The L Word," but the developers believe the site will eventually exist as a site for gays and lesbians rather than as a brand initiative.[31] Given recent research from Witeck-Combs Communications and Harris Interactive that finds gays and lesbians are heavier users of social-networking sites and other online activities, OurChart is well positioned for the market.[32]

Coke, Nike, and Showtime developed independent spaces, but brands with smaller budgets can still develop networking sites that are consistent with their brand image. Ning is a company that seeks to empower brands and consumer groups to do just that. Anyone can register at Ning and set up a community on any topic. The communities can feature video sharing, photo posts, discussion forums, blogs, and all the other features commonly offered by established social networks. Importantly, Ning offers the ability to brand the community space. If a friend visits Jeep's profile on MySpace, it is still clear that MySpace is the host. With Ning, brands can truly own the social-networking space. Ning has already registered 26,000 networking sites, including PezHeads (a networking site for people who collect Pez dispensers) and AdGabber (a site for people interested in advertising). While Ning is the only major service provider for independent social-networking sites, this is not likely to last long. Cisco Systems has announced that it will invest in the technology to enable large-scale clients to create social sites similar to MySpace.[33]

Sponsorship

Brands can create sponsorship relationships to accomplish online what brands have long succeeded in, off-line. When marketers use sponsorships off-line, the goal is to link the brand to something about which the target market feels passionately. Brand sponsorships of NASCAR are a classic example of this. Because NASCAR fans are passionate and they associate brand sponsorships with the potential success of their favorite drivers, they let the passion for the sport seep into passion for the brand sponsors. Other sponsorships are based on providing something of value to the target audience. Charmin, for instance, has been successful sponsoring concert events and festivals. Part of the sponsorship includes on-site luxury toilet facilities equipped with—you guessed it!—Charmin toilet paper. When the next best option is a "porta-potty," fans can get real passionate about the Charmin brand. Sponsorship of social-networking sites works the same way. Nikon has created a sponsorship of the Flickr social network. In this example, the choice is perfect. Flickr members are passionate about photography, capturing memories through photographs and sharing those memories with others online. Nikon, as a premium camera brand seeking to gain market share in the digital camera market, benefits from enhanced exposure to the brand name and the emotional connection between the site, the site's purpose for members, and the sponsor.

Social-network advertising provides an entire continuum of advertising devices for brands entering this online space, but brands should consider integrating a range of involvement opportunities in a site. Dogster clearly understands this as it offers "packs" or levels of advertising integration in its media kit. Dogster recommends including banner ads, information in its electronic newsletter, the use of a branded group, and a featured section on the Dogster home page. As with other advertising techniques, effectiveness is maximized when the target audience is reached with several devices, several times, with an integrated voice.

■ Quiz: Is the Brand Primed for Friendvertising?

Clearly, there is a lot to be gained for brands operating in social media, and from friending customers in social networks. Ask these questions before deciding whether friendvertising will work for a specific brand.

- Is the brand event set up for engagement? Mark Kingdon, CEO of Organic, Inc., a digital-marketing agency, had this to say about brands exposing themselves to social engagement:[34] "[Brands] have to allow for and anticipate dialogue, because consumers very much want to engage with brands and not all brands are set up for engagement. A lot of brands are simply set up to broadcast their message to an audience." Some brands will be safer with one-way communication.
- If the brand participates in social media, where should the brand be? Should the brand have its own dedicated social-network space (like Nike's Joga)? Or will the brand have the best chance at creating consumer dialogue and engagement by using an existing platform (like MySpace)? Is there a social-networking site that is well suited to the brand? For example, Purina is perfectly suited to advertising on Dogster but may not be as effective on MySpace.

- If an existing platform is selected, will the brand need to build profiles on several sites or will it focus on developing a network on one site that seems particularly well suited to the brand and its target market?

- If the brand develops a profile presence on one or more sites, how can the profiles be developed in such a way as to reflect the brand's personality?

- How will the brand nurture the relationships it develops on the site? For instance, will the brand send happy birthday messages to its "friends" on their birthdays?

- How will the brand address brand encroachers on social-networking sites? Even though telecommunications is one of the leading social-network advertisers, the brand name "Verizon Wireless" is used as a screen name by an individual who clearly does not represent the brand. Not only is this a wasted opportunity for Verizon, but it could also potentially dilute the value of the brand.

- If "fan pages" exist among brand loyalists on social-networking sites, how can the brand leverage the fan sites to better meet its objectives?

- How can the brand integrate its social-network presence into other campaign components? For example, Audi's Art of the Heist campaign for the Audi H3 utilized a phenomenal ARG to engage its target audience. Clues to the game were embedded in all forms of media. Could Audi have provided game clues or player information on a social-networking site? (Going back to the point about protecting social brand space, the Audi MySpace profile is registered to a teenager in Orange County, California.)

- How can the brand integrate itself fully into the social network it chooses to operate within? Should it use display ads, video, sponsorships, brand communities, co-branding, or some combination? As with any media plan, advertising is most effective when it utilizes multiple forms of media and vehicles. This does not change in the social-networking space.

Mark Drosos of *iMedia Connection* reminds marketers that social networks can meet several marketing objectives with social networking so long as the brand (1) designs a persona so that it drives value, (2) gives community members a reason to meet, communicate, and share, and (3) provides relevant content that offers the community value.[35] How can you give consumers a reason to communicate and share brand information? How can you foster the momentum effect? Social-network members share stories, tools, tips, and experiences. Offer branded assets like downloads, shareable widgets and wallpapers, and stories that invite users to cocreate branded content. Use the brand's profile as an information hub and announce new products, company news, contests and promotions, and career opportunities. Provide this kind of content and, assuming it is relevant to the target's interests, they will share it. Remember that content is the key to social-networking sites. Without content, social networks are nothing more than message boards. Social-network advertising is positioned to be among the must-use tools for brands in the foreseeable future. Most brands are not even in this space yet, and those that are still have a lot to learn. However, the potential to take branding and the use of brand personalities to an entirely new level does exist.

4 ▪ ▪ ▪

Advertising in the Imagination
Social Virtual Networks and the "Vlobalization" of Brands

In this chapter, we continue our discussion of social-media marketing. Recall that social-media marketing refers to a genre of online marketing based in and around social communities. Here, our focus will be marketing in virtual worlds. Nick Wilson offers this definition of a social virtual world on his blog, Metaversed, "A social virtual world has game-like immersion and social-media functionality without narrative-driven goals. At its core is a sense of presence with others at the same time and place."[1] In just a few years, numerous virtual worlds have emerged, collectively making up what could be thought of as a virtual globe, or vlobe, including Second Life, There, and Kaneva, among others. Some brands have focused on a single market, at least for now, while others have pursued a multi-market strategy, with entries that complement each other, developed for different virtual worlds. Estimates suggest that by 2011, 80% of Internet users will be active in one or more virtual worlds, which are already growing steadily in popularity.[2] Marketers are taking notice of consumer interest, and the potential for branding. Janet Meiners reports, based on figures from Parks Associates, advertising in virtual world will reach $150 million by 2012 (ten times the current estimate).[3]

Before we move forward, take a moment to consider the realm of social-media marketing, particularly as it relates to virtual worlds. Frequently, we tend to think of social-media marketing as a form of online advertising, but that is not always the case. There is no doubt that social-media marketing can be an effective and efficient form of online promotion—enabling marketers to communicate a brand's benefits, value proposition, and personality to its target audience. In many social-media scenarios, it would be more accurate to call this approach social-media advertising.

But when it comes to virtual worlds, the term marketing is apropos. Why? Marketing encompasses the development and implementation of pricing, promotion, and distribution of products to create exchanges that meet the goals of the parties involved. For commercial brands like Sony, IBM, and Coke, virtual worlds are mostly about branding—an aspect of the promotion component of marketing. Consumer-produced media, consumed online, is the soul of social-media marketing, again leading to an emphasis on communication over other marketing considerations. Still, it is worth noting that in virtual worlds, brands (entrepreneurial and "big brands") are doing more than just advertising.

Take, for example, Adidas. Adidas hosts a virtual retail store to distribute its branded virtual shoes (sold at a value price point for the budget yet fashion-conscious avatar) and promotes the brand in world with events and signage. There is probably a Tracy McGrady avatar shooting hoops in world, decked out in Adidas brand merchandise. Adidas is *marketing* in world—it has products developed for a target audience of avatars (integrated with its product line for real-life customers); the products are priced competitively given the brand's value proposition (and using a different pricing strategy than that used in real life); the products are distributed using a channel of virtual manufacturers and a virtual retail storefront; and the products are promoted in world using a combination of advertising and public relations tactics.

Adidas benefits from many aspects of its virtual-marketing strategy. It builds awareness through the publicity garnered from media outlets writing about business innovations in virtual worlds. It inspires word-of-mouth (and mouse) communication from brand enthusiasts and virtual enthusiasts. The strategy sells virtual shoes and can also serve as a direct response device for sales of real Adidas shoes. Thus, it serves to support an internal and external (the real-world) market. It drives traffic to the Adidas Web site. It promotes the brand as an innovative, tech-savvy brand. It differentiates the brand from other athletic and street wear brands slower to experiment with social media. It extends the opportunities for customers to interact with the Adidas brand and maintains exposure to the brand's message. Adidas' virtual-marketing strategy can be executed at a cost far below that required to launch a broadcast-intensive ad campaign.

We'll come back to the Adidas example shortly. The brand, along with others, can offer valuable lessons for applying social-media marketing to virtual-world communities. First, let's revisit the meaning and types of virtual worlds, and consider some of the most prominent options for marketing in metaverses. From there, we'll consider the virtual-market entry strategies brands might pursue and the stages they represent. Lastly, we'll view examples of virtual campaigns and the lessons to be learned from them.

■ Social Virtual Worlds

Virtual worlds, also known as "metaverses," refer to 3D communities that mimic the real world without its physical limitations. The concept was proposed by Neil Stephenson's (1992) book, *Snow Crash,* which went on to inspire Phillip Rosedale's creation of Second Life, arguably the most prominent of virtual worlds.[4] Virtual worlds include both social worlds and game worlds. Social worlds are game-like but lack the goal orientation of virtual games. Social virtual worlds offer opportunities for learning, entertainment, shopping, working and doing business, and socializing, but there are no objectives intrinsic to the community. Throughout the chapter, the focus is on social virtual worlds.

Virtual worlds are rich with possibility for brand engagement, sales, market research, facility utilization, and entertainment, but they are communities above all else. Participants interact with others using avatars as in-world representatives. Many forms of communication are possible (this varies depending upon the specific world), including text chat, voice chat, instant messaging, and electronic mail). Activities are seemingly endless. One can shop, work, tour an art gallery, take a class, drive (or fly) a car, meet with friends, exercise, and date. Involvement runs the gamut from those who poke around out of curiosity to those who purchase homes, decorate them, and spend time volunteering in their virtual neighborhoods.

■ Motives for Participation in Virtual Worlds

There are many contributing factors. For one, as a society, much time each day is spent with a screen, particularly a computer screen. Virtual worlds combine a sense of community and socialization to our screen time. They also enable "acting out" of fantasies, far-fetched and otherwise. In so doing, they build upon our imaginations and provide a more actionable form of daydreaming and computer-based entertainment. As we will discuss more below, virtual worlds provide a great deal of control over our in-world situation and environments starting with one's choices for the visual representation of one's avatar through the places we spend time, the visual construction of spaces in world, and our interactions there. Even our perception of self as we interact in world can be controlled in some cases in that perception of the environment can take place from the stance of first or third person. The context of a virtual world is rich with detail and encourages immersion by integrating sensory cues like depth, texture, sound, color, lighting, and movement.

In the best cases, the worlds feel like active, living communities with functional, experiential, and symbolic benefits. Functional benefits mean that participation in the world can serve some purpose in life such as being used to attend a distance education class, meeting with colleagues or clients who are geographically distant, or learning a skill through in-world simulation. Experiential benefits refer to the value of activity, of participation, of involvement in something that might be meaningful, memorable, or just plain fun. Symbolic benefits refer to the value of expressing ourselves, using the world and the way we construct that world (including the visual identities of avatars) as tools to express our thoughts, feelings, ideals, fears, and perceptions of self and the world around us. Before we delve into more on virtual-world branding, let's consider the relevance of the avatar in the virtual experience and the related brand opportunities.

■ Me, Myself, and I: Avatars as Self, a Virtual Dream Market

The phrase avatar refers to a god's physical manifestation on Earth. Now, the phrase also references one's digital self, a virtual alter ego. Virtual worlds offer an intoxicating amount of control to residents, and this sense of control and self-determination begins with the development of one's avatar. Virtual worlds typically offer a "stock" avatar to get new residents started, but customization of one's avatar is a cultural norm in virtual worlds. There is powerful normative pressure for new members, referred to as newbies, to develop a unique look for their avatars.

This cultural norm for avatar development creates a basis for marketing potential in world. Many of the brands we feature in this chapter serve, in world, as brand engagement tactics for real-life marketing objectives. Some, however, will seek out or simply leverage the trend of playing "dress up" with our avatars. These brands will offer hair styles, clothing, accessories like jewelry and electronic devices, cars, and even cosmetic enhancements for avatars. Internal product offerings may be linked to real-world products, too. Further, this market can easily grow as existing members create multiple renditions of their self-identities. Many residents in virtual worlds have more than one active avatar. Books like *Alter Egos: Avatars and their Creators* highlight the relationship between our "selves" and the avatars we create.[5] Individuals have actual selves that may or may not be reflected in their avatar, but many do develop avatars that are slightly more perfect representations of their real selves.[6] What does that mean for the avatars? Typically, avatars similar in visual identity to their real-life creators have physical augmentations. They might be taller, slimmer, more curvaceous. If the real-life individual is balding, the avatar may have a full head of hair. Overall, though, the visual identity is akin to that of the real person.

Others, however, develop entirely different visual identities for their avatars, switching genders or even delving into pure fantasy with a nonhuman identity. Residents do not even have to choose whether to augment or internalize their identity. Virtual worlds do not limit the number of avatars one can maintain, so there can be the like-me avatar, totally not-like-me avatar, fantasy avatar, dating avatar, working-stiff avatar, and so on. All of these avatar identities are likely to be constructed using products purchased or built within the virtual environment. Avatars are not limited by reality. They can be anything they choose to be. My personal favorite was a near-perfect rendition of Snoopy I met when visiting a virtual bank in Second Life. Truly, avatars can be anything from a rubber duck to a spoon, a giant, a couch, or something pretty human.

Further, avatars can have most anything they want to have. Even a luxury sports car that might be financially out of reach for the real person may be had for just a few dollars in the virtual world. The norms of status and hierarchy exist in virtual worlds, too. This suggests that even in virtual worlds, unrestricted by established norms, our accepted tools for promoting identity and status in the real world are brought to play in the virtual world. Brands, as a primary method of building and displaying identity and status, have the potential to thrive here.

In the article "Even in a Virtual World, 'Stuff' Matters," Shira Boss describes the fanaticism with which active avatars treat fashion and design and their enthusiasm for virtual material possessions.[7] Chronicling the consumption dreams and experiences of several Second Life residents, Boss makes it clear that the desire for status and popularity is prevalent in virtual life as well as in real life. Status symbols abound, but they are not necessarily real-life luxury brands like Hermes or Cartier.

Status symbols often reflect the design or programming complexity as in the case of virtual grunge clothing, difficult to create because of the programming required to offer ripped and stained attire. Second Life and other virtual worlds are built on a respect for aesthetics and style.

■ Marketing Potential In World

Consider again the view of virtual worlds as outlets for functional, experiential, and symbolic benefits. Companies have an opportunity to offer products in world that meet the functional needs of a target audience. For example, a Web-programming company could develop a line of virtual conference rooms to be leased by companies that periodically need virtual meeting and presentation space but do not wish to own and develop private conferencing facilities. There is more business promise in virtual worlds than just marketing and promotion. There are also training and education, communications (holding conference calls, conducting interviews with geographically dispersed job candidates), and more. For instance, Rivers Run Red, a marketing agency, uses a virtual facility in Second Life to meet with clients and partners around the world in real time.[8] Meeting in a virtual world saves time and travel expense.

Companies can also meet the experiential needs of consumers by offering brand-related experiences in world. This is a core tactic for leveraging the virtual environment for branding. Offering activities, games, concerts and events, and other interactive devices in a branded space serves to meet the consumers' experiential needs while reinforcing a brand's message. Lastly, brands can meet the symbolic needs of avatars and their real-life alter egos by providing merchandise with which identity can be constructed in world. All in all, the virtual world is filled with marketing opportunity.

■ The Vlobe

How can we categorize virtual worlds in a way that will help to simplify the branding opportunities that exist within this form of social-media marketing? There are several competitors in the field of virtual worlds already and, most assuredly, there will be more. As explained earlier, virtual worlds can be thought of as open or closed. They also tend to either target adults exclusively or children. The competitors in the kid-targeted virtual-world arena, though they meet the definition of a closed (or branded) virtual world, are so different from those targeting adults that they will be discussed in a separate chapter. Some "vertical" or category-specific worlds are beginning to emerge, like Football Superstores, which target people with a specific interest or hobby.

The open virtual worlds are hosted and managed by organizations whose mission is to provide an environment for members. An open world is branded (e.g., Second Life and There), but it is not exclusively sponsored financially by a consumer products brand as closed worlds are (e.g., MyCoke.com and Stagecoach Island). Brands that wish to market products (real or virtual) in world have a range of possible tactics available in open worlds. Closed worlds are developed, managed, and funded by a specific organization, and the offering is tied to the company's marketing objectives. For instance, Wells Fargo hosts Stagecoach Island, which is a virtual world open by registration at no cost to members, where residents can learn about personal finance and banking. Wells Fargo might selectively co-brand with other organizations, but it entirely controls what brands are affiliated with its world, if any. Because brands have more control over the environment, they narrowcast the offer to its target audience; also, given concerns for security, as well as the successes of closed worlds tied to toys targeted at children, we can expect to see an increase in the number of closed worlds.

▪ Virtual-Market Entry Strategies

Social-media marketers can benefit from the insights gained as businesses expand into new global markets. It is conceded that entering a new virtual world is considerably less risky than entering a new global market. There are fewer barriers to entry for companies to contend with when entering virtual markets than when entering new country markets, though barriers do exist. However, the methods companies can use for entry are similar. Companies can follow an exporting model, distributing products manufactured domestically to the market in question. Likewise, brands that wish to enter softly into virtual worlds may do so by offering branded virtual products through an in-world retailer. Exporting might also refer to companies that offer services and products for use in world without actually developing their own in-world presence. This is a possible entry strategy for services like those provided by Web developers, programmers, and marketing consultants. Companies may pursue internationalization through joint ventures and strategic alliances, and this is possible in virtual worlds, too. One example is Coke's Virtual Thirst campaign which was designed, hosted, and managed as part of an alliance with Coke's virtual ad agency, Crayon. For the most committed of brands, there is the wholly owned subsidiary. In virtual worlds, these are the brands that have bought land, designed and developed infrastructure, staffed their facilities, and continued to invest in developing the brand's business opportunities. Examples of brands following this vlobal market entry strategy include Reuters, Sony, Toyota, and Dell, among others. The most advanced point on this continuum is represented by virtual-world branding that is entirely developed for the brand in question. MTV's Virtual Laguna Beach exhibits this degree of commitment to virtual branding.

Each of these strategies can be thought of as residing along a continuum much like that proposed by S. Tamer Cavusgil in his Innovation-Related Internationalization Model, also known as international stage theory.[9] In that work, Cavusgil proposed that there are five stages to internationalization. Stage 1 is limited to conducting business in a domestic market with no international markets. Stage 2 is the pre-export stage. Stage 3 is export involvement. It is with stages 4 and 5, active involvement and committed involvement, respectively, that companies invest heavily with a commitment to endure in the international markets in question. Likewise, we can easily apply this commitment continuum to brand involvement in virtual worlds. There are those that do not, and will not, pursue social-media strategies, particularly strategies involving virtual worlds. There are those who are weighing their options and studying the landscape. There are those already working peripherally with virtual worlds and related others. And then there are brands that have invested in the market with land, builds, staff, exchange opportunities, and experience-driven benefits for avatars and their real-life alter egos.

Importantly, a brand can reach stage 5 and own and operate a wholly owned subsidiary in one world—if a single virtual world seems sufficiently profitable and appropriate. However, this is unlikely. For now, there are brands with a presence in one world, and most commonly that world is Second Life. But brands explore new international markets to generate new demand for its product, leverage assets that are applicable across borders and cultures, and gain access to scarce resources. Brands benefit further by identifying several such markets. In that same spirit, brands with an entry in one virtual world are likely to develop facilities in others.

■ Virtual Worlds

There are many players in the arena of virtual worlds. The Virtual Worlds Review Web site (www.virtualworldsreview.com) lists many virtual worlds, categorized by the primary target audience of the world.

It is clear that this is already a highly competitive landscape with numerous offerings for multiple target audiences. The field is ripe for consolidation or some form of integration given that participants may want portability that makes it easy to participate in multiple worlds. New worlds are also likely as organizations continue to learn of the benefits of virtual environments. Sun Microsystems will surely play a role in the growth of virtual environments for business and personal use. Its Project Wonderland initiative enables organizations to build their own 3D virtual worlds. Its Web site explains that the mission of Project Wonderland is extensibility noting, "Developers and graphic artists can extend the functionality to create entire new worlds, new features in existing worlds, or new behaviors for objects and avatars. The art path for Wonderland is also open. The eventual goal is to support content creation within the world, but in the shorter term, the goal is to support importing art from open source 3D content creation tools as well as professional 3D modeling and animation applications."[10] Sun Microsystems seeks to provide organizations using its tools a virtual world that is secure, scalable, reliable, and functional. Aside from the degree of innovation and technological superiority offered by Sun's tools, why is this considered a revolutionary project in the realm of virtual worlds? Project Wonderland is an open source, and free.

There are many developed virtual worlds, too many to highlight individually here, although there are two featured in this chapter: Second Life and MTV's Worlds.

Second Life

A virtual world launched in 2003 and hosted by Linden Labs (but developed by residents), Second Life is the most recognized of all virtual worlds. A Google search of "Second Life" results in more than 75 million hits! Stories about Second Life have graced the covers of *BusinessWeek* and *Inc.* magazines with features in other major media outlets, including the *New York Times, Financial Times,* and *Wired* among others. Basic membership is free, but there is also a premium membership. Second Life has a thriving economy with its own currency of exchange (Linden dollars). Linden Labs does not sell products or buildings in world, but it does offer "land" space. All residents have the tools available to create places and things, and this has resulted in a culture of user-generated innovation. Not all residents have the time or skills to design and create, which has fed demand. Entrepreneurs fostered a consumer culture, offering most anything that can be bought and sold in real life, from custom buildings and facilities to transportation devices to services to manufactured (virtual) consumer goods.

It is by far the largest world in terms of total population. It boasts just shy of 12,000,000 residents as this is written. This figure is inflated because many users have multiple avatars. Second Life's State of the Virtual World Key Metrics site estimates that 63% of its total population are unique users (currently about 7.5 million). The total population figure also includes avatars that were created (presumably out of curiosity) and since abandoned. Second Life's statistics count those with more than forty logged hours as active; 10% of its unique users. Thus, while the 12 million sounds impressive, the market of Second Life is more like 750,000. All worlds do suffer from attrition, but given the prevalence of Second Life in the media and its name recognition, the rate of attrition in Second Life is probably above that for other worlds. Branding in Second Life features prominently in this chapter.

It is not hard to understand why brands would be interested in Second Life. Its sheer size warrants attention, and it has received enormous media attention ranging from mainstream media to blog postings (at one point, Second Life was averaging 175 blog post mentions a day). Linden Labs does not restrict organizational activity in world, and there are no fees for organizations to be there, other than the fees associated with the purchase or rent of land. There is a segment of residents who are actively engaged in the site, with frequent and relatively long visits, suggesting that there is a substantial, measurable, reachable market in world. In addition to the age-old practice of marketing to people where they are, Second Life also plays host to a materialistic set of avatars with a zest for branded virtual goods. For example, residents can travel anywhere in Second Life by flight, arriving instantaneously at another geographic location. Yet, many residents do own cars. Toyota, Mercedes, and Pontiac have responded to the avatar need for virtual transportation. Likewise, residents do not need to sleep in Second Life, and so presumably do not need shelter. Still, many residents own property and have built lavish homes. Avatars do not need food to sustain themselves, yet there are popular restaurants in world so busy that reservations must be made far in advance.

Virtual worlds offer many business opportunities, and nowhere is this more clear than in Second Life. These opportunities include sales, brand engagement, market research, publicity generation, and facility utilization and management. Market Truths, a Second Life–based market research firm, developed a Second Life Brand Impact Metric to quantify the value of brand presence in Second Life.[11] The metric encompasses two key variables: the number of people who are aware of the brand's

Second Life activities and the influence of the Second Life presence on overall brand attitudes. The company concludes that most brands have benefited from Second Life involvement but the brands that benefit most are those that make the brand relevant to the Second Life community. How can brands enhance relevance? Brands do this by matching marketing strategy to virtual-world culture, offering interactivity, and providing customization options. For example, Toyota not only sells virtual Scions in Second Life—and the Scion is customizable—but even teaches residents how to "pimp their virtual rides."

How Are Brands Utilizing the Second Life World?

Second Life features both business-to-consumer brands and business-to-business brands. Bartle, Bogle, and Hegarty (BB&H) staffs a virtual advertising agency, realizing that, to include metaverse campaign components in client campaigns, it needs to truly understand the space and the behavior of residents. BB&H developed a Second Life brand presence for a client, Vodaphone. *Marketing Week* reported that BB&H developed an interactive island for Vodaphone.[12] Visitors to the island can become immersed in the brand experience by participating in "intense sensory experiences such as butterfly flights and a sound garden." Vodaphone's Second Life strategy is consistent with its real-life brand strategy: "Make the most of now." In a truly inspired example of linking innovative brand placements like this one with other brand touch points, Vodaphone offers virtual mobile phones, which Second Life residents can use to call each other but which can also reach contacts outside Second Life.

Others are pursuing the metaverse from a sales channel approach. This is the case with Dell, which not only offers engagement devices but also provides a direct sales link for real-world computers. Dell has developed a virtual personal computer factory in Second Life. Residents can buy virtual and real versions and arrange for the real computer to be shipped to the workplace or home. Visitors can tour the interior of a virtual computer as well as the factory. Importantly, Dell maximized relevance by offering avatars lessons on how to better operate their avatars. In so doing, Dell transferred one of the primary principles of sponsorship marketing to its social-media marketing strategy. When a brand offers something of value and relevance to people, they are more receptive to the brand message.

Businesses are using virtual space as conference facilities. Employee avatars can meet at a virtual conference table, while their human life forms type in chat conversation from physical office locations dispersed around the globe. Crowne Plaza offers free conference space to those who need in-world meeting space. Some media exist in world, like the newspaper for Second Life residents called "The AvaStar" developed and sold by Bild. T-Online, the largest entertainment portal in Europe.[13]

Starwood Hotels opened a hotel, Aloft, in Second Life. The hotel chain used the virtual construction and experience to gather consumer feedback for use in designing the real-world version of Aloft.[14] While Starwood was motivated primarily by a quest for consumer insight, its brand managers surely hoped that residents who visited the hotel in Second Life would be drawn to experience the hotel in the real world. The use of the world as a feedback and product development tool was an inspiration, but apparently the Second Life investment did not accomplish Starwood's marketing objectives. Recent reports indicate that the Aloft hotel will be closed and Starwood will no longer participate in Second Life.

The Coca-Cola Company was one of the early entrants in the virtual-world arena, offering MyCoke.com, a branded virtual world, years ago. MyCoke.com still exists (and reportedly boasts about the same number of registered users as Second Life) but has since developed a partnership for a virtual space within There.[15] This space is known as CC Metro. Coke utilized a cross-world strategy with a Virtual Thirst campaign in Second Life. Coke's alliance with There suggests a continued commitment to social-media marketing in virtual space, but it highlights the negative business experiences found in Second Life. Walt Disney is another early Second Life brand, which has gone on to focus on its own universe of virtual worlds, tailored to Disney properties. Wells Fargo set up the first Stagecoach Island within Second Life. Later it closed its Second Life island and developed its own virtual world, which is also named Stagecoach Island.

It was not long ago that Pontiac would have been hailed as an example of great branding in Second Life. One of the earliest big brands to commit to virtual-world promotion, Pontiac offered a customizable Solstice model for avatars (at a very affordable price). The campaign sought to aid in the launch of the new Solstice and to find a creative, tech-savvy way to position the Solstice as an affordable sports car with speeds akin to those of a Porsche. As the campaign developed, Pontiac dreamed of creating an entire "car culture" in Second Life by introducing car clothing, auto mechanic shops, drive-in theaters, and other car-enthusiast amenities.[16]

Prima facie, Pontiac seemed the perfect brand to fully examine Second Life's branding potential. Pontiac is one of a few brands on the forefront of social-media marketing, having also developed its own social-networking site, Pontiac Underground. In Second Life, like its other social-networking executions, Pontiac sought to reach a more youthful yet affluent market than it has traditionally.[17] Motorati Island, as it was known, resided on 96 acres of "land" in world. Pontiac challenged residents to a contest centered around its goal of developing a car culture. It offered free land for small businesses that contributed to Motorati Island's car culture. Early bets on Pontiac's success or failure tilted to Pontiac's favor. At the time the brand entered Second Life, $6 million in exchanges took place every month. Pontiac sold over 1,200 virtual Solstices (earning a revenue of about $3,000), won more than 30,000 unique visitors to Motorati Island, and many of those visitors returned.[18] There was no device in place to track real-world sales of the Solstice to the Second Life campaign, but measuring direct response is not what social-media marketing is about. The brand closed Motorati Island on December 31, 2007.

Why? It could be as innocuous as a planned end to the Solstice online campaign. Or it is possible that Pontiac simply decided that other online tactics offered a better return on investment. Second Life was not Pontiac's only social-media marketing tactic. As noted, it hosts a popular branded social-networking site. It has also used tie-ins to other products, including the recent Halo 3 game and online events, reportedly increasing traffic to the Pontiac Web site by 20% and to the Pontiac G6 site by 55%.[19] But, despite claims of Pontiac's success, Pontiac may have suffered a common fate in world. Was Motorati Island a virtual ghost town? The phenomenon of islands as ghost towns is ubiquitous in world.

No matter that Motorati Island is no more, Pontiac offers a case study of what's possible in world. Aside from sales objectives, branding in Second Life is a means of differentiating a brand from other less-innovative brands. Pontiac used Second Life and its other online advertising tactics to point to its differential advantage and build its brand image in the minds of its target audience. It also generated enormous media impressions for the minimal amount it cost to launch and manage its in-world campaign.

How Can Brands Optimize Their Marketing Efforts in Second Life and Other Virtual Worlds?

As noted, brands need to offer an engaging, innovative opportunity for brand-consumer interaction. The offer should be relevant. The brand's event and/or facilities should be well staffed and responsive. In addition to those best practices, brands need to think about how consumers find the brand in the context of the virtual world. Just as Web users will turn to search engines to find Web sites of interest, virtual-world residents will use the search function in world to find branded locations. Thus, there is a need for virtual-world optimization, which mirrors the goals of SEO for virtual worlds. SEO is the process of improving the volume and quality of traffic to a Web site from search engines like Google and Yahoo! through organic (those that are not purchased) search results for targeted key words.

The white paper "The Virtual Brand Footprint," written jointly by DMD, Combined Story, and Market Truths, identifies several tips for virtual-world optimization.[20] These tips include the use of title tags, the addition of key-word descriptors, the use of link optimization strategies, and advertising on in-world ad networks. To make good use of title tags, the title of the virtual location should include important key words. For example, the WWF's Conservation Island could be named WWF's Green Training Ground. The idea is to offer a title in the search listings that will allow the location to get a search ranking even if the brand name is not mentioned. Toyota's site might be labeled Toyota Scion custom cars so that searches for cars result in a link to Toyota's in-world location. Key-word descriptors act like descriptions and meta tags for Web sites. If American Apparel's store in Second Life includes a description like "clothing for young, hip avatars specializing in jeans, jackets, and t-shirts," then a search for jeans will include the American Apparel site. Link optimization in world means offering transport options directly to other sites, possibly affiliate sites or co-branded sites. Of course, traditional advertising in world, primarily limited to virtual billboard space, can also promote site traffic.

What Are the Limitations of Second Life for Businesses?

Some brands, like Pontiac, seek to differentiate themselves, and some are simply exploring the possibilities. Many of the brands brave enough to enter are leaving. Those yet to act are wondering whether to consider social-media marketing in virtual worlds. There are definitely reasons to be in this space. There are also reasons to forgo virtual-world promotions or to limit those promotions to worlds with high levels of control and other desirable commercial benefits.

Second Life has its benefits and drawbacks, and other worlds share some but not all of them. Consider some of the reasons, despite the potential for marketing, Second Life specifically may not be the right channel for your brand's social-media marketing strategy.

- Second Life is complex and user unfriendly. *Time* magazine called it a case of Fortune 500 companies' trying too hard to be hip. A recent report from

Forrester suggests that marketing in virtual worlds is still too complex for broad adoption as a business strategy but that this is likely to change in the next five years. Complexity is an issue, not only from the marketer's perspective but also from the consumer perspective. Complexity is one of the primary characteristics that can slow the rate of adoption for innovations. Some virtual worlds are easier to learn than others; Second Life is likely the most difficult to learn.

- Second Life, and some other virtual worlds, requires users to install its software. Software installation could be a deterrent to growth beyond the innovators and early adopters already a part of the virtual-world phenomenon.

- Second Life does not have the reach that other online advertising venues garner. Despite the claim of millions of residents (with continual growth), under a million are active and engaged.

- Residents are known to dislike and distrust big brand promotion. "Griefing," vandalizing and harassing in world, is a common problem for brands. Linden Labs takes a hands-off approach to managing griefer attacks, relying instead on resident governance. How bad is the griefing? A helicopter crashed into a Nissan building, starting a fire that left a couple of dead bodies, and American Apparel customers were attacked by members of the Second Life Liberation Army who were armed with virtual guns.

- Related to the above, Second Life offers publicity and the value of free media impressions as social and other media cover new developments. However, when the media report attacks on customers, the publicity does not build brand equity.

- Aside from the security from griefers, Second Life has struggled to provide security to the real-life people behind the avatars. In 2006, hackers obtained credit card information for some residents.

- Second Life's infrastructure limits the capacity at some events. Your brand might do a phenomenal job of planning and executing a relevant brand experience with an outpouring of enthusiasm only to find the system crashes when more than seventy avatars are present at a time.

- Of course, you will only have the problem of too many people at an event if things go very well. Spend some time walking or flying around Second Life. It is filled with exquisitely detailed representations of real and fantasy locations. Yet, seeing other avatars is rare, unless one is spending time earning free Linden dollars (the currency of Second Life) at Money Island.

- Some brands have sold digital versions of their products. Toyota, Reebok, Adidas, and Dell are all examples. No brand has yet announced success at using the in-world branding site as a direct response tool for real-world sales. Bob Tedeschi, in his article entitled "Awaiting Real Sales from Virtual Shoppers," explains that brands experience little measurable influence on real-world sales that can be tracked to virtual branding efforts.[21]

- There are still a limited number of media outlets and advertising opportunities (beyond supporting retail space, experiential facilities, and events). NPR and Reuters are there, along with the AvaStar newspaper, but for brands accustomed to buying ad space in hundreds of television networks, consumer and trade magazines, and national, regional, and local newspapers, this is not a rich media landscape. Ad inventory will develop over time. A "MetaAdverse" network has been established to provide in-world billboard advertising.[22]

- It is difficult to gain economies of scale in branding initiatives. One cannot lower the average costs of products by making mass amounts of products and there are no huge media buys to lower the costs of advertising.

- There are expenses to brand building in Second Life. Linden Labs sells land and then requires ongoing maintenance fees. Those are minimal compared to the design expenses brands encounter. Alex Veiga points out that brand building requires artists, designers, writers, and marketers to develop all aspects of the brand's identity in Second Life.[23] Scion City, a Toyota initiative, took about ten weeks and probably cost about $100,000. Importantly, brands that enter Second Life must be committed to operating there. It does no good (and in fact could harm a brand) to have a presence there that is not manned, managed, and leveraged toward accomplishing the brand's objectives.

In open worlds, economies are free markets. Brands are welcome to compete, and the spoils go to the brands with the best strategy, the best targeting, and the best engagement propositions for their target audiences (mindful, of course, to ensure the strategy is suitable for the virtual culture in question). The brands with the wherewithal to strategically plan a social-media marketing campaign will also know that they must commit to the campaign and provide ample time for the strategy to work prior to making judgments of success or failure and redirecting resources to other marketing executions.

MTV's Virtual Worlds

Second Life is a behemoth among virtual worlds, but much can be learned from one of the closed virtual worlds, MTV's Virtual Worlds. In fact, MTV's offering is not so much a single world as its own universe of individual worlds, each one tied to an MTV program. MTV's Virtual Worlds include the following unique worlds: Virtual Laguna Beach (the first venture), The Virtual Hills, Virtual Kaya, The Virtual Real World, Virtual Newport Harbor, Virtual Pimp My Ride, and Virtual Skate Park. There is even an avatar model search, sponsored by Mariah Carey and the Ford model agency, and a virtual MTV video music awards. MTV began its foray into virtual-world branding with Second Life but recognized the value of maintaining total control over its brand and its fan interaction. Consequently, MTV created a virtual world for its popular program, Laguna Beach. Since then it has developed virtual worlds for several of its programs, as noted above. Daniel Terdiman, a staff writer for CNET News.com, explains that MTV is pursuing a cross-platform strategy, known at MTV as "4D."[24] The concept focuses on overlapping content from the television programs with the 3D experiences possible in virtual worlds.

MTV's concept benefits from consumer interest in celebrities and their lifestyles. In the MTV virtual worlds, members can interact with the program's characters, celebrity avatars, and even experience virtually the life of a celebrity. Virtual Laguna Beach boasted impressive registration figures within one month of launch, and registrations have continued at a quick clip. MTV's Virtual Worlds offers two enormous branding benefits for the MTV brand and the specific branded programs featured in the worlds. First, the world is filled with branded content. The MTV brand and the specific program brand are ubiquitous in world. Second, the nature of the interaction ensures that participants are engaged in the brand message throughout each and every visit. A virtual Laguna Beach in Second Life would be wasted on many residents who would not fit the target audience for the program. Even for those who do fit the target, MTV would face the challenge of making the residents aware of the site in world and encouraging visits and brand interaction. Whether in an open world or in its own closed world, MTV must develop and maintain virtual facilities and programming so the challenges across worlds are quite similar for resources required. By developing and managing its own worlds, MTV maintains control over the brand message, prevents potential equity damage from associations with other brands, and benefits from the collection of user data.

MTV made an impressive strategic move by developing its own series of worlds. That is not all the company did well. It also created numerous benefits that result in high levels of involvement, stickiness (a site is sticky when site content results in an increase in the length of time spent per visit), and return visits among its user base. What did MTV do? Membership is free, but premium memberships can be had for a fee. This makes the world easily accessible while still producing revenue. The sites offer many features important to those who interact with social media: personal profiles, avatar representation, shopping, member groups, video, and music. The worlds feast on celebrity interest by bringing cast members to life as avatars. Cast avatars interact with viewer avatars, appealing to those who dream of meeting a favored celebrity. It recognized that while there is some duplication in the viewership for its shows, there are also viewers who watch only a specific show or a specific set of shows, but not all shows. For this reason, MTV's Worlds include specific worlds geared for its most popular shows. To accommodate those who do view multiple shows, avatars can teleport from world to world with a single click. If an avatar is participating in Virtual Laguna Beach but then wants to visit a location in Virtual Hills, teleporting is as simple as it would be to stay in a single world. The worlds feature virtual locations that mirror those on the television shows. Residents can do all the things in an MTV world as in other virtual worlds.

Wired magazine, reporting on the launch of the first MTV world, noted that MTV needed a strategy to rejuvenate its position as a cutting-edge entertainment property.[25] Registration figures suggest that its target audience is responsive to the offering. Within one month, MTV's Virtual Laguna Beach had more unique users than Second Life did in its first three years! Further, the award of an Emmy suggests MTV is doing just that. "Virtual Laguna Beach" virtual world won the National Academy of Television Arts & Sciences' Technology & Engineering Emmy Award for Outstanding Achievement in Advanced Media Technology for Creation of Nontraditional Programs or Platforms. It is the first major entertainment company to earn an Emmy for a virtual property.[26]

Clearly, MTV has designed a series of worlds with great appeal to its core target audience for each show. The design, interactivity, and relevance all add to MTV's success in developing virtual worlds that are effective brand engagement devices. Importantly, MTV also incorporated other components that make its virtual worlds revenue generating or, at a minimum, a good return on investment. Richard Siklos, author of the *New York Times* article entitled "Not in the Real World Anymore," pointed out that MTV wisely aligned advertising into its virtual-world model.[27]

As in Second Life, avatars in Virtual Laguna Beach crave fashionable attire and other virtual products. They can earn the currency for these consumer wants by watching an infomercial in world. Avatars can also purchase real-world versions of the digital products they buy. Finally, even though MTV is a closed world created to maintain brand control, MTV hosts relationships with other brands. Current brand partners include Pepsi, Secret, and Paramount Pictures. These partner relationships provide a source of revenue and enable the brand to plan events and activities that can benefit from the expertise associated with other brand messages. For example, Secret invited Laguna Beach users to submit "secrets" in a co-branded contest. This is an ideal example of co-branding in a closed world. The campaign was interactive and intriguing. The activity matched the image of the show, Laguna Beach, and that of the virtual world—a space where secrets are prevalent. It encouraged participation and linked well to the sponsoring product's brand name—Secret. Closed worlds solve many of the problems associated with virtual worlds like Second Life while maintaining a high degree of flexibility.

■ Branding in Virtual Worlds: Final Thoughts

Brands considering either a closed or an open virtual world for branding should first consider these questions:

- Does the virtual world of interest offer access to a primary target audience and a branding opportunity not available elsewhere?
- How will the virtual campaign contribute to accomplishing real-world marketing objectives?
- What is the competition doing?
- Can the brand commit for the long term?
- How can the brand make itself relevant in the virtual worlds in which it chooses to participate?
- How can, and how will, success be measured?

Answering these questions will enable brand managers to ensure that virtual-world marketing is the right approach for the brand.

Social-media marketing is still early in its development cycle. Social virtual worlds as branding opportunities are even newer. This chapter reveals some of the possibilities for brands in virtual environments and also warns of the limitations and challenges. Brands, at a minimum, can establish a social-media presence to differentiate themselves and to reach consumers in yet another environment. What is yet to be seen is whether brands can use these platforms to truly engage consumers on a wide-scale basis. Participation in social virtual worlds has not yet reached the "tipping point" for consumer involvement. In any case, it will be interesting to see how brands will initiate a digital dialogue with consumers using these innovative environments.

5 ▪ ▪ ▪

From Moments to Minutes
Advertising with Social Play

Virtual worlds are a rapidly growing social-media platform, and this is particularly true for kids. Thought of by many as 3D renditions of 2D social networks, virtual worlds supply many desirable features for the youth market still unavailable in the realm of social networks. Among these are a sense of immediacy, unparalleled media richness, and the heightened interactivity possible in the virtual space. Young consumers respond to the immediacy of communications, meaning that communications occur in real time (while social networks still primarily provide asynchronous response). Real-time response adds to the sense of contact comfort participants feel. Media richness is embellished with the enhanced visual representations of virtual worlds as well as the ability to chat using instant messenger, electronic mail, and sometimes voice chat features. Lastly, social networks like MySpace are limited in what can be offered for participants in terms of entertaining and interactive pursuits within the space. It is no wonder then that young consumers are enamored with virtual worlds. eMarketer estimates that 24% of the 34.3 million child and teen Internet users in the United States used virtual worlds on at least a monthly basis in 2007 and this figure is expected to rise rapidly over the short term.[1]

For marketers, social virtual worlds represent an enormous opportunity for branding by extending the time consumers spend with a brand's message from moments to minutes. Indeed, the average amount of time spent per session in social virtual worlds ranges from as little as twenty minutes to more than two hours—substantially more than the typical thirty seconds of attention garnered by a television commercial. This advantage accrues simply from the time spent with the message. In addition to increases in the time spent elaborating on a message, there is added value in brand-consumer interaction. Nowhere is this level of interaction more possible than within the confines of a social virtual world. Reuben Steiger, CEO of Millions of Us, acknowledges the importance of brand-consumer interaction when he notes that the most successful advertising approaches in these kid-targeted virtual worlds will be those that use participation programs to enhance a child's experience in the space, rather than intruding the way typical television advertising might.[2] In this chapter, we'll explore the types of virtual worlds targeting children and the possible revenue models, identify reasons for the growth of this platform among a younger demographic, and consider the challenges and best practices for advertising to young consumers using this platform.

■ Marketing and Revenue Modes for Youth-Oriented Virtual Worlds

Youth-oriented virtual worlds can be classified using several categories, from the specific youth age group targeted, the world's purpose, or the degree of branding exclusivity to the world's revenue model. Worlds do tend to target first on specific age group. Gaia Online, for example, targets 13- to 18-year-olds, while Disney's Pirates of the Caribbean targets those ten years and older. Webkinz and Nicktropolis target kids aged seven to fourteen. MyePets.com, another Webkinz imitator, seeks an even younger audience of 4- to 7-year-olds. Like adult-targeted virtual worlds, virtual worlds for kids can be categorized as open, meaning that the site is not affiliated with an exclusive, sponsoring brand, or closed, meaning that the site is exclusively branded. The open-world model is more common for adult-targeted sites, while closed worlds are more heavily utilized when targeting children. Whyville and Doppelganger are examples of open, youth-targeted sites; Webkinz is a premier example of a closed world. In both cases, opportunities for branding and advertising exist for nonaffiliated brands, but in Webkinz (and other similarly branded worlds) the underlying mission of the site is to foster involvement with and drive sales for its own brand.

The worlds also vary based on the purpose they purport to serve for their members. The primary offerings promoted thus far include "play" with a focus on toys, entertainment, and education (or edutainment). The "play" offer is the most prevalent thus far with many worlds affiliated with a toy, stuffed animal, or product of some sort. Be-Bratz offers a line of dolls sold with a pink, pet mouse and a flash drive that links to the Bratz virtual world. BarbieGirls.com is bundled as part of a BarbieGirls doll-shaped MP3 player which links to the site and provides access to free features like clothes and other virtual goodies.

The virtual-world marketing approach is especially appealing to media companies, offering entertainment value to the target market, which can leverage the platform to build interest in a media franchise and loyalty to franchise-related products. A media franchise is a set or series of components based on an original work, generally fiction, such as film, literature, television programming, or video game, involving a story, characters, and setting. The franchise may include multiple install-ments of the story as well as the merchandising of related products and endorsements. The Matrix franchise is a great example of the power of media franchising, with multiple films, branded video games, merchan-dise, online sites, and more. The media franchise is at its core a brand, and the more valuable the franchise, the more valuable the brand's equity. Past successes lead to future successes for new components of the fran-chise. Consequently, media companies recognize that there is great opportunity for building media franchise value by building virtual-world portfolios. Involvement in the world heightens involvement in the franchise, breeding future success. What's more, this approach can be among the most efficient techniques. The cost to launch a world might run, for a company like Disney, $5–10 million. But its maintenance costs once launched are miniscule. Thus, Disney is pursuing a virtual-world portfolio strategy, which is useful for matching themes to its entertain-ment properties and for matching activities to specific age groups. Its Pirates of the Caribbean world will be complemented by other worlds themed for Cars and Tinker Bell among others. Ultimately, every fran-chise in Disney's portfolio could have a corresponding virtual world. Preschool children can begin with Pixie Hollow, move on to Club Penguin and then Cars, and graduate to Pirates of the Caribbean. Warner Brothers plans a similar strategy with worlds for Looney Tunes, Hanna-Barbera, and DC Comics. Entertainment companies view the popularity of virtual worlds as a new entry into the minds of children. Once upon a time, these companies would have turned to Saturday morning cartoons, but the pro-liferation of the Internet results in a need to rethink the best way to reach young consumers. Whyville is a leader in the realm of edutainment, offering social networking in an immersive, virtual environment with opportunities for members to learn about and identify methods of response to pressing environmental issues like the effects of viral diseases in dense populations.

These worlds also vary based on revenue model. There are four possible business models: (1) the product tie-in model, (2) the fee-based model, (3) the ad-supported model, and (4) the hybrid model. Some worlds, the worlds emphasizing "play," are funded with product tie-ins (especially stuffed animals). Webkinz, Neopets, BarbieGirls, and many more have found initial success using the product tie-in model. Many worlds have sought to imitate the success of Webkinz by offering stuffed animals or other toys. A related revenue source is the sale of virtual goods for members.

The fee-based model is primarily marketed as the non-advertising model with the worlds emphasizing their "no-ad environment" as a selling point for parents. Nickelodeon's Nicktropolis promises no advertising as does Disney's Club Penguin. Club Penguin earns revenue from subscriptions ($5.95 per month) and merchandising Club Penguin clothing. Based on Club Penguin's membership figures, the subscription fees would result in revenues of more than $50 million per year.

Whyville and Gaia Online follow an advertising revenue model but emphasize that branded events or sponsorships perform better for brands than do display advertising. Toyota Scion has been applauded for its promotion, in both Gaia Online and Whyville, which offered virtual Scions to participants. This promotion was successful in terms of direct participation (with thousands of virtual Scions given away) in the promotion and generation of in world buzz and chatter about the virtual Scions. The children participating in these promotions are not old enough to drive yet, but Toyota recognizes that it has an opportunity to build a relationship with them now and maintain that relationship until they reach driving age. This tactic is not uncommon; it is known as "growing a consumer." Toyota's use of the Scion promotion is a great example, but in-world sponsorships are not always commercially focused. Whyville designed a simulated ecological catastrophe to promote the children's version of Al Gore's book, *An Inconvenient Truth*. Whyvillians are encouraged to identify ways to deal with environmental issues like tropical storm damage.

Webkinz serves as a good example of a well-developed business model for virtual worlds. Members are introduced to the Webkinz World through the purchase or gift of a Webkinz stuffed animal. The plush animals come with a code for membership in the Webkinz World, an online play area for members complete with its own economy and currency (KinzCash). Once in world, the stuffed animal is transformed into a virtual pet. Kids are taken through an adoption process through which they name the pet and learn about the Webkinz World. There, members care and provide for these virtual versions of their stuffed animals by building rooms to their pet's homes, decorating the homes with furniture and accessories, buying food, clothes, and toys for the virtual pet, and more. Members pay for these purchases with KinzCash which can be earned by adopting new pets or buying accessories like lip gloss, trading cards, and backpacks, playing games on the site, answering educational questions, and participating in a range of Webkinz World activities. The need to continue earning and spending KinzCash is the critical motivator to ongoing and lengthy visits to the site. Webkinz offers a premium level for enhanced tools for a fee and also sells advertising space in the form of display advertising occasionally on the site. Finally, Webkinz access codes expire after one year, requiring kids to purchase additional toys (ensuring that there is an ongoing source of revenue) if they want to continue playing in world. Thus, the Webkinz revenue model is primarily focused on the product tie-in, but there is a hybrid component in that additional revenue is generated from fees and advertising.

■ The Growth of Youth-Targeted Virtual Worlds

Virtual worlds targeting the underage demographic are definitely in a growth stage. There are few barriers to entry in this market. New entrants in the youth-targeted virtual-world arena are being devised and created and participation across the board continues to increase. Despite Second Life's position as the media darling of social virtual worlds, virtual worlds targeting the youth market far outpace Second Life and other adult-targeted worlds in terms of traffic. In fact, the top ten virtual-world sites all target kids and all trounce Second Life on traffic statistics. According to eMarketer, Webkinz, BarbieGirls, and Club Penguin all boast users upward of 5 million each.[3]

Why are these youth-targeted worlds so magnetic? We typically think of advertising and other forms of marketing communication as a device for informing or persuading consumers of the availability of a specific product that can meet a need they have. In the case of virtual worlds (and also social networks), the device itself meets the need of consumers—a need for social interaction.

Jim Bower, CEO of Whyville, makes this point saying, "It turns out there is a significant difference between the way adults use Second Life and other social-networking sites and the way that kids use Whyville—Whyville isn't their second life, it is their first life."[4] According to Bower, the majority of Whyvillian interactions are with real-world school friends or with distant relatives. While adult social worlds meet other needs, including esteem needs (to be something other than one's actual self, to acquire a degree of status unattainable in the real world, and to meet new people), kid-focused social worlds enhance the ability of the children to interact with the same people they would communicate with anyway. The world simply acts as a different, albeit immersive, visually stimulating, and sometimes goal-oriented, channel.

Some of these worlds, particularly Webkinz, have taken on fad status much like that of Beanie Babies in years past. Webkinz differentiates itself from others with its plush and cuddly stuffed animals and certainly benefits from a first-mover advantage, being an early entrant in the toy-tie-in virtual-world model. But more so than its distinctiveness or first-mover advantage, Webkinz and other top kid-oriented worlds meet specific criteria that make them go-to sites for their target markets. These criteria include relative advantage, simplicity, trialability, and observability. These factors help to explain the rapid growth of social virtual worlds for children.

First, these sites offer some relative advantage over other virtual worlds, social networks, and even other forms of entertainment like television programming. Matthew Nelson of ClickZ points out that youth-targeted virtual worlds offer parents a relative advantage by offering virtual worlds with controls and protections for children in place.[5] For the children, the relative advantage depends upon the perspective. Virtual worlds are more interactive than television and more immersive than social networks. Within the virtual-world arena, different worlds offer a relative advantage by focusing on toy tie-ins (e.g., Webkinz and Neopets), entertainment (e.g., Disney's Pixie Hollow), or edutainment (e.g., Whyville). Second, the sites are simple to use. Most worlds do not require (Doppelganger is an exception) special software to be downloaded from the virtual world to make the world compatible with the user's computer hardware and software. Tutorials are available to encourage new participants to feel comfortable interacting as quickly as possible. Third, the worlds offer trialability for both parents and their children. This means that people interested in the site, trying to understand how it functions, can take a tour to explore prior to committing to a membership. Frequently Asked Questions pages are generally available for parents to alleviate concerns about their child's interactions. Some sites have affiliated message boards for parents to ask questions of each other, which also enhances the perception that they are able to try the world before making a commitment to membership. Fourth, and most importantly, the popular kid-targeted virtual worlds have harnessed the influence of observability. That is, worlds like Webkinz, Club Penguin, and Stardoll benefit from the "networking effect."

As membership in the world grows, the value to members increases. The greater the number of people involved in the world, the more likely it is that a new member will have friends in the world. There is more social proof that the world in question is a good place to be in, as a member. Social proof is an influential tool for persuasion that occurs when a person uses the choices of others as evidence of how he or she should also behave. The more members affiliated with a virtual world, the bigger the buzz about participating in that world, and the more the social proof for participation. The world is increasingly observable in that members are likely to talk about their in-world activities at school or on the telephone as a part of their real-world social interactions. These characteristics—relative advantage, simplicity, trialability, and observability—explain the success of kid-targeted virtual worlds.

There is one characteristic that has thus far limited these worlds, with the exception of MTV's Worlds: compatibility. The extent of duplication in the membership of these youth-targeted virtual worlds is unclear, but anecdotal evidence suggests that many virtually active kids participate in more than one world. It may seem wise to create perceived investment and switching costs for participants to inhibit their interest in other social environments. However, members will appreciate having the benefit of portability for their avatars and profiles. MTV's Worlds promote portability across worlds (at least within the MTV portfolio), allowing members to shift from world to world and communicate across worlds to friends without shifts in virtual location. Google's OpenSocial project seeks to offer portability for social-networking sites; hopefully, similar progress will be forthcoming for virtual-world environments, too.

■ Challenges Facing Youth-Oriented Virtual Worlds

Social virtual worlds offer young people many opportunities for entertainment, socializing, communicating, and learning. For these reasons, they have largely been embraced by parents and teachers who recognize the potential benefits. For example, Todd Copilevitz, commenting on his daughter's enthusiasm for Webkinz, writes, "My daughter is now scheming ways to afford her next Webkinz, #17 if I'm not mistaken. Each has an online counterpart that has friends, a home, a mortgage, and rich world of imagination. That's something the PowerRangers never managed to deliver."[6] Still, these worlds have also come under criticism for promoting consumerism, materialism, and an artificial version of reality. Could the slogan for BarbieGirls.com be a line from Madonna's *Material Girl*?

Virtual worlds walk a fine line in this regard. They cannot exist without revenues to support the costs of developing and maintaining the sites. Admittedly, many if not all were created for marketing purposes. Stephanie Olsen, staff writer for CNET News.com, reports that executives at companies like Whyville and Gaia Online understand the unprecedented opportunity to market to children in an engaging and immersive fashion using virtual-world platforms but that they also acknowledge there are minimal standards in place to protect children.[7] Kathryn Montgomery, author of *Generation Digital: Politics, Commerce, and Childhood in the Age of the Internet*, explains that digital marketing taps into the developmental needs of young people.[8] By blurring the lines between content of interest to young consumers and product marketing, brands are able to reach young consumers with high levels of motivation to elaborate and act on the brand's message. The only regulation in place to protect children online is the Children's Online Privacy Protection Act of 1998. This legislation requires Web sites targeting children under the age of 13 to post a detailed privacy policy and obtain parental permission prior to collecting any personal information. The legislation does not directly address advertising and was developed before the concept of Web 2.0 and virtual worlds existed.

Advocacy groups exist to promote and protect the rights of children. For instance, Common Sense Media (see www.commonsensemedia.org) maintains a well-developed scorecard-style review system on Web sites, movies, television programming, games, and books targeting children. Its ratings include categories for violence, language, sex, and message. The message rating includes subcategories for social behavior, commercialism, and drug and alcohol usage. Parents and children are invited to submit ratings along with Common Sense Media professional raters, resulting in recommendations, including appropriateness by age. Webkinz's review on the Common Sense Media Web site provides a good example of the organization's approach to educating parents and their children on the benefits and drawbacks of participating in specific virtual worlds. Webkinz received a positive endorsement for kids ages eight and above. Common Sense Media's review of Webkinz reminds parents that the fun environment and online activities make it necessary to maintain time limits for users noting the addictive quality of the virtual world. The review cautions parents that fake ads (encouraging kids to eat fruit, for example) are sometimes intermixed with real ads (for age-appropriate products like movies) and that the activity of earning KinzCash that can then be spent in the W store promotes consumerism. In addition, the site access granted with purchase of a toy expires after one year. To maintain access, kids will need to buy a new pet. However, Webkinz is also applauded for teaching kids about monetary exchange and shopping, and the care of pets.

Reviews like those provided by Common Sense Media help to minimize the need for legislation to protect children online. In addition, groups like the Campaign for a Commercial-Free Childhood have been active monitoring advertising on many virtual-world sites. In particular, this advocacy group garnered parental and media support against advertising on the Webkinz site when advertisements for the "Bee Movie" and "Alvin and the Chipmunks" were spotted. Webkinz responded promptly by eliminating the offending ads. A Ganz spokesperson, Susan McVeigh, told *Brandweek* that Ganz, the owner of Webkinz, considers third-party advertising cautiously and allows minimal advertising with no advertising that would drive children outside the Webkinz Web site.[9]

The sites that promote themselves as environments with no advertising certainly seek to appeal to parents and child advocacy groups. Still, it is important to note that these "no-ad" virtual worlds are still branded. Club Penguin is a Disney brand. Nicktropolis promotes the Nickelodeon family of programming. These worlds may not sell traditional display advertising or interactive sponsorships to external brands, but their own ads are there, embedded in the worlds themselves.

Other worlds, like Neopets, have addressed privacy and safety concerns by restricting certain areas of the world based on age unless parental permission is given. Neopets (as do some other worlds) also has regular patrols around the world to monitor language, violence, and other possible inappropriate social behaviors. The key for these worlds and for marketers using the worlds as a promotional platform is to balance the commercial components with valuable benefits for the users.

The potential for regulation and legislation to protect children is not the only challenge facing social virtual worlds for kid. Others revolve around the psychology of trends. In fact, one could say that the biggest challenge for social virtual worlds for kids is that they target kids! Brooks Barnes points out that being able to create and play with an avatar cannot serve as a company's long-term differential advantage.[10] Kids do show excitement for creating their own online identity and interacting with others using avatar representations. But it is not a competitive advantage because there are numerous other sites that offer a 3D world for one's self-designed avatar. As long as children turn to this form of media, many competitors can succeed in the field. However, kids have a reputation as fickle consumers who will follow the next fad when it appears. It is difficult to predict how long kids will choose to spend their leisure time socializing in these virtual-world environments.

Related to this concern is the issue of how to maintain the desirability of virtual worlds, especially when investing in specific worlds. Webkinz, for instance, successfully created a perception of scarcity with parents going on hunts to find specific Webkinz toys like the alley cat or bull frog. Robert Cialdini's *Influence: The Psychology of Persuasion* identifies scarcity as one of the six principles of persuasion.[11] Related to the theory of psychological reactance, perceptions of scarcity work to incite an intense drive to have something that one believes is less available. Scarcity is powerful in part because people assign more value to things that are difficult to attain. Item availability can also be used as a proxy for product quality much the way price is sometimes used as a quality indicator in the absence of other information. Finally, when people experience a sense that something is unavailable, there is a feeling of lost freedom associated with the sensation. People naturally resist restrictions on their personal freedoms and will make decisions designed to protect their freedom. Lastly, people respond most fervently to scarcity when it requires that they compete with others to acquire the item in question. When applied to the use of scarcity as a marketing tool, the result is a preference for hard-to-come-by items perceived as desirable and of high quality due to their scarcity, with an inclination to protect one's rights to the product by seeking it out and making a purchase. Webkinz has utilized scarcity as a marketing tool brilliantly, particularly given that it is more influential for children than for adults. Cialdini suggests that teenagers are particularly sensitive to restrictions on their freedoms because that period of time is characterized by explorations of individuality.

Webkinz initially utilized the scarcity principle of influence by releasing only limited numbers of its plush toys and distributing the toys through specialty retailers. However, more recently, Webkinz increased its supply substantially while shifting to convenience model of distribution intensity. Not only did more Webkinz toys reach stores, but they are now distributed in warehouse clubs, gas stations, and roadside eateries, too.[12] As the availability becomes apparent, the sense of scarcity dissipates, and the positive effect on the Webkinz brand fades. Granted, virtual worlds offer value for young consumers, aside from the enhanced sense of equity produced from influence tactics, and the product (whether it be stuffed animal, toy, or MP3 players) bundled with virtual-world access provides a tangible unit of value for consumers. But, as Emily York of *Advertising Age* emphasizes, Webkinz stuffed animals are likely to be found tossed aside and forgotten because kids want them for the ID tags not for the toy itself.[13] As virtual worlds for kids shift from a growth stage where competition is easy and everyone can win because demand is strong to one where the market is saturated, it will be increasingly important to monitor popularity, traffic on competing sites, and new competitors. Social virtual worlds will need to seek out ways to promote a sense of exclusivity in a market that is just not that unusual any more.

■ Leveraging Social Virtual Worlds for Kids

What will social virtual worlds need to emphasize? Any product must always focus on its benefits to the consumer regardless of its life-cycle stage. Youth-oriented virtual worlds should continue to promote themselves with their benefits, including tangible goods like stuffed animals, dolls, and MP3 players, access to popular communication channels for socializing with friends, entertainment value, and educational opportunities. These worlds should also consider finding a way to create a portability option that would enable kids who are members of multiple worlds to interact easily between worlds. Portfolios should be developed when applicable to the brand assets tied to the virtual worlds. Disney and MTV have both illustrated the advantages of using a portfolio of social virtual worlds to appeal to kids of different age categories, to maintain a relationship with kids as they shift from category to category, and to build on the media franchises already in place. Virtual worlds should remember that children respond to scarcity in product marketing. But at the same time, children also respond to social proof, the influence of knowing that other people have made a certain decision or behaved in a specific way. They will need to balance the influence of social proof (e.g., more than 5 million have already registered for BarbieGirls.com!) and the influence of scarcity (e.g., where can I get a Webkinz alley cat?). Lastly, social worlds will need to strategically lobby advocacy groups to acquire endorsements. With so many competitors in the virtual space and growing parental concern for children's online activities, offering parents unbiased, well-evaluated assessments from advocacy groups like iParenting Media and Common Sense Media about the appropriateness, safety, and value of specific virtual networks will be important. Doing so will promote a sense of trust and credibility among parents.

How can marketers advertise in social virtual worlds for kids? There are three primary vehicles within this social-media platform: (1) traditional advertising in world, (2) branded sponsorships, events, and experiences in world, and (3) branding an exclusive virtual world from scratch. First, most of these worlds will sell display advertising space (like billboards) in world. This is an easy approach to testing social-media marketing in a virtual-world space. Unfortunately, it does not take advantage of the level of consumer involvement offered by virtual worlds. It also is quickest to garner criticism from advocacy groups. This is because display advertising is easily identifiable. Display advertising also fails to provide value to the members exposed to the message. In social media, part of the culture is cocreation of content. Simply purchasing access to child consumers is inconsistent with the context.

Second, brand sponsorships and events enable the brand to be embedded within the world's network. In other words, the target audience can be immersed in the advertising. This route is superior to the first if the brand has devised an experience that will give members of the world a reason to participate in the brand experience and share their experience with others. For example, Nike sponsored a competition called Zwinky Field Reporter Quest in Zwinktopia that offered members the chance to interact with Nike athletes Maria Sharapova, Kobe Bryant, LeBron James, and Serena Williams. Members answer questions and solve clues that lead them to the athletes' avatars. Ultimately, members can win Nike items and participate in an in-world Nike press conference. The Zwinky-Nike partnership exemplifies how brands can build an experience that is engaging, immersive, and fun. Participation in a branded experience results in that mother of all marketing benefits—extending brand exposure from moments to minutes.[14]

Brands that choose this route should remember another tool of influence touted by Cialdini, reciprocity. Reciprocity influences relationships in all areas of life. It works by activating one's acceptance of the rule of reciprocity, which states that a person must try to repay another for something he or she provided. Once obligated, the initial recipient will seek to reciprocate the kindness. The rule of reciprocity is a common technique in marketing, and is the foundation of the use of sales promotions (marketing offers like coupons designed to encourage a consumer response within a designated time frame). When marketing in social virtual worlds, the rule of reciprocity can be easily initiated with the offer of incentives for participation in a branded event. For example, a successful promotion on Gaia Online for the New Line film *The Last Mimzy* offered Gaia members a virtual magic stuffed rabbit for their avatars similar to the one in the movie. Widgets, also known as mini-applications or gadgets, are another wonderful engagement device that can be offered as an incentive and can serve to maintain interest in the brand over time. People can embed the widget onto social-networking pages, blogs, or computer desktops. Some are purely promotional, while others are functional like the successful Weatherbug widget, which offers a desktop preview of the weather.

Third, the brand can develop its own social virtual world. As discussed in chapter 4, apropos social virtual worlds for adults, developing an exclusive branded world requires the greatest commitment of resources but also offers many benefits. The brand can control the messages consumers see in world, and information on consumer behavior can be tracked and mined. More so, building a branded virtual world can result in the world as a profit center rather than a cost center as the world earns revenues from product sales, fees, and selling advertising space to other vendors. Branding a virtual world exclusively also positions the brand for transmedia storytelling. Transmedia storytelling is an approach to branding that utilizes multiple media platforms and multiple story angles and plot lines to engage the target audience. With a virtual world in place, transmedia brands have another channel for their stories and the opportunity to invite members to participate in the story dialogue.

What of the ultimate value to marketers for branding in youth-oriented social virtual worlds? Debra Aho Williamson, author of the report "Kids and Teens: Virtual Worlds Open New Universe" and senior analyst for eMarketer, acknowledges it can be difficult to assign value to a marketing campaign launched in a virtual environment. She asked, "What value is there in a person's avatar drinking a Pepsi?"[15] This begs the question, what is the ultimate measure of effectiveness for marketing in virtual worlds (or for that matter, using any form of social-media marketing)? It encourages us to reiterate the reasons for being in this space to begin with. Is it to sell more cans of soda (if Pepsi), or more cars (if Toyota)? For some brands, the result will be direct. Disney will likely sell more movie tickets to future installments in the Pirates of the Caribbean franchise, more DVDs of the three installments now available, and more branded merchandise by involving young consumers in the Pirates virtual world. Ganz counts on Webkinz to sell more toys. For others, the point is indirect. The point is to find another point of attraction between the brand and the consumers, encourage the consumers to elaborate on the brand's message a little longer and more often than they may have before, and to enhance recall and recognition of the brand and its message. The distinction is not unlike that of the early days of the Internet when critics harped on the uselessness of banner advertising with miniscule clickthrough rates. Yes, there is value in conversion. But there is also value in exposure to the message. Bowers, of Whyville, had this to say,

"This is a very powerful medium for marketing because it involves this huge engagement. It's more powerful than a sugar cereal commercial."[16] The power comes from the consumers' degree of involvement and engagement in the brand's message, the sense of relationship, the interactivity and cocreation that exist between the brand and the consumer, and the frequency and length of exposure to the brand's message. For these reasons, marketing via virtual worlds, particularly to youth-markets, will continue to develop over the coming years.

6 ▪ ▪ ▪

Influence the Influencers
Building Brands with
Social News Media

Social-media marketing embraces many possible techniques for advertising and branding across a wide array of online communities from social networks—including sharing sites for photos, videos, and bookmarks, virtual worlds, micro-communities—to social news sites. Brand marketers can purchase ad space for online display advertising using banners or rich media on community sites and can create brand personas that live among the community and contribute to it by offering resources and activities to members. Building brands with social media by leveraging social media's potential for engagement is a key message. But social media also enables an online version of publicity generation that can play a valuable role in meeting a brand's communication objectives.

Communication plans generally encompass a range of goals, like increasing brand awareness, improving brand likability, and improving sales conversions. Conversions refer to shifting viewers of an advertisement to the next stage in the buying process. The traditional conversion thought of online is the clickthrough rate, which documents the percentage of viewers who were exposed to the ad who then clicked on the message to learn more. Online sales conversion is the percentage of people who then continue to complete an online transaction. Online advertising formats are almost always empowered with direct-response options for consumers exposed to the messages, enabling various levels of conversion and accountability for the advertising expenditures. Even the emerging approaches to social media frequently have a direct-response device embedded in the promotion in order to enable conversion. For instance, retail stores in Second Life include link to retail Web sites and online order forms. Social media is increasingly a part of strategic media planning given its ability to increase brand awareness, brand liking, and brand engagement.

There are other goals social-media marketing can be used to address in a brand's marketing communication plan. These include building credibility, driving Web site traffic, and influencing and encouraging word-of-mouth communication. Importantly, when these goals are accomplished, all are likely to generate incremental sales.

How can social media be utilized for these purposes? Social news marketing campaigns, a type of social-media marketing, accomplish these goals by leveraging the power of referrals from influencers in the social news arena to highlight branded content. The results can include (1) an increase in traffic to the brand's Web site, (2) improved perceptions of the brand's credibility, reputation, and quality, (3) improved search engine rankings, (4) lifts in word-of-mouth communication about the brand, and (5) sales.

■ Social News and Bookmarking Communities

When it comes to news, social media enables the creation of news stories by citizen journalists and the sharing and distribution of those stories virally. The shared distribution model is facilitated by a host of players, including content providers (e.g., corporate Web sites, bloggers, and publishers), participants in social news and bookmarking sites, known as influencers, and the universe of Internet users. Social news Web sites are social communities that allow its users to submit news stories, articles, and multimedia files, including videos and pictures so the submissions can be shared with other users and the general public. Submissions can receive enhanced attention and visibility based on votes from users.

The value offered by the social news and bookmarking communities is clear. The online social news media system is one characterized by enormous amounts of information and content. Technorati, a blog search engine, reports more than 112 million blogs active at the end of 2007. That's just blogs! There are also corporate white papers, articles from online publishers, and other valuable content available online. Thus, the average online information consumer could easily be overwhelmed or simply miss valuable sources of information. Enter social news communities. Participants in these communities facilitate access to the most valuable information online by recommending content to other users.

These communities uphold the principles of media democratization. Individuals determine what material is disseminated throughout the community as well as the value ratings associated with the material. Users act in an editorial capacity, identifying what material should be pushed to the featured areas of the site. The process supports the wisdom of crowds in that individual users recommend and vote on submissions. Submitted content is filtered using an algorithm to determine the popularity of a story. The algorithm includes number of votes received as well as other factors like the richness of the discussion related to the story. The system ensures each individual has a voice, if he or she chooses to use it, but it also enables some voices to be heard louder than others. The most active and respected participants, the influencers, come to hold positions of high authority in the community. Manipulation of the voting system is minimized with the internal algorithms that help to identify voting campaigns (in which voters are incentivized to vote for a story). In addition, some social news Web sites have editorial staff who review stories and award featured positions for relevant, newsworthy stories. Social news Web sites can be general or narrow in scope. Digg is the most popular and well-known social news site. Other popular social news communities include Reddit, Mix, and Propell. Sphinn is an example of a site specific to Internet marketing resources.

Social bookmarking communities are similar to social news communities in that users can share material from around the Internet with each other and the size and influence of a user's network affects the ultimate influence of the resource in question. Users store and organize bookmarks (using tags, one-word descriptors that enable easy search and retrieval of related items) to online source materials with the social bookmarking site (instead of storing bookmarks with one's Web browser). The community aspect comes into play with the network of users. Within each community, users can share bookmarks with friends and colleagues, resulting in a shared wisdom effect. The leader among social bookmarking sites is del.icio.us.

Regardless of the community type, note that there are three key layers necessary for the community to function and benefit. First, there must be *content creation*. In the past, content was created by professional writers and journalists. In this age of media democracy, anyone with something to say can create content. Second, the content must be *shared*. Again, there was a time when society relied almost solely on editors, publishers, and large media outlets to distribute content. With the advent of social media, anyone can act as an editor and distributor of content. Third, content must be *consumed*. If there is no demand for the content, the content is without influence. Its creator might experience value in creation for the sake of creation, but the influence we associate with content exists only when content is consumed. Social media also supports the content consumption process by filtering the mass of content available such that the most desirable, relevant, and consumption-worthy content is featured.

■ Power in the Social News Community: The Influencers

Social media is applauded for its democratization of media, such that everyone and anyone can create, disseminate, and critique content. At the same time, social news communities are hierarchical with some users gaining positions of authority and power. These powerful users are known as influencers. Influencers have long been a subject of interest in marketing. Referred to as market mavens and opinion leaders, influencers are people who are seen by others as knowledgeable sources of information with a strong communication network that results in their ability to affect purchase decisions for a number of other consumers, directly and indirectly.

Ed Keller and Jon Berry propose five characteristics common to influencers. They are (1) activists, (2) well connected, (3) capable of making an impact, (4) mentally active, and (5) trendsetters.[1] In other words, influencers develop a network of people through their involvement in activities. They are active participants at work and in their communities. Their social networks are large and well developed. Others trust them and find them to be credible sources of information about one or more specific topics. They tend to have a natural sense of intellectual curiosity, which may lead them to new sources of information. They set trends by being among the first to adopt new innovations. Typically, influencers are not innovators, a term used to describe the very first group of consumers to adopt a technological innovation. Rather, influencers belong to the early adopters group, the second group to adopt innovations. This is an important distinction as innovators are thought to be too different from the general population to be influential.

Influencers exist in all social communities. It is a natural pattern for some to be more active and acquire positions of authority within a community. Influencers have a strong network, which means there is a channel in place for the distribution of the influence they have to wield. The source of influence itself, however, originates from the power bases refined by the influencer. How can someone acquire power? As French and Raven explained in their classic article, "The Bases of Social Power," several sources of power individuals can accrue in organizations.[2] These sources of power include reward power, coercive power, legitimate power, referent power, expert power, and information power. Reward power is associated with one's ability to provide others with what they desire. Coercive power is the ability to punish others. Legitimate power is organizational authority based on rights associated with a person's appointed position. Referent power is authority through association. Expert power is based on others' recognition of one's knowledge, skills, and ability. Information power is based on one's control over the flow of and access to information.

For influencers within social-media communities, several forms of power can be developed (and, importantly, anyone willing to invest time in accruing power can become an influencer). Influencers begin by actively participating in the community, submitting high-quality content (and possibly also writing original feature content). Over time, the user will develop a reputation as an expert. The user will also spend time commenting on the submissions of influential others. This will build referent power by association. Likewise, the user community will recognize the investment in time and energy heavy users are making to benefit the community, resulting in legitimate power. Eventually, as a user gains power, he or she will begin to influence access to content (information power) and can reward or punish others (reward and coercive power) with the decision on whether or not to support new submissions. Ultimately, the influencers are critically important to the success of a social news marketing initiative. Without support from one or more influentials, the incremental traffic resulting from a social-media campaign would be inconsequential.

■ The Value of Social Media for Achieving Marketing Objectives

These communities can draw attention to branded content and drive traffic to the source of that content. Social news marketing campaigns are designed to facilitate exposure of the brand's content to the social-media communities targeted. Clearly featured links on social news community sites will increase brand awareness, but there are other marketing benefits as well. First, links from the social news and bookmarking sites will lead to an increase in traffic to the site hosting the original content. In addition, after promotion on a social news site like Digg, other Web sites might also link to the branded content. These links result in referral traffic from secondary Web sites.

Traffic to the brand's Web site will also increase as a result of higher search engine rankings which occur because of the large number of links developed through the social news community. Search engines refer to the number of natural, permanent links from nonrelated Web sites in determining organic search rankings.

Traffic from organic search engine rankings and from influential members of the social-media community in question is enhanced with the credibility and trust associated with the referral source. Of course, some traffic will be unproductive. However, some of the prospects will visit the site with the understanding that a search engine or referral source on the news community site recommended the brand's content. Referrals are recognized as among the most valuable source of new prospects for any business. Prospects who originate from a referral have a predisposed positive attitude toward the brand. They view the referral source as unbiased and credible and are likely to internalize the referral's opinion of the brand, making it their own. It is for this reason that word-of-mouth marketing has received so much attention in the past. Social media makes this use of referral marketing efficient as well as effective.

In addition to Web site traffic, brand awareness, and borrowed credibility from trusted sources of information, social news marketing is inexpensive. The costs are limited to the time and manual labor necessary to create content and promote the content to the social news communities. It is, in essence, quite similar to the role played by public relations specialists. Press releases about a brand are prepared and pitched to news media that are thought to have an audience with and influence over the target market. This approach cannot be the only one used in a brand's marketing communications campaign, or perhaps even in a social-media marketing campaign. But it can be an effective and efficient complement to other tactics.

▪ Marketing with Social News Communities

Social news marketing begins with the development and offer of content. This content is designed to pique the interest of the target audience such that once aware of the content, people visit the site hosting the content, read the content, and perhaps even stay to browse the site, make a purchase, or return another time. Social news and bookmarking communities facilitate this process by promoting high-quality content among their users. Getting content noted as popular on a social-media site leads to a high clickthrough to the content itself and, if things go according to plan, the other benefits noted. There are three key strategies to getting content rated on social-media community sites, and they will be described in detail shortly. All of the strategies presented assume that the brand has high quality and interesting, engaging content to share.

Social news and bookmarking communities are unlikely to vote an online sales catalog to a position of popularity. These communities do not exist for the purpose of marketing. Rather, they exist for the value of the members to meet their needs for social and intellectual stimulation. Consequently, using a social news marketing campaign requires a brand to create content. This content can be in a number of forms. Blogs, white papers, video tutorials, and articles are all possible forms of content, which can ultimately lead interested consumers to a brand's Web site. When preparing content for this purpose, quality is more important than quantity. The goal is to generate a credibility rating through the "popular" designations offered on social-media community sites and to parlay those ratings into site visits. Having a lot of content of mediocre quality will not be as influential as having less frequent, highly engaging pieces.

This notion of creating an engaging piece of content is a key tactic in generating votes for content. Content should be constructed with "link-baits" that will work to intrigue potential readers. Andy Hagans' blog, Tropical SEO, provides a detailed account of linkbaiting, explaining that linkbaiting is essentially packaging the content in a desirable and interesting package.[3] The most important piece of linkbait is the content's title. For example, Hagans' entry on linkbaiting is called "Andy Hagans' Ultimate Guide to Linkbaiting and SMM," but it could have been called "Basics of Linkbaiting." The title is critically important to social news community because this is the primary bit of information seen about the content. It should do all it can to garner attention and interest in the piece itself.

Hagans also identifies several "hooks," which can be used in positioning content for a target audience, including the resource hook, the contrary hook, the humor hook, the giveaway hook, and the research hook, among others. The resource hook is common, but appreciated, among social news addicts. It refers to content written with the intent to be helpful to the target audience. For example, the Serta mattress company might create an article entitled "5 Methods to Ensure a Restful Night's Sleep." The contrary hook is used to refute some accepted belief. Challenging the belief incites people to read the content if only to argue the point.

For instance, Weight Watchers might post an article entitled "Is It Possible to Lose Weight with Chocolate?" recognizing that this will spark an interest from those who believe chocolate cannot be part of a weight loss plan. The humor hook is designed to show that the content will entertain. The giveaway hook promises something for free. In other words, it embeds a sales promotion, an incentive offered to encourage a specific behavior response in a specific time period, into the content. For example, our Weight Watchers' article could have been titled "Save $50 Doing What's Good for You!"

Lastly, the research, or statistic hook, offers some claim about something of interest. All of these hooks can act as successful forms of linkbait, encouraging submissions to social news sites, links from bloggers and other Web sites, and clickthroughs from those exposed to the links. Regardless of the degree of linkbaiting incorporated into the brand's content, it should be relevant to the audience and relate back to the brand and the brand's message.

■ Strategies for Social News Marketing

There are three primary approaches to marketing with social news media: (1) influence others, (2) develop a large network, and (3) influence the influencers. The first approach, influence others, requires that the brand representatives establish themselves as an influencer within the social-media communities targeted. This approach will take time to participate and gain the respect of the community. Social-media communities do tend to show respect to those who have been involved the longest and invested the most time in the community. Once the power is established, the influencer can market content from one or more specific brands (and even draw negative attention to competing materials). The time investment necessary is a drawback to this approach, but the relationship between the influencer and the branded content is a limitation, too. Other users are likely to discount repeated recommendations of branded content once it is common knowledge that a relationship exists between the brand and the influencer promoting the brand's content.

The second approach is to build support from the "grassroots," developing a large network of supporters. With this approach, it is not necessary to garner the support of influentials because the sheer number of votes for the branded content will ensure a featured placement on the social news site. How can you acquire so many votes? Develop a voting network. Solicit friends and colleagues to register for the social news site targeted for the campaign, and then collectively vote. Some companies have attempted this model even paying users for voting up specific stories, but this is frowned upon by social communities as it undermines the intent of the social news community. Acquiring large voting blocks can be difficult to accomplish and, even when large numbers are generated, it can backfire if the site's algorithm targets artificial voting patterns.

The third approach is to influence the influencers. Just as journalists receive pitches for content from public relations specialists pitching stories that promote specific brands, influential social news users can receive pitches for branded content. This is basically public relations for social media rather than traditional media. This method is less time consuming than the first option and also offers the added value of leveraging the credibility of the influencer recommending the content. The influencer acts as a referral, providing an unbiased, third-party word-of-mouth endorsement of the content.

The process of influencing the influencers follows the public relations model. The key to success is to ensure that the content pitched is relevant for the influencer targeted. The better the pitch is targeted to the right person, the higher the rate of success. Remember that influentials gained power within their community by making good recommendations to the community, consistently. Consequently, influentials will be cautious in making endorsements.

There are several steps in the process: (1) setting objectives for the campaign, (2) targeting the social news communities, (3) targeting the influencers within each targeted community, (4) networking with influencers, and (5) pitching content. Begin by setting objectives for the social news portion of the campaign. What is it that needs to be accomplished? Is it brand awareness? Does that brand seek to build a reputation or enhance its image? Is there a desire to drive more traffic to the brand's Web site? Is there a need to increase search engine rankings? In the second step, the specific social news communities to be targeted will be identified. Digg, Reddit, and Propeller are the most popular communities, but depending upon the brand's industry and the type of content the brand has to promote, a niche site may be more effective. In selecting the communities to target, there should be a match between the brand's target audience and the characteristics of the community population. Ask, will this social news community provide the kind of audience needed to meet the campaign's marketing objectives?

The community should also be evaluated for quality and engagement. Inactive or weak communities will not offer the social support necessary to propel a successful social news marketing campaign. Consider this list of community characteristics when evaluating the desirability of a community target:

1. What is the community's focus (general news, specific topics)?
2. How many active users are involved in the community? What kind of traffic does the site receive?
3. How active are the top users on the site?
4. How many comments on average are generated for each new submission?
5. How many votes are required to earn front-page status on the site?
6. Are stories on the site's front page recent? How rapid is story turnover?
7. Are there limitations for branded content in the community's Terms of Service?
8. What have others (such as bloggers) said about the social news site?

In the third step, the specific power users, or influencers, are identified. These will be the heavy users on the site that might ultimately support the desired content. In selecting the influencers to target, one must first identify the influencers and then profile those influencers to determine who is best to target.

How can one find the right influencers? It is easy to identify the power users for most sites. There is a list of top Digg users, for instance, that ranks power users by order of influence along with the number of submissions made and the number the user made popular. However, it is not sufficient to simply target the top power users. Power users gained power by making good recommendations to the community. Consequently, they protect that reputation by resisting pitches unless they believe that the content will further their power base in the community. In other words, the content must be relevant (as well as high quality). Once the list of power users is identified, visit the profiles of these users. The goal is to match the content's topical area to an area of interest noted in the user profiles. Doing so will enhance the chances that the influencer will perceive the content as worthy of recommending. Another technique is to simply search the news site for other submissions on the same topic. The top users submitting on the topic will appear with the search results. This step is critical to a successful social news marketing campaign. Without identifying the right target, the content will not receive the best promotion on the site.

The fourth step is to develop relationships with the targeted influencers on each community site in the campaign. Just as most people do not appreciate hearing from a friend only when in need of a favor, influencers as a group are unlikely to respond well to obvious pitches from social-media marketers. Some care must be taken to introduce oneself, acknowledge the contributions the influencer makes to the community, and flatter the influencer's judgment and expertise in making high-quality content submissions. The influencer will be helping the brand by virtue of the content submission and vote, so it can be useful to help the influencer by offering other content that will be perceived as desirable prior to pitching the branded content.

In the final stage of this process, the pitch is made. While traditional public relations practitioners might make a pitch using a standard press release, this is not the case with social media. Interestingly, there is a social-media press release template publicly available online. This approach can be considered when attempting to get attention from a social news sites' editorial staff. However, when approaching influencers, the use of a standardized social-media press release could be considered social-media suicide. Instead, a more personal pitch that emphasizes knowledge of the influencer's recommendation patterns and the marketer's relationship to the branded content is likely to be effective.

■ Search Media Optimization

Rohit Bargava coined the term *social-media optimization* to refer to the need to optimize a site so that it is more easily linked to, more visible in social news and bookmarking searches, more visible on custom search engines like Technorati, and more frequently included on blog posts.[4] Based on the general concept of SEO, which recognizes the need to ensure a site garners the best organic search engine ranking possible, social-media optimization enhances the visibility of content in the realm of social media. Since the introduction of Bargava's rules for optimizing social-media marketing, several other rules have been proposed resulting in a list of best practices for social-media optimization, and these are detailed at the Influential Marketing Blog. For search news marketing campaigns, embrace these best practices for optimization.

- Provide content. For a site to gain incremental traffic from social media, it needs to offer content to the social-media community. This content can be in the form of blogs, white papers, or thought pieces, or even summarize or index other published content.
- Encourage others to tag or bookmark the content. Make it easy for others to link to the site by including "add to del.icio.us" and "digg it" buttons to the contents page.
- Include Trackbacks to promote those who promote your content. The term trackback refers to posting links to other sources of content that links to

original content. It can be a method of communication between bloggers but, importantly, it provides a method of acknowledging those who are sending traffic to the brand's site while reciprocating the kindness.

- Promote valuable content. When a site has valuable content of interest to a group of readers, encourage influencers to acknowledge the material so a wider audience can benefit from the material.
- Syndicate content with an RSS feed. Enhancing the ease of content distribution with an RSS feed makes it easy for others to consume new content as it is offered.
- Participate in social news and bookmarking communities. Social media is a conversation. It should not be limited to anonymous submissions of content. The more the brand is engaged, the more likely it is the consumers will reciprocate.

Social news marketing campaigns can accomplish challenging marketing objectives with amazingly little in terms of financial resources. Still, there are limitations. It is not appropriate for brands whose prospects and customers are unaware of social media or do not use social news sites. It also requires that the brand offers content, not advertising but real content that can inform and/or entertain the target audience. Without content, there is nothing to share through the social news communities. Patience is required. Results are not typically as rapid as with paid forms of promotion, though they do tend to accrue rapidly once content is designated as popular on a social news site. Social news marketing campaigns can build brand awareness, word-of-mouth communication, and Web site traffic, ultimately resulting in additional sales.

7 ▪ ▪ ▪

Citizen Advertising
Consumer-Told Brand Folklore

Media democracy is the underlying philosophy driving the participatory Web. It has driven the development of participatory, conversational, and fluid social communities, which encourage and enable members to produce, publish, control, critique, rank, and interact with online content. The lessons provided in *The Tipping Point*, which are applicable to understanding the influential network effects possible with social network advertising, are again applicable here.[1] Gladwell advocates that viral spread is partially a function of the concept's stickiness and the application of the law of context. Stickiness is the degree to which the message inspires action. Context is whether the message has sufficient "legs" to inspire others to develop a community around it. Can brands inspire a community? If so, will community members, brand enthusiasts, be inspired to produce and cocreate brand content, which can then be published and shared with others? The development of CGM, especially consumer-generated advertising, suggests the answer to these questions is a resounding yes. Brands can leverage media democracy for their own marketing objectives when engaged consumers are motivated to create and cocreate branded messages for a public audience. The result is consumer-generated advertising, a brand-centric type of user-generated content.

User-generated content, also known as CGM, user-created content, and conversational media, encompasses any content produced by end users and made public (typically online). The report "Participative Web: User-Created Content," prepared by the OECD, defines user-generated content as content that (1) is made publicly available online, (2) reflects some creative effort on the part of the user, and (3) is created outside professional practice.[2] Thus, it is a broad range of content which can be classified as user generated, including videos, photos, blogs and vlogs, comments and responses to other content, podcasts, forum discussions, online product reviews, wiki contributions, and consumer-generated advertising. Content creation is not uncommon. According to Deloitte & Touche's "The State of the Media Democracy" report, 40% of Internet users create some form of content, whether it is editing videos, posting photos, or writing blogs, and 51% acknowledge reading and watching the content of other users online.[3] With younger consumers, the consumption of user-generated content is even higher with 71% reporting watching and/or reading user-generated content online.

The lexicon of online marketers includes many commonly used phrases and accompanying acronyms related to CGM.[4] *Consumer-generated media* is the catchall phrase for user content, but primarily is meant to reflect first-person commentary about brand experiences that consumers may produce and publish online in a variety of venues, including blogs, message boards and forums, online product review sites, product rating areas, social-networking sites, and photo- and video-sharing sites. CGM functions like publicity, intercepting consumers during product information search activities, whether through search queries or serendipitous discovery. The following terms identify specific types of CGM.

Consumer-generated multimedia (CGM2), a type of CGM, refers to content that includes audio, video, and perhaps animation. It is better able to capture an attentive audience due to its enhanced entertainment value, and enables visual demonstrations. YouTube's success is tied directly to the prevalence and popularity of CGM2. CGM2 is thought to reflect primarily organic content. It may or may not be citizen advertising. Citizen advertising is content created by consumers using verbal and/or visual imagery to inform, persuade, or remind other consumers about a brand, resulting in an ad unit, which can be disseminated electronically or otherwise. Such ads are sometimes called V-CAMs, viewer created ad messages. CGM2 can refer to user videos that do not advocate for or against a brand, as well as citizen advertising. Perhaps the most famous example of citizen advertising is the "I Love My iPod" YouTube post from an Apple brand enthusiast. His YouTube video generated thousands of ad impressions and Apple applauded it, acknowledging that the creativity and strategic positioning outpaced much of that in its own official campaign. The video promoted a brand but was totally organic. User content is organic when its creation was motivated by an intrinsic intent on the part of its creator rather than incentivized or guided by the brand itself. Organic, citizen advertising, at least when promoting the brand in a favorable light, is valuable and suggests highly engaged customers.

Consumer-solicited media (CSM) captures invited but non-incented citizen advertising. Sometimes called participatory advertising, brands invite content, setting mandatory guidelines and specifications and possibly also providing participants with selected brand assets. The most frequently used manifestation of CSM is the "create your own ad" contest, which has been used by numerous brands, including Frito-Lay, Dove, and Chevy. This form of citizen advertising has some degree of authenticity, although less than that of purely organic forms of consumer-generated advertising.

Incentivized consumer-generated media (iCGM) is CSM that is also incented by the sponsoring brand. It functions just as non-incentivized citizen-advertising campaigns except that the sponsor encourages submissions with incentives such as prize money, the chance for the winning entry to be broadcast on television (possibly during high-exposure events like the Super Bowl and the Oscars). Doritos used this approach with its Crash the Super Bowl campaign.

Consumer-fortified media (CFM) captures the phenomenon of consumer content that is created around the existence of some other content. The Dove Evolution commercial is a prime example. The spot was created professionally for the Unilever Dove brand, but much of the media value generated came from consumer conversation about the spot. Thousands discussed the ad in online forums and posted commentary and embedded links to the ad in blogs. Again, the result is like a credible, trustworthy form of publicity generated through consumer-controlled media.

Compensated consumer-generated media (cCGM) refers to paid consumer content. Consumers are paid for their content creations, and brands may actively seek out certain people like bloggers, videographers, and artists to participate in the campaign. For example, the company Pay-PerPost pays bloggers to endorse products. The Lonelygirl15 YouTube phenomenon was a planned, strategic marketing ploy to promote the capabilities of its producers. There are less malicious variations to this CGM model in that some content-publishing sites, primarily Revver, but also YouTube, offer to share revenues with authentic consumer content producers. Essentially, this form of CGM is counterfeit content—

nothing more than paid rich media advertising posing as authentic consumer expressions of their brand perceptions and posted on social-media community sites.

■ Citizen Advertising

Citizen advertising encompasses three of the categories of CGM reviewed above: (1) CGM2, (2) CSM, and (3) iCGM. All three forms capture the phenomena of consumer content creation and brand enthusiasm. When solicited (whether incentivized or not), the concept relies upon a process by which a company invites consumers to submit ads to a Web site. Engaged consumers, the brand enthusiasts and/or those with creative skill who dream of fame and fortune spend time with the product, thinking about the brand, developing the ad submission, and hyping the contest to their friends and family. The ads are shown online to encourage brand chatter to develop and spread. They also go through a review process, often involving a vote by other engaged consumers, whereupon the winners are awarded prize money and widespread distribution of their winning ad. Assuming there are quality entries, the brand then broadcasts the winning entries using a mass medium.

The CSM process embraces many of the characteristics of successful social-media marketing. The brand issues an invitation to consumers (and sometimes personal invitations to particularly talented brand fans) to engage with the brand by creating branded content. The act of inviting participation and dialogue serves to trigger the brand *democratization* process. Turning to the public for professional services is the essence of *crowdsourcing,* one of the outcomes of media democracy. Recall that *engagement* occurs as a "subtle, subconscious process in which consumers begin to combine the ad's messages with their own associations, symbols, and metaphors to make the brand more personally relevant."[5] Brand democratization occurs when the brand acknowledges the value of consumer cocreation. The invitation is the source of *stickiness* Gladwell advocates is necessary to spark the spread of an idea. Engagement is the outcome of that democratization and the foundation for brand communities, another critical component of viral marketing. The content produced is from the consumer perspective, based on their values, wants, needs, and brand experiences. Thus, it should resonate with the target audience and benefit from their perception that the message is authentic. All the while, the campaign builds buzz on- and off-line, including word-of-mouth communication and publicity from stories published about the contest. Sarah Fay of Isobar reveals what could be thought of as the mantra of effective citizen advertising: "Brands whose consumers tell the best stories to each other win—not those whose brands tell the best stories to consumers."[6]

In the short period of time that citizen advertising has been utilized as a campaign strategy, it has generated enormous value. Listed below are several possible benefits that can accrue to brands that successfully incorporate citizen advertising into their integrated marketing campaigns.

- Increased customer engagement
- Enhanced interactivity for campaign
- Improved brand image
- Increased brand loyalty
- Access to new ideas from users
- Buzz generation and publicity
- Increased site traffic (on microsites and primary brand Web sites)
- Increased insight into target markets (including how consumers perceive the brand and its positioning)
- Lower production costs for creative content

Brands like Doritos, Dove Cream Oil Body Wash, Pontiac, and Oreos have successfully driven traffic to their Web sites, spawned buzz and word-of-mouth communication on- and off-line, and benefited from a new source of creative talent, all for an efficient cost. Consumer-generated advertising is thought to cost 25%–30% of the amount required for agency work. Big brands recognize the potential of citizen advertising, but the costs of execution make it a natural alternative for small- to medium-sized businesses.

■ Creative Control and Distribution Approaches

As noted, citizen advertising exists along a continuum, progressing from totally organic contributions (pure citizen advertising) to mechanistic contributions (solicited and incentivized campaigns). The notion of a continuum helps to reflect the relative degree of control over the resulting ad and source of motivation for creating content. At one extreme, totally organic media tantalizes content producers with complete control over the message strategy, creative execution, and distribution of content. These ads can appear on video-sharing sites like YouTube, and links to them may be embedded in blogs and on social-networking sites. Their distribution grows virally, determining their success or failure in terms of viewer impressions. Consumers of organic citizen ads are influenced by the credibility and authenticity that accompanies communication that is not sponsored by a commercial entity but offered for consideration from one consumer to another. Chances are that brands that become the subject of organic citizen ads are either "lovemarks," a phrase coined by Kevin Roberts to capture those brands that inspire emotional attachment with their customers, or hated by customers, who use citizen advertising to terrorize the brand. These citizen ad producers are known as brand terrorists because they create content as an attempt to harm a brand's equity and position in the marketplace. Search "iPod" on YouTube, and many examples of organic citizen advertising created to educate consumers about iPod's battery life and disappointing customer service will appear. The now infamous video of a person using a Bic pen to open a Kryptonite brand bicycle lock is another example of organic CGA used to harm a brand's position, or at least warn fellow consumers of a brand's limitations. Organic ads reflect media democracy, but (even for the positive, brand advocacy ads) they are not being actively leveraged by a brand to accomplish marketing objectives, including the almighty goal of brand engagement.

Solicited and incentivized citizen-advertising campaigns are more mechanistic because they typically restrain the participating consumers by requiring that certain mandatory elements be included (for instance, the brand's tagline might be a required element of the ad), specifications be met (such as a set length of exposure time), and brand assets (such as the brand's logo and even specific imagery and music) be utilized. The degree of control varies from campaign to campaign, however, with some encouraging extensive creative freedom (as was the case with the Converse Brand Democracy campaign) and others soliciting very narrow creative components (as with Mastercard's Priceless execution). The Dove Cream Oil Body Wash promotion spawned ads more closely approximating organic ads in that the contest guidelines did not limit participants to brand-approved assets like specific slogans, copy, images, or music.

Brands that seek greater control over messaging can limit contributors to packages of brand-endorsed assets, including audio, video, copy, and imagery. Called "mash-ups," users build their advertising messages from "ingredients" or "kits" provided on the brand's Web site. A key benefit of limiting participants to marketer-provided ingredients is the ability to increase the likelihood that the resulting ads will be consistent with the brand's positioning strategy. Consistency with brand positioning strategy is a frequently cited concern for brands considering citizen advertising. Heavily restricted creative specifications help to minimize this concern.

Mastercard's citizen component to its Priceless campaign illustrates the control brands can maintain while inviting consumer participation. It requested only copy lines from consumers. However, using this limited form does not preclude consumers from creating organic ads. There are numerous spoofs of the Priceless campaign on YouTube and Google Video.

Chevy Tahoe's Apprentice contest used the packaged approach. Participants could select from several scenes, mix the order and number of scene shots, and add music. In terms of imagery, every consumer-generated ad created showed gorgeous shots of the Tahoe driving in rural landscapes. If one were to look only at the scenery, the implication is clear—the Tahoe is a desirable, sleek SUV with the ability to take its driver wherever he wishes to go. However, even with a packaged approach complete with brand assets, Tahoe did not eliminate the risks associated with citizen advertising. Contributors wrote their own copy for their ads, and it was with the copy that contributors shared their criticisms of Tahoe, and SUVs in general. Should Chevy have limited contributors with copy choices, too? Doing so would have minimized some of the parodies created during the contest. But it would also have limited the overall impact of the campaign. Because Chevy provided some freedom of expression for participants, its campaign promotion became viral with users posting their ads on YouTube and bloggers providing links to the Chevy Web site and to videos posted elsewhere. The sheer controversy over whether it was a smart marketing move or not resulted in valuable publicity for the Tahoe brand.

The degree of citizen control on the continuum of organic to mechanistic is one factor that must be considered by brands, but an equally important aspect is the distribution method. Consumer-generated ads may be shared with others via online space that is primarily user controlled (like YouTube and other file-sharing sites) and/or through brand-controlled outlets.

Pontiac has created just such a site and named it Pontiac Underground (visit http://pontiacunderground.autos.yahoo.com/). The site is provided through a partnership between Pontiac and Yahoo! but allows users to post photographs, share videos, and discuss opinions and information through forums and opinion polls. It is a brand-controlled space that still allows users a great deal of freedom. Even the slogan encourages Pontiac enthusiasts to contribute material, "Where Passion for Pontiac is Driven by You." As such, it successfully leverages CGA as a builder of brand equity.

The Converse Brand Democracy campaign invited films inspired by Converse for posting on its Converse Gallery microsite. The Converse submissions allowed a high degree of creative freedom with the only limitation being a requirement that submissions be twenty-three seconds in length (to easily enable Converse to use submissions for television commercials). Nikon sent one of its new digital camera models to several users of Flickr, the photo-sharing social network, and invited them to use the camera and submit their pictures. The best photos were then used to create a three-page insert in *BusinessWeek*. Southwest Airlines used a different tactic by distributing ad submissions to its Wanna Get Away campaign extension contest, posting them on YouTube instead of on a Southwest microsite, but it screened all submissions first, allowing only those deemed consistent with the brand's strategy online.

In solicited and incentivized campaigns, the shared distribution system must recognize that while video files will be posted on the sponsoring site they will also likely spread as a result of the use of video-sharing networks by the citizens themselves. When brands systematically expose an audience to citizen advertising through traditional media channels, like television and online vehicles, in branded spaces (e.g., www.jinglesforpringles.com), they are maximizing the reach and enhancing the opportunity for the campaign to engage others. Brands may attempt to restrict distribution of submissions in the contest rules, an important choice given the potential for poorly executed concepts and damaging content, but even then it would be shortsighted for brands to fail to recognize that there is an "underground" where such content, whether organic or packaged, can thrive.

■ Heed the Warnings

Of course, as with any developing tool, there are risks to brands that invite their customers to contribute CGA. Perhaps the most salient risk to brands is the potential for contributors to highlight negative attributes of the brand. Chevy Tahoe experienced just this when it invited consumers to create their own Tahoe ads using a mix of images and music provided on its Web site. Tahoe, like many other brands, limited contributors to "mash-ups," meaning that contributors could select only images and music provided on the site. Tahoe's risk arose from allowing contributors to write their own copy for their ads, and it was the copy that revealed the views of consumers. The Web site used for the CGA promotion, www.chevyapprentice.com, is no longer active, but some of the ads created are still available on YouTube.

A more recent promotion from Dove Cream Oil Body Wash did not inspire parodists to the same degree, but consumers who wish to parody brands do not miss out on such opportunities. The "winning" consumer-generated ad is available for viewing on the Dove Cream Oil Web site, www.dovecreamoil.com. But spoofs also appeared in response to the citizen solicitation on YouTube.

Another potential hazard exists in how consumers view the brand's use of the tactic itself. A survey conducted by the American Marketing Association found that while consumers over the age of 25 felt that companies using consumer-generated advertising were "more creative, customer-friendly, and innovative than companies using only professionally creative advertising," those under the age of 25 felt just the opposite.[7] Why might perceptions of brands using citizen advertising vary so extensively? Execution is the key. Younger consumers are more literate than older consumers when it comes to engagement tactics. CGA promotions that fail to be executed in a manner consistent with the target market and the brand's image or those with questionable authenticity will not resonate with consumers high in social commerce literacy. Take, for instance, Buick's attempt to pass off a video on YouTube as footage captured by a bystander. This video was quickly identified as a fake on blogs like Straightline (on the www.edmunds.com Web site) and even by viewers commenting on the video on YouTube. Is it any wonder that consumers are a bit cynical? A trust mark or some kind of label guaranteeing authenticity may be necessary to reassure suspicious consumers.

Volkswagon is a brand that has suffered some harm to its brand equity from an organic citizen ad that featured a VW Polo minimizing damage from a terrorist bomb attack. The bomb exploded in the car, but the strength and indestructibility of the car prevented damage to the would-be innocent victims. The citizen ad featured Polo in a positive light, but the ad set off cries from critics who thought Volkswagon endorsed the ad, saying the ad was insensitive and politically inappropriate. Volkswagon's public relations staff was placed in the undesirable position of creating a crisis communication campaign to repair the damage to its reputation. One point of discussion in the industry is whether negative GRPs (gross rating points, a measure of the weight of a brand's communication vehicles in the media market for a specific period of time) should be assessed against marketing communication campaigns that suffer from negative publicity and perceptions when citizen advertising works against a brand's image.

There are legal issues at play, too. Consumer content producers might use content that is not original, posing copyright threats. Known as indirect product placement, the threat occurs when the video created includes other brands as backdrops or inadvertent setting props (such as having the main character drive a Toyota to purchase the bag of Doritos when

Doritos is the sponsor but Toyota is not). Brands involved in this way could insist that they be compensated for use of their trademarks or that the video distribution be halted.

Bigger legal concerns are already emerging from a suit filed by Subway against Quiznos and iFilm, the Web site that ran the contest.[8] The feud began with Quiznos' implementation of a contest, which invited consumers to submit commercials that showed Quiznos sandwiches as superior to Subway sandwiches. Specifically, the Quiznos sandwiches should be shown as meatier. Subway's suit claims that the resulting videos contain false statements and that the microsite developed for the contest, called meatnomeat.com, depicts Subway negatively. The case poses a legal question of critical importance to brands considering this approach: if a sponsoring brand's specifications call for making potentially false claims about a competing brand, resulting in consumer ads produced and distributed publicly, but the sponsoring brand itself did not make the false claim, should it be held liable for the user-generated content? The outcome of this case, scheduled for trial in 2009, could end this form of community promotion, making solicited citizen advertising too great a legal liability.

Overall, it is a good idea to remember the motives consumers might have for submitting content to brand-sponsored contests. Are they semi-professionals hoping to parlay a win into a career in film production or advertising? Are they after a simple fifteen minutes of fame? Are they truly brand evangelists eager for an opportunity to share their brand enthusiasm with others? Are they frustrated customers tired of poor customer service? Or is it just about the money, winning the big cash prize that accompanies some incentivized campaigns?

Speaking of cash incentives, there is also a risk that these content providers might begin to demand serious compensation for their idea generation and creative execution. Brands protect themselves to some degree with the fine print in the contest guidelines and rules, but over time this could be an issue.

Even the open distribution systems could limit the effectiveness of citizen advertising as a credible communication device. YouTube and other video sharing sites host a mix of organic CGM2, parody responses to incentivized campaigns, and solicited campaign ad units along with professional videos. What if the ratio of paid to organic placement shifts over time such that YouTube becomes nothing more than a broadcast channel for paid sponsorships?

Perhaps the most important concern is determining whether a consumer-generated ad will be consistent with the brand's strategy. Participants in these campaigns do not necessarily understand the brand's history, its positioning statement, its creative strategy, or even the characteristics of the target market. The vast majority of ads submitted in response to invitations are at best inconsistent with the brand's strategy or, at worse, totally inappropriate and offensive.

Lastly, brands must remember that while consumers create the content, content creation is not the only task necessary to use the resulting content. Someone has to sift through the entries, respond to queries, deal with public relations, and manage the legal issues that surface.

■ A Burgeoning Support Industry

Brands have many options for entering the arena of consumer-generated advertising. They may follow a limited approach of requesting ideas or copy like Mastercard's Priceless campaign. This can be as simple as integrating the invitation into other media exposures and providing a link online for submission. Other brands, such as Southwest's Wanna Get Away campaign, work with a provider like YouTube to promote and enable submissions and viewing of submissions. Brands can also develop fully interactive sites dedicated to citizen advertising, as Converse did.

For companies that need a more managed solution, there are service providers like ViTrue. ViTrue offers three primary product solutions: branded video communities, its AdMixer program, and Sharkle, a site that hosts citizen-advertising units (organic and mechanistic). The branded video communities are sites developed and hosted by ViTrue, which enable video posting, video sharing, and other social-networking aspects all in a branded format. Pringles' Jingles for Pringles Web site is an example of ViTrue's branded video communities (www.jinglesforpringles.com). The communities encourage brand loyalists (and aspiring creative directors and film producers) to post video advertising and other forms of CGM. ViTrue's AdMixer program (see image 3) is a "mash-up" software that enables brands to invite packaged content drawing upon brand-approved assets. Lastly, organic and packaged content can be submitted to ViTrue's Sharkle (see image 4), a video community that accepts citizen ads for any brand, not just those that use ViTrue's services. Like other communities, Sharkle offers many social-networking features, including messaging, blogging, and file posting.

XLNTads.com is a start-up company designed to host contests for brands sponsoring citizen-advertising campaigns. Brands subscribe to the service, which includes management of the content submissions. XLNTads promotes all the contests live on the site, offers a cash prize for winning submissions, screens submissions that are objectionable, recommends winners, and hosts the ad units.

Current TV is another innovative player in the citizen-advertising niche market. Current TV is an independent television network, cofounded by Al Gore, that features viewer-created programming and citizen advertising. Brand sponsors like Toyota, Sony, and L'Oreal have invited consumers to submit their ads to Current TV. Content is incentivized with viewers whose spots are chosen to run on the network receiving $1,000.

■ The Decision to Engage with Citizen Advertising

Consumer-generated advertising will continue to grow in the short term as brands become accustomed to working with consumers to create brand messages. How can brands make the most of this approach? This list of questions can assist in determining whether to pursue a CGA strategy.

- Is the target market for the brand likely to respond to CGA invitations?
- If so, what might they say?
- How likely is it that the messages provided by consumers will be consistent with the brand's intended positioning strategy?
- How much freedom is the brand willing to provide to consumers generating content? Will organic or packaged contributions be encouraged?
- How will the "invitation" be promoted to the target market?
- How will submissions be judged?
- Will all submissions be shared or will there be a screening process?
- Should the brand collaborate with a site like YouTube to gain increased awareness of the CGA promotion and a distribution outlet?

If the answers to these questions lead the brand to the use of participatory advertising, there are several guidelines for maximizing the potential for effectiveness. First, integrate the CGA promotion with other aspects of the brand's communications plan. Contests and other CGA executions will be most effective when they are embedded in a brand's messaging strategy. Second, don't let fear guide the brand's response to citizen ads. Even submissions with off-point messages can act as an engagement device and result in benefits to brand equity. Remember that spoofs are not always meant as insults. Third, collect biographical sketches on the consumers submitting advertising. There are many reasons for this. As consumers become more aware and increasingly cynical due to counterfeit citizen ads and shilling practices, being able to talk about the creators of citizen ads will offer a counter to suspicions about the authenticity of the program. Plus, the stories about contributors could easily be fodder for engaging other consumers. The insights from film contributors on the Converse Gallery Web site are great examples of this. Fourth, do encourage submissions from amateurs. If CGA gets a reputation for being created by brand professionals, it will backfire. Already there is a perception that winning user-generated advertising tends to come from professionals or semiprofessionals looking for a career break. If this trend continues, everyday contributors—the true amateurs—may lose interest in participating. While amateurs should be encouraged, a professional context for the contest should be created to promote high-quality content. Consider issuing personalized invitations to highly talented and/or highly involved brand fans. Fifth, remember the motives that drive citizen submissions. Content creators likely want fame or fortune, or both. Offer incentives and promote the winners. Feed their desire for recognition and reward. Lastly, remember that organic CGA is a source of insight into the consumers' beliefs about your brand. If consumers develop ads with a certain brand message, there is a good chance others in your target audience feel the same way.

What are the characteristics of successful citizen-advertising campaigns? They can be summed up with a few key words.

- Consistency: The framework for the contest ensures the resulting ad submissions are consistent with the brand's positioning and strategy.
- Democracy: The brand managers must be prepared to accept the work of the participants. Brand democracy is meant to be democratic, with a voice to those who choose to use it.
- Authenticity: Consumer content creators and content recipients appreciate more fluidity and creative freedom. The closer to pure organic the submissions are, the more valuable the message the ads promote will be.
- Participatory: The campaign enables participation from many consumers, not just those who wish to create content. Others can engage by voting for favorites, critiquing submissions, and sharing content with "send this to a friend" capabilities and by embedding links on blogs and social-networking sites.

Marketers who recognize the value of CGA understand that an inherent trade-off is accepting that not all the consumer dialogue created will be positive or on point with a brand's positioning strategy. They understand that there is a net gain to engaging consumers and that even parodies serve to provide brand exposure. Ultimately, the goal should be to create and nurture a relationship between consumers and the brand. Relationships are not perfect. They have their ups and downs, but valuable relationships offer more good to the parties involved than bad. This is a basic principle of citizen advertising and the philosophy of brand democratization.

8 ▪ ▪ ▪

In My Opinion
The Social Influence of Consumer Product Reviews

In the virtual environment of social media, consumers have a platform for producing content, distributing content, and interacting with content provided by others, consumers, professional media, and commercial entities. The social Web invites conversation from those who might otherwise never connect due to dispersed geography, interests, and intent. The social influence of the Internet enables people, citizens of the Internet, to share control over the creation and distribution of information and entertainment. Content distribution is no longer limited to organized commercial media outlets that determine what should be shared, how, and when. Instead, media institutions coexist alongside vast social networks of consumers who exercise their influence over the spread of content. This is the essence of media democracy, one aspect of which is the democratization of brand messages. Manifestations of media democracy include the rise of citizen journalists reporting on news events without the potential philosophical biases sometimes attributed to organizations, citizen advertisers embedding their creative ideas about a brand's appeal in videos, and citizen product experts voicing their satisfaction with, concerns about, and experiences with branded products.

The last results in a plethora of product information available online in the form of product reviews on review Web sites like Epinions.com, retail Web sites like Amazon.com, and in millions upon millions of posted comments (in blogs, in response to blogs, on message boards, and in chat rooms), as well as through conversations that take place among socially networked friends and acquaintances. It is word-of-mouth communication, the sharing of information from person to person, spread not to the few one could reach using one-to-one communication but to the masses using online vehicles, which are available to millions of consumers and which exist in perpetuity due to the nature of the Internet.

Arnold Brown, writer for the *Futurist*, captures the displacement of product experts by the everyman, stating, "I call it Zagating the marketplace—a term from the Zagat hotel and restaurant guide that polls the opinions of actual diners and hotel patrons, rather than 'expert' reviewers." He insightfully concludes, "The individual consumer, alone or collectively, no longer needs or accepts being told by any aspirants to higher authority what to do, what to think, what to buy."[1]

Opinions of products are a form of user-generated content and can be categorized as either CGM or CFM. CGM is an umbrella term for user content but primarily refers to first-person commentary, brand essays, about brand experiences that are published online in blogs, on review sites or review sections of retailer sites, on message boards and forums, and elsewhere. CFM includes opinionated responses to content. For example, a video ad may be posted on YouTube. In the comments section, consumers can voice their opinions of the video as well as relay product information, experiences, and attitudes toward the brand. Responses might also be issued through consumers' own blogs or on social-networking profile pages. Whether through CGM or CFM, the consumer opinions become part of the public discourse about the brand. The difference is simply whether the consumer voiced the opinion by initiating the conversation or responding to some existing piece of communication.

Either way, the publication of consumer opinions is a powerful and influential form of user-generated content. In fact, one could claim online word-of-mouth communication of product reviews and opinions are the most influential form of user-generated content. They arise as typical people are empowered to express themselves and share these expressions with others using the Internet as medium and social-media outlets as vehicles, and typical consumers seek out unbiased, credible information to aid in decision making. The two forces push from opposite sides (informant and information seeker) to manifest a shift in the relative influence of marketing product information. It would be shortsighted for any brand not to consider how to manage these conversations to build brand equity.

This shift in the authority attributed to product experts was perhaps first witnessed in the areas of film, theater, music, and literature. Critics still review creative works and publish these reviews in traditional media outlets. However, word-of-mouth opinions by laymen who consumed the creative product tend to be more influential on sales of these products than are good reviews from the critics. As Watts admonishes in his book, *Six Degrees*, when it comes to spread of information online, anyone can be influential.[2] Watts explains that influence takes place as people with opinions to share do so with their network of friends, family, and colleagues, who may then in turn influence their network, and so on. The spread can begin with anyone, but the degree to which the information spreads relies upon the receptiveness of those receiving the information and the size of their networks. Online, the cascade effect, the widespread propagation of influence through networks, is more likely to occur because of the critical mass of people and the ease with which information can be published, shared, searched, and retrieved.

■ The Influence of Online Product Opinions

There is a critical mass of opinion givers and takers. Data from Nielsen Online suggests that 74% of online adults have participated in the following activities: commented on a blog, posted an online product review, participated in an online discussion, or used online opinions to research a product purchase.[3] Access to online product reviews on retail Web sites is the most demanded Web site feature, behind search functionality.[4] A research study by eVOC Insights indicates that 48% of online shoppers seek out product reviews before buying.[5] Even more moving is this factoid from the E-tailing Group: 92% of online shoppers say that reviews are helpful to them.[6] Jupiter Research claims that 77% of online shoppers use reviews and ratings when purchasing.[7] The following story illustrates the influence of user-generated reviews perfectly. A reviewer described "how Burpee's Sea Magic Organic Seaweed Growth Activator perked his spider plant up 'just like a light socket.'"[8] Sales of the product doubled following the post! Quite simply, consumers trust information from other consumers. One study reports that the most trusted form of product information consists of recommendations from other consumers (cited by 78% of survey respondents). Another finding in the same study: consumer opinions posted online was noted by 61% of the survey respondents.[9] Consumers trust information provided online by other consumers more than television, magazine, radio, or Internet advertising, more than sponsorships, and more than recommendations from salespeople or paid endorsers. Online product reviews may appear on many types of Web sites. They may appear on formal review sites like Epinions.com or Uncrate.com, on retailing Web sites, in comments posted to social community sites, and on blogs. While product reviews on review, retail, and social community sites have high levels of credibility, blog posts do not. *Brandweek*, reporting on a study by Jupiter Research, notes that only 21% of consumers feel that they can trust product information found in blogs.[10] Some wary consumers might feel that blog reviews lack integrity; one possible explanation is the affiliate relationships some bloggers have with manufacturers and retail Web sites. Another is the prevalence of splogs, spam in the form of a blog, which are used to promote products or Web sites. Still, the presence of citizen reviews and their influence cannot be denied.

Why are citizen reviews such powerful sources of influence on consumer shopping behaviors? It comes down to five key factors: (1) accessibility, (2) trust, (3) perceptions of authority, (4) similarity, and (5) the consensus effect. Online shoppers appreciate the value that reviews offer in terms of a decision heuristic. Reviews make it easier for shoppers to narrow their decision sets, and shoppers trust other shoppers more than information provided by marketers. The information is easily accessible to online shoppers who use the Internet to find product-related information prior to purchase. As shoppers enter search terms for product information, reviews, blog posts, and other content are easily indexed and retrieved. Others come across product information by serendipity, as they shop.

Attribution theory offers an explanation of the trust factor. Consumers tend to discount opinions or recommendations offered by paid endorsers, whether they are celebrity brand endorsers or salespeople who serve as brand agents. They attribute the recommendation to the relationship between the agent and the brand. In other words, they discount the value of the opinion because it came from someone who is paid for the opinion. However, citizen endorsements are not motivated by the brand that stands to benefit from the recommendation.

While citizen endorsers are not paid agents representing a brand, they do hold a position of authority in the minds of other consumers. When an expert, someone perceived to be an authority on some topic, makes a recommendation, people who are relying on heuristics, or mental shortcuts, to make decisions will tend to follow the expert recommendations. Professional experts and reviewers, whether book critics, movie critics, doctors, or lawyers, have authority in specific, relevant product categories, but so do citizen endorsers who have actually used the product. In other words, one's experience with the product serves as the source of authority.

This effect is heightened by a perception that citizen endorsers are more like us. Consumers tend to be more influenced by people who seem similar than those whose lives and experiences seem vastly different. We seek out people with like fields of experience and states of need. Celebrity endorsers benefit from attractiveness, likability, and the dream many have to live the good life. But they tend to lack the characteristic of similarity. How similar is Oprah's life and situation compared to that of the average working woman? How alike is Tom Hanks to the average middle-aged father? Ultimately, celebrities have resources and lives so far beyond the realm of everyday life that, while capable of generating product awareness and trial, they can fall short compared to the influence of a credible opinion offered by a product user deemed similar to the information receiver. Citizen endorsers benefit from perceptions of similarity that are typically absent from celebrity endorsers. Likewise, product experts have credentials that enhance perceptions of authority in the product category, but detract from the sense of similarity. BizRate found 59% of users considered customer reviews to be more valuable than expert reviews.[11]

Lastly, shoppers seeking out product information online can be influenced by consensus. It is human nature for people to seek consistency with the beliefs of referent others and to tend to respond to the bandwagon effect, going along when it seems like everyone else is, too. People tend to act and believe as others do. Jen-Hung Huang and Yi-Fen Chen examined this phenomenon in the context of online shopping and confirmed that "herding" does occur. The study found that consumers shopping online were more influenced by other consumers than by recommendations from experts.[12]

Product opinions affect shoppers, but that is not the only benefit to accrue to retailers. Online reviews generate increased sales by bringing in new customers. Further, people who write reviews tend to shop more frequently and to spend more online than those who do not write reviews. A report from Jupiter Research and Bazaarvoice reveals that while active reviewers account for just 20% of online shoppers, they are responsible for 32% of online sales.[13] If those who offer reviews tend to be among the most active online shoppers, it makes sense to offer that option on a Web site. Traffic can also be driven to the retail Web site through organic search. Organic search results improve because reviewers tend to use the same key words (tags) in their product descriptions that searchers will use. For example, Petco, a pet supplies retailer, found that customer reviews generated five times as many site visits as any previous campaign.[14] Feedback areas are also an effective conversion tool for Web sites. Reviews also result in better site stickiness—customers reading reviews will stay at a retail site longer than they would otherwise. Lastly, the reviews and opinion posts become a source of research data highlighting consumer opinions in a frank yet unobtrusive fashion. Some businesses believe the data resulting from online reviews to be more valuable than data from focus group research. Businesses can learn whether consumers like a competitor's brand better and why, how consumers are reacting to positive or negative press, what stories are being spread about the brand, and which customers are being evangelical and which ones are acting as "brand terrorists."

What does this mean for brands? Brand strategy must be twofold. First, brands must be prepared to ensure high standards when it comes to product quality and service if they wish to survive in the world of social reviews. It is now so easy for anyone to tell everyone about their brand experiences, whether good or bad, that it behooves brands to ensure that those experiences are good—very good. Organizations that fail in satisfying customers with product and service quality risk having citizen reviewers share negative word of mouth with the world. What's more, those reviews will magnify the negative aspects of the brand while devaluing the positive, ultimately reducing brand equity and any competitive advantage that brand might have had.

Second, brands should embrace, not hide—because there is really no place, online, to hide from consumer opinions. Instead, organizations can engage in word-of-mouth marketing by actively giving people reasons to talk about the brand while facilitating the conversations. The Word of Mouth Marketing Association (WOMMA) identifies five key components of word-of-mouth marketing on its Web site (www.womma.org), all of which can be applied to managing online product opinions for brand value:

- Educating people about your products and services;
- Identifying people most likely to share their opinions;
- Providing tools that make it easier to share information;
- Studying how, where, and when opinions are being shared; and
- Listening and responding to supporters, detractors, and neutrals.

This means encouraging the conversation by informing consumers about the brand, offering consumers a forum for expressing opinions about the brand, and responding (making the communication a two-way process) to comments consumers make on the forum and elsewhere. Brand enthusiasts can be invited to offer reviews, resulting in more engagement from brand fans and the propagation of positive word-of-mouth communication about the brand. Perhaps, most important is the final component of word-of-mouth marketing—listening. There is valuable information about the need for product improvements like product features and service quality embedded in consumer opinion posts.

Third, brands should recognize that the influence of consumer opinions can be propagated by the development of a community that encourages and rewards participation from brand fans. Social communities will support citizen reviews—they already do so, as evidenced by the plethora of reviews posted on social-networking sites. But the brand can better participate if it backs this form of social media with a branded platform.

■ What Are the Deterrents to Leveraging Citizen Opinions?

With statistics like these, it seems clear that e-retailers should utilize online opinions as a form of influential brand communication. Although most consumers want reviews available on retail Web sites, they still are not a standard feature of such sites. Why? Aside from the problem that marketers and advertisers have overlooked their value and influence, the most commonly cited reason given for not allowing online reviews on sites is the fear that dissatisfied customers will use the review feature as a venue for flaming a brand. Given the old adage that negative word-of-mouth communication is more damaging than positive word-of-mouth communication is beneficial, some retailers have erred on the side of caution when it comes to offering a review feature.

The sheer ratio of negative to positive reviews found on various sites suggests that this fear is unfounded. Macy's reported that of the more than 9,000 product reviews posted on www.macys.com, 72% of them were positive, and Bazaarvoice, a firm that provides a customer review and rating service for e-tailers, has reported that 80% of its user-generated reviews are positive.[15]

Sam Decker of Bazaarvoice points out that retailers can benefit from negative reviews and should welcome them.[16] Consumers want to see negative reviews to be able to accurately assess the degree of product risk they face when purchasing. They seek to minimize perceived performance and financial risk associated with purchases. Negative reviews give them the information they need to assess risk. The negative reviews also provide a sense of credibility. Consumers abide by the assumption that if the reviews seem too good to be true, they probably are. Lastly, negative reviews give valuable information to the retailer on products that should be improved, augmented, or discontinued.

The other primary deterrent for e-retailers is more operational in nature. There are challenges related to acquiring and managing reviews and the review process as well as site maintenance. Fortunately, there are companies, like Bazaarvoice and PowerReviews, which service retailers by providing the technology for capturing and displaying customer feedback. Citizen reviews can become part of the companies' review databases, which may be shared (at the discretion of the client) with other clients. Customers may view the reviews on the client's Web site or at the service company's portal.

PowerReviews maximizes the effectiveness of user-contributed reviews by providing several unique features like PowerTags (a feature that allows reviewers to select from tags offered by previous reviewers), PowerSummary (a feature that allows readers to see easily, rather than scrolling through numerous reviews, what reviewers have agreed upon), Merchant Response (a feature that allows manufacturers and retailers to respond to comments made by a reviewer), and Verified Purchaser (a feature that highlights whether a reviewer was actually a purchaser of the product in question). Bazaarvoice manages a team of editors who read every review submitted to its clients' Web sites. Editors do not change the meaning of a reviewer's submission but clean up mistakes and inappropriate language.

Companies like PowerReviews and Bazaarvoice earn revenue using a pay-for-performance system. Portals reveal snippets of a review, but readers are directed to a retail client's Web site to read the full review. Thus, companies like Bazaarvoice provide the benefit of driving traffic to retailer Web sites.

Sites with review features need to remember that when inviting consumers to contribute marketing messages, they are basically inviting consumers into a conversation—and conversations should be two-way communication. There is value in responding to user-contributed reviews. It illustrates the company's appreciation for consumer input and provides an opportunity to point out product improvements or other steps that may be taken to improve a product offering. However, this means that companies must allocate financial and human resources to the ongoing dialogue with consumers. Some organizations hesitate to allocate such resources.

■ What Are the Deterrents to Using Citizen Opinions?

From the perspective of the shopper being influenced, the greatest limitation of online reviews is the potential for the reviews to actually be stealth-marketing attempts, when marketers post content disguised as consumer generated, or shill reviews, when a person pretends to be independent but actually serves as a paid agent for the product in question. PayPerPost, an agency that matches bloggers to brand sponsors who pay for brand mentions in the blogger's commentary, brought the issue of shilling to the forefront. Consumers look for clues to identify unethical word-of-mouth marketing practices. For example, overly positive reviews can tip off consumers to a fake review. In addition, the presence of pitch diction, language that sounds too promotional, is an indicator. For example, consider this review found on a retail Web site for watches: "This watch is an exquisite beauty, a finely crafted automatic timepiece coupled with the accuracy and reliability of quartz." Pitch diction uses industry jargon and oversells the product's features and quality. It simply isn't believable as a citizen opinion.

Amazon's review editor has noted that most of its online reviews are not paid advertising, but it can be difficult for users to distinguish between reviews that are genuinely user generated from those that are marketing generated.[17] Some sites, especially those exclusively for reviews (like Epinions.com), do not allow manufacturers to submit reviews. For instance, www.expotv.com does not allow company submissions. Another review site, www.shopwiki.com, does allow such submissions, but any affiliations must be transparent to site visitors.

Sometimes, though, it can be difficult for consumers to detect the presence of stealth marketing or the work of a shill. BzzAgent, a word-of-mouth marketing agency, recruits and assigns "buzz agents" to learn about products and share product information with others. Buzz agents are people who have volunteered to actively discuss products with others. Agents are not compensated financially, but they receive product samples, discounts, and special offers. One of the primary motives for becoming a buzz agent is the social capital the agent gains by always being the person in the know. The company offers word-of-mouth marketing assistance, physically and virtually. The BzzAgent Frogpond service is offered to companies seeking to develop a citizen presence online.

Companies that practice unethical word-of-mouth marketing techniques may find themselves victim to a backlash from consumers in the form of credlining, whereby consumers analyze product information, identifying the truthful from the false and the positive from the negative, ultimately publishing a scorecard of the results online.

■ Best Practices for Leveraging Citizen Opinions

Ultimately, it is important to remember that users read online reviews because they want to know what people like themselves think of a product. Brands should strive to achieve these characteristics in any word-of-mouth marketing program determined to generate citizen-generated social influence:

1. *Authenticity:* Accepting organic word of mouth, whether positive or negative.
2. *Transparency:* Acknowledging opinions that were invited, incentivized, or facilitated by the brand. Both authenticity and transparency build credibility, and the more trust consumers have in citizen opinions about the brand, the more influential the opinions will be on purchase behavior.
3. *Advocacy:* Enabling consumers to rate the value of opinions offered on the site. These ratings aid consumers as they seek to efficiently process a mass of product information.
4. *Participatory approach:* Encouraging consumers to offer posts. Many consumers who would not submit something as effort intensive as citizen advertising will post a review or comment. Give them a voice with reviews.
5. *Reciprocity:* Acknowledging the value of the opinions offered by brand customers. It takes effort to review a product and post an opinion. Citizen endorsers should be thanked, and their efforts on behalf of the brand (even if the review is negative) acknowledged.
6. *Infectiousness:* Sharing of reviews. Brands can syndicate opinions by making it easy to send reviews to friends or embed links to reviews on blogs and social-networking profiles.
7. *Sustainability:* Ensuring the reviews remain available. One of the reasons opinions online are so influential is because they live on in perpetuity. If a consumer tells a friend about a satisfying brand experience on the phone, the story once told is no longer retrievable or trackable. Online stories can live on forever, and their field of influence tracked.

Consider these specific guidelines for making the most of customer-generated online reviews:

- Ensure the review and editorial system in place can operate sufficiently and rapidly. Customers like to see their reviews posted right away.
- Editing should be limited to minimizing the use of inappropriate language. Customers should not feel that their views are being altered by the site.
- Solicit reviews from buyers; encourage those shopping on the site to review the products. This offers several benefits: it provides an additional touch

point with the customer; it suggests that the company cares about customer opinions; it enhances site stickiness; and it increases the likelihood that those customers will shop again on the site.

- Increase the ego benefit for users posting reviews. Reviewers are, at least in part, responding to a desire to see their opinions published. Enhance this benefit of reviewing by enabling reviewers to post their picture and other methods of leaving their "signatures." Several product review sites, including www.expotv.com, www.shopwiki.com, and www.ciao.co.uk, are encouraging reviewers to post video product reviews.

- Consider using trust marks to authenticate organic product reviews from those that are incentivized or scripted.

- Consider offering an incentive for reviews. Offering an incentive, even a simple thank you, can trigger a reciprocation response in a reviewer by creating a sense of relationship with the site and emphasizing the value the site places on reviews.

- Enhance credibility by providing links to other reviews. Don't require readers to do background checks on products; make the information readily available to them.

- Disclose the source of the review. Don't make users wonder where the information came from and whether they can trust it.

Brown[18] perhaps said it best, "Understanding that public-opinion trends are driven not by a few influentials influencing everyone else but by many impressionable people influencing one another should change how companies incorporate social influence into their marketing campaigns."

9 ■ ■ ■

Social Fiction
Branding with Alternate Reality Games

> If I had a world of my own, everything would be nonsense. Nothing would be what it is, because everything would be what it isn't. And contrary wise, what is, it wouldn't be. And what it wouldn't be, it would. You see?[1]

Brand engagement starts with a desire to do more than just push brand messages through traditional channels to a target audience. Today, consumers want to be involved. They want to cocreate a brand's message. They want interaction with the brand and with others who are interested in the brand. Brands that understand this opportunity for consumer involvement are energizing their brands using many of the devices we have discussed already: social networking, consumer-generated advertising, and viral video. But many are also exploring other forms of social communities. One such community is that of the players who participate in ARGs. As a form of social media, ARGs begin with a scripted scenario but become a form of CFM as the network of gamers participate in the game by discovering clues, sharing information with others, and changing the structure and plot of the game with their responses. In this chapter, the focus is on the communities that surround the play of ARGs.

■ What Is an Alternate Reality Game?

What does Alice know about branding? It seems she understands the very philosophy behind this relatively new entertainment (and branding) genre. In fact, Alice's fall down the rabbit hole inspired the terminology for the official start to a game. Alternate reality gaming, which is also referred to as immersive fiction, is, at its core, gaming, but the term gaming doesn't begin to capture the intricacies of this genre. Unfiction.com (www.unfiction.com/glossary), a leading Web site for the ARG community, defines an ARG as "a cross-media genre of interactive fiction using multiple delivery and communications media, including television, radio, newspapers, Internet, email, SMS, telephone, voicemail, and postal service."[2] This definition points to the truly cross-media, cross-channel (all-wheel network) communication structure of ARGs.

ARGs are interactive narratives that comprise fiction and nonfiction, mystery and detection, and scripted and unscripted scenes played out by characters and real people. The games unfold over multiple forms of media and utilize many types of game elements, each tailored for the media platform used. ARGs may utilize telephones, e-mail, outdoor signage, T-shirts, television, music, and more to reveal story clues, compose scenes, and unite gamers. It would be impossible to solve the puzzle alone; hence, the term "collective detective" acknowledges the need for a team approach in solving the mystery. It is this reliance on social networks and collaboration necessary to share clues and scenes quickly and efficiently that ensures online communication is the primary outlet for uniting geographically dispersed players. Thus, despite the use of so many media channels, the Internet is the central channel by which gamers share information and collaborate to solve the pieces of the puzzle.

Jordan Weisman, creative director and cofounder of 42 Entertainment (arguably the leading company for the development of ARGs for branding), emphasized that the Internet was the inspiration for his experimentation into ARGs, saying, "The experiment was to develop a narrative structure that was organic to the web. In looking at the web, I realized that it had been and still is used primarily for distribution of narrative formats that existed prior to the web—audio, video, written word, etc. There wasn't a narrative structure that embraced the chaotic and frustrating nature of the web."[3] Weisman's experiment has subsequently inspired several audacious brands to develop games to engage consumers in the story guiding the game and, importantly, in the brand's story.

Games (and their stories, scenes, and characters) are written and controlled by writers and directors known as puppet masters. Teams of players may work together to find clues, analyze what's happened so far, and further the story by communicating theories about the plot and the game's meaning. By the way, despite the references to gaming, ARG enthusiasts live by a basic mantra established during the original ARG, the Beast: *This is not a game!* These stories seek to involve people in becoming game participants, but even spectators can feel involved by monitoring advances and developments in the game.

Take, for example, the start to the "I Love Bees" ARG used to promote the launch of the video game "Halo 2." According to the Web site, "I Love Bees Quick Start Guide" (see http://www.mirlandano.com/quickstart.html), this ARG began when several people received a Fed Ex package of honey. A few days later, the promotional trailer for Halo 2 referenced a Web site, ilovebees.com/xbox.com. This Web site provided lists of pay phone numbers, GPS coordinates for the phones, and a time each number would be called. More instructions and clues were then delivered via calls to the pay phones.[4] From the start of the game until its conclusion (with players earning a preview experience of the Halo 2 game), players and observers visited the I Love Bees Web site for updates on the narrative and new clues. In addition to material posted on the official Web site, numerous Web sites and forums developed for those following the game. Just in this brief summary of the start of I Love Bees, the characteristics of the ARG genre are apparent.

- ARGs are based on a fictional story. Game characters, events, places, and plot are imagined and explored by the game writers, known as puppet masters.
- The story unfolds as a mystery, which invites players to solve clues before more of the narrative is revealed.
- Story clues are offered using a variety of media, ranging from traditional media like television and newspapers to text messages and messages hidden in code in movie trailers or even concert T-shirts.
- The story is fictional, as are the game characters, but the game space is not. The players are real people, and the clues are revealed in real time. Consequently, real life is a medium. This characteristic has led to the ARG "TINAG" belief—"This is not a game!" Telephone numbers, Web sites, and locations revealed in game are all real and functioning.
- Players collaborate to unravel the meanings of the clues offered.
- The story unfolds, but typically not in a linear fashion. The speed of disclosure is influenced by the player's success and speed in solving clues and sharing them with the player population.
- Even the story may not unfold as initially conceived. Because players interact with the game, and player response can dictate the next scene in the story, stories are fluid, organic, and unpredictable.

- Players rely on the Internet as the hub of communication.
- The desire that players share information with each other and even that the story be followed by observers attests to the viral nature of ARGs.
- ARGs are not exclusively designed for marketing purposes, but the most successful ARGs to date have been affiliated with brands.

ARGs are mystery-based narratives designed by game architects and revealed via multiple media platforms to encourage players and observers to collaborate online to solve the mystery. Although the experience of playing the ARG may be its primary mission, ARGs are often created and executed with the goal of engaging consumers with a specific brand sponsor, as was true of I Love Bees.

■ The Vocabulary of ARGs

ARGs have their own vernacular—understanding the lingo is the first step in understanding the culture of alternate reality gaming. This list, adapted from Unfiction's glossary (www.unfiction.com/glossary), presents the basics of the lexicon of alternate reality gamers.

- Puppet master: The authors, architects, and managers of the story and its scenarios and puzzles.
- Curtain: The invisible line separating the players from the puppet masters.
- Rabbit hole: The clue or site that initiates the game.
- Collective detective: A term that captures the notion of collaboration among a team of geographically dispersed players who work together to further the story.
- Lurkers: People who follow the game but do not actively participate.
- Rubbernecker: A person who does not actively play in the game but may participate in forums about the game and contribute to the game's solution.
- Steganography: The tactic of hiding messages within another medium such that the message is undetectable for those who do not know to look for it.
- TINAG: This acronym stands for a defining mantra of ARGs—This is not a game!
- Trail: A reference index of the game, including relevant sites, puzzles, in-game characters, and other information. Trails are useful for new players coming late into a game and to veteran players piecing together the narrative.

■ ARGs as Transmedia Stories

Henry Jenkins, author of *Convergence Culture,* notes that ARGs are one manifestation of a new form of storytelling, transmedia storytelling.[5]

He defines a transmedia story as one that "unfolds across multiple media platforms with each new text making a distinctive and valuable contribution to the whole."[6] Transmedia stories are not necessarily branded, at least not beyond the brand of entertainment itself. The Matrix, for instance, is offered in *Convergence Culture* as an example of transmedia storytelling. The Matrix did not simply offer merchandising through co-branded goodies distributed via fast food merchandise and toys modeled after story characters. As a transmedia story, The Matrix utilized three films distributed via movie theaters and DVD, a comic series, a series of film shorts, a video game, and a multiplayer online role-playing game. Each component could exist on its own, and fans could enjoy the story without all the components offered, yet the story held more depth, richness, and opportunities for involvement because of the synergistic effects of the multiple platforms. Indeed, entertainment properties like The Matrix are well suited to transmedia storytelling because the story is a brand.

We can conclude that an ARG is a form of transmedia storytelling in that the use of multimedia is one of the defining elements of an ARG, with each clue or story scene contributing to the game as a whole. But ARGs differ from other forms of transmedia storytelling. First, an ARG is not simply a story told via a variety of media platforms. Rather, the story behind any ARG is in part influenced and scripted by the players. Other forms of transmedia storytelling exhibit a greater degree of control over the narrative. Second, transmedia storytelling utilizes multiple platforms, but an ARG is more likely a single technique, albeit a complex one, in the arsenal of a transmedia story.

Jenkins, among others, has acknowledged that transmedia storytelling lends itself to transmedia branding—building a multimedia story, backward and forward, to promote a brand among its target audience. Nowhere is this potential clearer than in the case of entertainment brands like the Halo series of games, television programs such as *Lost*, or even novels like *Cathy's Book*. Each has included an ARG in its promotional campaign.

Grant McCracken likens the value of transmedia storytelling for brands to that of soap operas for Proctor & Gamble.[7] He points out that a loose association between P&G and the soap operas it sponsored was quite effective in building the P&G brand. As "cadet narratives," as McCracken calls these loose associations, the narrative is tied to the brand by association more than it would by building stories directly related to the brand itself. How is risk minimized? Because the story (or, in the case of ARGs, the game) is not acknowledged as a branding mechanism or tied solely to other components of a brand's marketing campaign, decisions can be made to distance the brand from the ARG or heighten the relationship between the brand and the game. Importantly, ARGs accomplish this same benefit by providing an intriguing story with which to engage consumers and brand loyalists while providing brand managers the necessary distance from the brand meaning to minimize risk to the brand's equity.

Importantly, while some of the most well-known and successful ARGs are associated with story-centric entertainment brands, ARGs have also been embraced by other products, including goods (like The Art of the Heist ARG affiliated with Audi) and environmental movements (like the World Without Oil ARG, which sought to bring about awareness of the potential for a global oil crisis). These brands have shown that ARGs can be used successfully as a transmedia device for nonentertainment properties.

■ Branding Via ARGs

Again, not all games are brand sponsored, but to date the most successful ones (based on participation statistics and online dialogue) have been. The movie launch of A.I. started it all with the development of "The Beast." Since then, some of the brands that have used ARGs as branding devices include General Motors, Audi, Nine Inch Nails, and Microsoft's Xbox, among others. The prevalence of brand-initiated ARGs is at least in part due to the funding necessary for building an intricate, multimedia, multichannel narrative with characters and clues spread on- and off-line. For instance, David Kiley reports that Audi spent $5 million to run its Art of the Heist ARG.[8] Compared to traditional advertising, the cost of an ARG is minimal. However, the resources required are sufficiently substantial to warrant the need for a brand sponsor. Game architects have sought to develop player-funded games; Perplex City's Receda Cube is an example. It was launched in 2005 and ended when a player found the Receda Cube in early 2007. Thus far, player-funded games have not gained the traction (or been capable of generating resources) necessary to compete with branded games.

The value of branding for the ARG genre is not limited to resource generation. In addition to covering the development costs, a brand sponsor provides for the ARG's foundation or story context. Brands help establish the in-game characters, set the scenes, establish the plot, and identify the meaning of signs and symbols used in clues. The brand's history lends itself to the ARG's back story. Further, brand enthusiasts bring to the game knowledge of the brand, which can assist in the discovery and interpretation of game clues.

The relationship between brands and ARGs are mutually beneficial. The reach and ability for an ARG to engage those it reaches is undeniable. Those who are curious about the reach and effectiveness of ARGs are encouraged to visit Christy Dena's site (www.christydena.com). Dena maintains a Web site detailing the statistics for several ARGs on her site.

Brand enthusiasts are likely to participate in an ARG affiliated with a favored brand, but they are by no means the sole target. ARGs also attract game enthusiasts who seek a game opportunity and, through interaction with the brand, may become a customer. Players may come from either group—game or brand enthusiasts—but ARGs extend beyond active players to reach passive observers. Consider this common line from brand-sponsored sweepstakes, "you don't have to play to win." ARGs attract attention from people who choose not to play. They stay involved as "lurkers," defined by unfiction.com as people who follow the game through posts online but do not directly participate, or "rubberneckers," defined by unfiction.com as those who attend chats online, post on game boards, and even contribute to the solution of the puzzle through their participation in the game dialogue, but do not have direct contact in the game. From a branding perspective, lurkers and rubberneckers are just as critical to the success of an ARG as are the active players. Unfiction.com estimates that the ratio of lurkers to active players can range from 5:1 to 20:1, depending upon the game.

There is a clear branding implication here: the reach of the game is far greater than the number of active players. For instance, Audi claims that 500,000 consumers, in its target audience of 25- to 35-year-old, upper-income males, participated in its Art of the Heist ARG with average exposure of four to ten minutes spent on numerous Web sites and pages used to embed game clues.[9] Did the ARG pay off for Audi? Kiley reports that hits to Audi's Web site were up 140% during the game with the most hits originating from game sites; its dealers earned 10,000 qualified sales leads, and 3,500 test drives could be attributed to the game.[10] Xbox's ARG for Halo 2, "I Love Bees," performed even better, attracting 750,000 active participants, and another 2.5 million casual players.[11]

There is no doubt that ARGs have value as reach vehicles. Frequency of exposure is high because the engagement devices pull enthusiasts (players, lurkers, and rubberneckers) into the story and encourage them to seek out new information as it is presented in the game. ARGs are welcomed brand messages among gamers because they do not invade people's space with a brand message. Instead, the rabbit hole and all subsequent clues are passive. They only take on meaning as they are discovered and pursued by consumers who seek them out and make them a part of their lives. The length of exposure, especially compared to other online advertising, is also high with most participants spending several minutes over several weeks and even months with game-related Web sites.

That's not all. Once involved, ARG enthusiasts are not just thinking about the brand when exposed to specific brand messages. They are cognitively involved in the story even when they are away from the game, doing all the things they typically do in their daily lives. Because ARGs are puzzles, they invite the gamers to cognate on the messages. Experts believe there is also long-term value to the players' involvement. For instance, John Hegarty, one of the principals of BB&H, referred to this as "seed branding." He went on to say, "if you develop a brand from the ground up like this, you encourage the customers to be evangelists."[12]

Yet another benefit to ARG sponsorship is the value of unpaid media coverage that brands earn when ARGs are revealed in news stories. Perhaps there will come a time when ARGs are so mainstream that they do not warrant media coverage, but for now press coverage of ARGs provide enormous value in terms of media impressions. For example, consider the ARG used by the band Nine Inch Nails to promote the launch of its latest album, *Year Zero*. Speculation about the ARG inspired numerous stories about the band, its tour, and album; a typical album launch for a less-than-mainstream band is unlikely to capture such media attention. Additional coverage and buzz is provided as bloggers talk about the game. The greatest advantage of all, though, is the ability for an ARG to engage. Perhaps Jonathan Cude, creative director of the McKinney agency, which developed Audi's Art of the Heist ARG, captures the advantage of ARGs best, "Marketers are realizing that in this landscape you are not competing against other luxury auto manufacturers. You are competing against pop culture for people's mind space."[13]

■ Games for All Brands?

Are there any drawbacks to using ARGs? Every strategy has some negative potential, and ARGs are no different. ARGs can only be used by brands whose target market enjoys the aspects of an interactive, online, complex game. Commenting on why "I Love Bees" was so successful James Hilton, the creative director of AKQA, the agency that developed the ARG, emphasized, "I Love Bees worked very well for Xbox because its audience is far more inclined to investigate further, hack into sites and solve problems."[14] ARGs have a great deal of potential for many brands, but there must be a good fit between the brand, the meaning the brand wishes to communicate, the target market, and the story and plot that form the foundation of the ARG.

ARGs are not without substantial work from the initial conception of the ARG, planning, and execution. Further, because the story line can change depending upon the response from players, ARGs require active writing and responsiveness from the game architects through and even beyond (as players are debriefed) the game's end. Because the game can evolve in ways the architects did not originally plan, there is a risk involved. Like the cocreation of brand meaning that occurs when brands invite consumers to generate their own branded advertising messages, ARGs are cocreated. Some brand managers might think the engagement power of ARGs is not worth the risk of damage to an established brand's meaning. For some brands this may be true, but those brands ready to embrace Web 2.0 and beyond recognize the desire among today's consumers to drive their own brand experiences.

This point also highlights a related dilemma. Brands with a loyal base can enhance their relationship with an ARG, but the loyalists may resent the influx of new people brought about by interest in the game. Nine Inch Nails experienced this criticism from longtime fans when it used an ARG for the launch of its *Year Zero* album. Still, the criticism does not appear to have negated interest in the band, its album or tour, or participation in the ARG.

Another limitation of ARGs is in its potential for impact. Compared to some options, an ARG's reach is small. For instance, measures of Audi's ARG success referred to a reach of 500,000, but a display ad on MySpace's home page could reach millions. Of course, the attention and involvement components are entirely different for these two examples, and it is important to consider the entire range of benefits and disadvantages associated with online advertising choices.

■ Evaluating the Effectiveness of a Brand-Sponsored ARG

How can we measure the effectiveness of ARGs as a branding tool? ARG effectiveness measures are similar to those used for other Internet-based branding tools such as social networking with an emphasis on site traffic and participation. The most common indicators then include number of players, number of active players, number of lurkers and rubber-neckers, rate of player registration from launch or from specific game events, number of player messages generated, traffic at sites affiliated with the ARG, number of forum postings (at sites like unfiction.com), and average play time. In addition, ARGs should be evaluated by the media impressions made through publicity generated about the ARG. For instance, The Beast generated more than 300 million media impressions in magazines, news programs, newspapers, and Web sites like Wired and Slashdot.

Ultimately, ARGs used for branding should consider how success will be measured in the initial concept and planning stages. When the purpose of the ARG is marketing, achievement of specific marketing objectives should be tied to the effectiveness measures used to evaluate the ARG itself. For instance, Audi's Art of the Heist sought to generate interest in the U.S. launch of its Audi A3. But Audi did not simply want to generate awareness of this new model, but it also needed to generate leads for dealers as well as some action on the part of prospects (i.e., test drives). Thus, Audi's measures of effectiveness included the number of queries about the car generated from qualified prospects (over 16,000), the number of quote requests on car pricing (over 13,000), leads to dealers (over 10,000), number of test drives (4,000+), and number of cars sold (1,025).[15] In addition to measures based on prospect responsiveness to the product, Audi also measured the ARG by media impressions (over 45 million), visits to the AudiUSA.com Web site (2 million, representing five times the average traffic to the site), number of active players (500,000), and posts to the unfiction forum (204,622 posts), among others.[16] There are many possibilities when evaluating the success of an ARG, but success is not simply audience engagement and player enthusiasm—the ARG should drive achievement of the brand's marketing objectives.

■ Using Brand-Sponsored ARGs

By now it should be clear why ARGs are a growing tool for branding. They engage brand enthusiasts, gamers, and drive publicity and buzz for brands. They are interactive—a characteristic consumers favor. They enable a brand to build a story backward and forward and to be woven tightly or loosely into the story's fabric. ARG participation spreads virally, and so playing (or at least lurking) encompasses a social component that provides for the "contact comfort" so many consumers find appealing. Below are guidelines for developing a successful brand-sponsored ARG.

- Have a story to tell. ARGs are first and foremost an interactive story. This story may be closely related to the brand's meaning or may be a "cadet narrative." In either case, it should be captivating, dynamic, and inviting.

- Ensure that the story and the notion of interacting in a game with geographically dispersed players are appropriate to the brand's image and its target audience. Audi's Art of the Heist targeted affluent, technologically savvy, Web-centric young men. There was a clear match between the Audi brand, the ARG, and the target audience.

- Plan, plan, and plan more. Begin by assessing how the ARG can facilitate accomplishment of the brand's marketing goals. Then figure out the back story (the pregame narrative), the primary narrative, and the forward story (if appropriate). Perplex City (http://seasonone.perplexcitystories.com/story.html) offers a detailed overview of its architects' planning process, including the pregame back story, the game overview, and flowcharts of game segments.

- Reveal the story narrative over time using obscure clues and messages that will require player interaction to decipher the scenes. This will encourage collaboration among players, incite buzz, and generate more interest in the game.

- Include plot lines that are nonlinear and can be revealed sporadically. The development of the narrative must not be predictable and must not rely on a linear unfolding of events to make sense.

- Design a story that will enhance the sense of reality in the story. Players should not be reminded of the game but should be invited to make the game part of their reality.

- Break the narrative into fragments, which can be reassembled by the players.

- Layer the story, and layer the clues. Figuring out each step in the game should not be obvious and easy for every player—if it is, players will be bored and attrition will occur. But some players must be able to decipher clues for the game to continue. Using layers of clues at various levels of complexity invites collaboration among the players and allows players to play at different skill levels.

- Utilize a variety of media, and carefully design game elements to leverage the characteristics of the delivery medium. There is no limit to the delivery choices. Past ARGs have utilized code on T-shirts and posters, Web sites identified in video trailers, posts to blogs, e-mail, text messages, and mass media advertising.

- Chart the flow of the story, clues, and media used for each as a planning tool.

- Be prepared to change the direction of the narrative in response to player input and response to past clues and events.

- Don't overcommercialize the ARG. Most ARGs are brand sponsored, and ARG enthusiasts understand this. Still, players want to immerse themselves in a mystery. If the ARG unfolds like a consumer-interactive advertisement, it will offend the ARG community, and much of the value possible will be lost.

- Commit to the ARG and its management. Although the expense is minimal compared to many advertising options, it can be a substantial portion of a brand's ad budget. ARGs take time and continued involvement and management as the story unfolds. The pace of the story may need to be revised, new scenes may need to be developed, and responses to player actions may be necessary—the game requires active management throughout.

- Use an agency with ARG experience. Brands would be wise to use experienced agencies like 42 Entertainment, Mind Candy, and McKinney & Silver when developing and executing ARGs.

- Measure the effectiveness of the ARG based on the objectives for the promotional campaign, not just according to game participation, site visits, and other traffic-based statistics.

■ A Case Study: Nine Inch Nails' *Year Zero* Launch

Inasmuch as people play games, alternate reality gaming is best understood with a story. Let's take a brief look at some highlights from the rock band Nine Inch Nails. The band formed in the late 1980s, fronted by Trent Reznor, the band's vocalist and director. On April 17, 2007, the band released its twenty-fourth album (but only its sixth major commercial release) entitled *Year Zero*.

In a prepared statement, Reznor said,

> This record began as an experiment with noise on a laptop in a bus on tour somewhere. That sound led to a daydream about the end of the world. That daydream stuck with me and over time revealed itself to be much more. I believe sometimes you have a choice in what inspiration you choose to follow and other times you really don't. This record is the latter. Once I tuned into it, everything fell into place...as if it were meant to be. With a framework established, the songs were very easy to write. Things started happening in my "real" life that blurred the lines of what was fiction and what wasn't. The record turned out to be more than just a record in scale, as you will see over time.[17]

This quote sets the stage for the band's use of an ARG to promote the album's launch. Who knows whether Reznor's statement really referred to the creation of music that ultimately inspired the ARG or reflected instead Reznor's marketing prowess. Either way, blurred lines between real life and fiction are prevalent in ARGs.

Reznor went on to describe the album as being about the future. He stated, "It takes place about fifteen years in the future. Things are not good. If you imagine a world where greed and power continue to run their likely course, you'll have an idea of the backdrop."[18] Players in the game found clues (and are still finding clues), which linked to Web sites, phone calls, and images from "the future." The clues found were consistent with Reznor's depiction of the future, bleak and disturbing. The "rabbit hole" in the game, the first clue, was discovered on the back of a shirt promoting Nine Inch Nails' current European tour. On the back of the shirt, several letters are highlighted, which spell out, "I am trying to believe." The words led fans to the Web site www.iamtryingtobelieve.com, which describes a drug named "Parepin" that, in the story of *Year Zero*, is being added to the water supply to dilute people's minds. The site also contained a blurred image of a hand-like figure reaching down from the sky. This was the first sighting of the image, later tagged the "presence," but it would not be the last. The image of the "presence" has served as a primary symbol for gamers tracking clues. It is also the image on the album's cover.

Several of the clues link back to the band. For instance, at the February 12, 2007, Nine Inch Nails' concert in Lisbon, Portugal, a USB flash drive was found in a bathroom stall. It was later found to hold a single audio file with the title "My Violent Heart." Later, it was discovered that "My Violent Heart" is a track from the yet-to-be-released *Year Zero* album.

The clues are well integrated. For instance, gamers noticed static at the end of the audio file found on the USB drive at the Lisbon concert. Using a logarithmic spectrometer to analyze the audio file, the gamers discovered an image embedded in the file. The image was the "presence." The "presence" is also described, though not directly mentioned, in phone calls which are accessed by dialing numbers found through various sources and Web sites. One such telephone number was delivered through another leaked song from the album "Me, I'm Not." Like the image of the "presence," the number was embedded in the file and visible when analyzed with the spectrometer. Several Web sites were used to provide additional game information. Clues lead to the various sites, among them www.anotherversionofthetruth.com, www.churchofplano.com, www.uswiretap.com, and www.artisresistance.com. The Art is Resistance Web site provided several downloaded items for fans, including icons, printable stickers, stencils, and posters. Physical renditions of these items have since appeared as street art in several locations around the world.

The ARG concluded around the album's release date with players registered at the Open Source Resistance site invited to meet in Hollywood. There, some players were given cell phones. Days later, the phones rang and gave the players instructions to meet again, where they were loaded on a bus and delivered to an abandoned warehouse—the site of a brief performance by Nine Inch Nails.[19] The games end? Prerecorded messages to the phones reportedly relayed this message: "we've got to go dark for a while, but that is ok—you don't need us anymore." Susan Bonds, president of 42 Entertainment, the agency behind this ARG, noted in an interview that this ARG might continue, particularly given that Reznor conceived *Year Zero* as a two-part album. Because the cell phones are still in the hands of the players and the forums are still active, reactivating the game is a definite possibility.[20]

While many brands use ARGs as brand-building devices, Nine Inch Nails used its ARG to advance album sales by generating enthusiasm among fans, both music and game enthusiasts. Puppet masters, agencies, and brands involved in ARGs are notoriously secretive prior to the conclusion of a game, so it is no wonder that we have not seen any measurement statistics on the effectiveness of this ARG (e.g., number of hits to the various game Web sites, increases in traffic to the main Nine Inch Nails Web site [www.nin.com], and estimated number of players, lurkers, and rubberneckers). The album and tour were acknowledged for their commercial success, and the ARG gained much media attention.

The Nine Inch Nails example is a well-designed ARG. It featured all of the components of well-designed games, including a good fit between brand, target audience, and plot. The clues were leaked in innovative ways using multimedia and multichannels. The symbols, including the image of the "presence," the Web site URLs, and the songs leaked, were all integrated into the meaning of the album and into the ARG plot. Players were so anxious that bathrooms were stormed when concert gates opened during the *Year Zero* tour with players searching for flash drives that might contain clues. Message boards about the ARG were active, and there was press and blog coverage of the tour, album, and ARG. Importantly, this ARG can be reactivated at any time, and it seems the players are clamoring for just that.

ARGs, as illustrated in this case study from Nine Inch Nails, are an emerging form of social media with extensive opportunities for engaging audiences and building a branded community. What is yet to be seen is whether social fiction can develop the scalability necessary to make it a form of social advertising that can rival other techniques like social-network advertising. As a platform, social fiction has great potential but has not yet been adopted widely even by marketers actively involved in social-media marketing. In any case, it will be interesting to see how brands will initiate a digital dialogue with consumers using these innovative approaches.

Ads in Play
Immersing Brands in and around Social Games

At least once a week, 89% of Americans watch prime-time television. It is the ubiquity of television in American lives, along with its media richness, that has made it the core of media plans for virtually all types of brands, decade after decade. When marketers think of video games, it is unlikely that they consider game media to have the potential for reach we attribute to other mainstream media. Yet, 58% of Americans play some kind of video game every week, and 63% have played at least one video game in the past year.[1]

With worldwide revenues estimated at about $25 billion in hardware and software sales, video games are a powerful entertainment medium. Revenues for games surpass (individually) box office revenues for movies, movie rentals, book sales, and music sales. Industry revenues in United States alone reached nearly $18 billion in 2007.[2] As an advertising medium, games offer much to advertisers looking for new access to consumers, particularly in places where there is limited clutter, little multitasking, and high levels of engagement.

Game-related advertising is not new. Early Sega games for the Atari 2600 console featured Marlboro cigarette ads on the raceway. So why the recent surge in games and game advertising? The medium's growth in recent years is associated with advances enabled by Web 2.0. In a report from eMarketer, Paul Verna estimates that game advertising is already valued at over $1 billion in annual expenditures.[3] He anticipates spending will grow at a compound annual growth rate of 23%, reaching nearly $2 billion by 2011. eMarketer's estimates include advertising expenditures from static, dynamic, and rich media in-game ads, product placements in games, and advergaming. Noting the many opportunities for game-related advertising as well as its benefits, Parks Associates confirms eMarketer's bullish estimates predicting that overall game-related ad spending will grow from $370 million in 2006 to more than $2 billion by 2012.[4]

In the United States alone, video game advertising ran $502 million in 2007 with just under half that being spent to develop branded advergames, games that are entirely developed by and tied to a brand.[5] Advergaming accounts for $207 million of game advertising expenditures in the United States, and is expected to hit $344 million by 2011. Some analysts predict a growth curve for in-game advertising that outpaces the growth of online advertising.[6] In fact, the compound annual growth rate of game advertising is expected to be much higher than that of any other major media, including television, radio, print, and the Internet.

■ Gaming Platforms and Audience Involvement

Video games as a whole include different platforms and genre. Each category offers somewhat unique advertising opportunities and appeals to different demographic groups. Video games are offered across three hardware platforms: game consoles (interactive, electronic devices used to display video games like Sony's PlayStation3, Microsoft's Xbox 360, and Nintendo's Wii), computers (either online, or games installed on the computer's hard drive), and on portable devices like the Sony PSP, Nintendo DS, or wireless handsets.[7] Overall, then, there are four platforms: (1) console games, (2) CD-ROM games, (3) online games, and (4) mobile games. Gamers have a high rate of crossover platform use, most of them playing games on two or more platforms.

Gaming experiences can be categorized as casual or core/enthusiast. Casual games target a mass audience. They are addictive, fun, easy to learn, and require time investments of less than thirty minutes per game. Core games, sometimes known as real games, are highly immersive, realistic, and require periods of extended game play. Game sessions may last more than ninety minutes, and some games take more than twenty hours to complete. Others have no real end and can be enjoyed for years.

Theoretically, casual and core games can be delivered using any of the four platforms. However, casual games tend to be more prevalent online, while core games more frequently rely upon a console platform. Nintendo's Wii system is an exception to this assumption. The Wii encourages casual gamers to accept a console platform with many family-friendly games as well as more intense core games. Casual games are offered to consumers using a number of revenue models, including try and buy, ad-supported free games, subscription, pay per play, and skill based. Core games are typically purchased but may also generate revenue through advertising support. Even within the categories of casual and core games, there are many genres, including casual, strategy, action, sports, adventure, shooters, and simulation. Of these, casual games are noted by 29% of gamers as their favorite genre.[8]

Once upon a time, advertising via games was thought to be appropriate only for a young male audience, but that belief is changing as more information on the demographics of gamers emerges. It is true that games are a good choice for reaching teenagers and young adults. About 90% of consumers aged 12–17 and about 80% of those aged 18–24 years have played a video game in the last year.[9] But coverage is strong for older adults as well, with more than 70% of those aged 25–34, more than 60% of those 35–44, and 50% of those 45–54 years playing video games. Overall, games are only slightly more popular with males than females; though there are clear age and gender preferences in the types of games pursued.

For instance, among online casual gamers, eMarketer claims that 80% of gamers are female with a median age of 47; 33% with children under 18 years in the home. Of the worldwide casual gaming audience of more than 200 million unique players, 71% of casual gamers worldwide are 40 years and older—and 47% are 50 and older.[10] Traffic at online casual game sites like Pogo and Yahoo! Games is at its peak between 8 a.m. and 2 p.m., Monday to Friday, but there is also traffic late at night, suggesting that many casual gamers play at work and during bouts of insomnia. Hard-core gamers skew younger and male. The IAB's Marketer & Agency Guide to Online Game Advertising describes the demographic market for console gamers (typically reflecting core games) as 68% male with a median age of 26.[11] Similarly, CD-ROM gamers are thought to be 66% male with a median age of 32. The demographic makeup of gamers suggests that gaming is a viable medium for advertisers targeting several markets from teens to middle-aged mothers to families.

It is not just the demographic diversity that appeals to advertisers. Gamer behavior matters, too. Games have a high degree of stickiness. Stickiness refers to the ability of a medium to attract an audience and keep that audience once there. Gamers as a cohort tend to be dedicated hobbyists, spending countless hours embroiled in intense games. People are passionate about games. In fact, gamers spend more time gaming than they do on the Internet in all other activities. Casual gamers do spend less time on games each week than do core gamers, but even then eMarketer estimates that 34% of gamers spend more than four hours a week playing games, 8% spend about three hours, 17% spend about two hours, and 9% spend one hour. The remaining gamers, primarily casual, report spending less than one hour per week.[12] Not only do gamers spend ample time consuming the medium. Gaming requires attention and active involvement. Players are not likely to be multitasking during a game or consuming multiple forms of media simultaneously. Gamers are not texting, talking, or using the remote to channel surf during an active game. For games played through game consoles, it is important to remember that game consoles are permanently connected to televisions in 86% of U.S. households. If the game console is on, television programming is not. Game advertising provides an opportunity to recapture that audience.

■ Other Factors Driving Growth in Game Advertising

The video game industry continues to grow and can now be considered a mainstream entertainment medium. All of the criteria for good market segments are met with games. The market is substantial (there is a large number of consumers involved in gaming). It is reachable (through the games themselves as well as through other media). It is measurable (particularly given the prevalence of online games and broadband-connected console games). The gaming demographic has broadened such that games are now considered viable vehicles for reaching women and older consumers as well as young males. Gamers spend sufficient, dedicated time with games to achieve valuable ad impressions. These factors alone would be sufficient to explain the surge of interest in gaming, but there are other reasons for considering game advertising as part of a brand's media strategy.

First, gamers appear to be open to advertising associated with the games they play. A study conducted by Nielsen Entertainment on behalf of Massive, Inc., a Microsoft-owned in-game advertising specialist, revealed that after exposure to in-game ads dynamically placed on Massive's advertising game network, brand familiarity, a measure of brand recognition, increased 64%. In addition, the study found that positive attitudes toward the brands studied increased by 37% and purchase consideration increased by 41%. The advertising itself also performed well with an increase in advertising recall reported and a positive attitude toward the ads.[13] These results are consistent with other research on the effectiveness of ad placement, which found that placing ads in creative locations like games over traditional placements like magazines resulted in positive feelings toward the brand. Zachary Glass examined the attitudes players had toward brands embedded in games.[14] Participants played a video game that featured branded products, and then took an implicit associations test to determine whether they had more positive attitudes toward the brands in the game than toward a set of equivalently rated brands. Players rated in-game brands more positively than those that were not embedded and did so more quickly.

In part, this acceptance of game advertising can be attributed to the desire for realism in the game environment. Adverts are ubiquitous in society with some events and experiences like racing and sporting events saturated with advertising. Stadiums are wallpapered in brand logos and symbols. A sports-themed game without branding would seem artificial to gamers who want to immerse themselves in the experience. For example, Groove Media recently introduced two skill-based video games, one a golf simulation. The golf simulation emulates the feeling of playing in a PGA tour tournament, compelling advertisers like BMW to seek out advertising opportunities in the game environment.[15]

Because brands seem a natural part of game settings, they easily benefit from association with the game itself. Brands accrue transference effects when associated with popular games and exciting and interesting game environments. When people are immersed and engaged in the game, the sense of preference for the game should transfer to the brand. This is a common benefit associated with event sponsorships. Brands seek to associate with sports, arts, and music events in order to gain residual benefits from the brand-event association. Likewise, it is possible for game advertisers to leverage the law of association by branding in and around games. The difference is simply that the "event," the game, takes place in a more intimate setting with a greater sense of one-to-one rather than one-to-many promotion of the brand-game association. Like event sponsorship, a prerequisite for success is congruence between the brand's image and the image and atmosphere associated with the game. In other words, there must be a good fit in order to maximize the value of the association. To pick the right game, Josh Larson of *iMedia Connection* encourages advertisers to think of choosing the right game for a brand as they would choosing any other vehicle.[16] One should consider the game's demographic target, its market size, and the quality of the game franchise. The game should be a great fit for the brand and its product category.

Not only do brands benefit from association with the game, but they can also achieve outcomes similar to using celebrity endorsers. Celebrity endorsers provide a form of association effect, the goal being the internalization of the endorser's brand beliefs by the target audience. Internalization occurs when members of the target market accept the beliefs of an endorser as their own. In a game context, the characters in the game's story and setting can act as brand endorsers. Grant McCracken explains the effectiveness of endorsers with his Meaning Transfer Model.[17] Consumers associate meaning with the endorser and then transfer the meaning to the brand in question. The consumer first chooses to assign the meaning associated with the endorser to the product or brand. Thus, meanings attributed to the endorser become associated with the brand in the consumer's mind. For game advertisers, the Meaning Transfer Model suggests that a character's attributes can be transferred to a brand that is used by the character in the game as part of an in-game product placement. The key to using character endorsers successfully parallels the choice of celebrity endorsers. The character endorser should have the appropriate set of characteristics desired by the brand.

Game character endorsements can affect consumers' brand attitudes.[18] One of the biggest determinants of increased positive brand attitudes is perceived trustworthiness and credibility. This finding mirrors the research on celebrity endorser effects on brand attitudes, which shows that, especially when consumers have little brand experience of their own, they are positively influenced by character endorsements. Their results imply that consumers who are new to a brand but see it being used by someone they consider trustworthy, even if that someone is a character in a video game, will form more positive opinions about that brand.

Game characters can act as product endorsers in the game, but game players can also identify directly with brands placed in the game. Many games function by casting the player into a character role in the game. Glass explains that game players may then imagine themselves as active characters in the game.[19] For example, a popular genre is that of "first-person shooter" games. In first-person shooters, players take the perspective of their character, which creates a certain bond between the player and the character. Character development also occurs in MMORPG. In these large-scale games, players are particularly invested in their characters, because they spend weeks, months, and even years to build their character identity and develop the attributes that will enable the character to compete at the highest possible level of the game. Even the name of the genre itself, "role playing," implies just how involved players are with their characters. When brands are embedded using immersive techniques like enabling players in a racing game to choose their brand of race car, the players can actively interact with brands during the game experience, resulting in a heightened sense of brand identification. Recognizing and leveraging the players' high sense of involvement enables advertisers to maximize the power of the game as an advertising medium. If the player in a sense becomes the character, he or she takes over the role of endorser or spokesperson for any brand the character uses. If we follow this line of reasoning using what is known about celebrity endorsements and message internalization, a virtual extension of the player that serves as the spokesperson for the brand should create strong, positive brand attitudes.

Game producers are actively investigating new and innovative ways of encouraging character immersion in games. At the 2008 Game On Finance conference, the focus was on learning about alternatives to packaging video game experiences. A possible development in the industry is the use of online social networks and virtual worlds tied to console games. The industry hopes to model the success of youth-oriented virtual worlds like Webkinz, which generate revenues through product sales.[20]

For all the discussion on the benefit advertising offers players by enhancing game realism, games build on the narrative structure of literature and film. In many ways, games approximate the immersive experience of watching a movie. Games, like movies, are capable of transcending barriers of class and culture. This is a valuable attribute given the goal of encouraging players to share identity with their game character. However, games offer more than stories told through film and literature in that games include elements of interactivity. Interactivity should lead to improved brand attitudes. Jennifer Escalas posits that even imagined interaction with a brand can produce more positive attitudes and purchase intentions.[21] If one considers the narrative transportation theory, it is clear how imagination can build brand attitudes. This theory proposes that mental stimulation through narrative storytelling encourages the player to become lost in the story. Once immersed in the plot, players are distracted from advertising embedded in the game. They do not elaborate on the message but rather rely upon the positive feelings evoked by the mental stimulation of the story to make determinations about the brand. So long as the stimulation of the game is positive, the attitudes toward brands embedded in the game should also be positive. Games can go even further than simple imagination because of the degree of interactivity and immersion possible. In addition, if the game is fun and the player is having a good time, positive feelings about the game should extend to the products advertised in the game.

All of this suggests that the basic characteristics of the medium offer great potential, but the industry is developing in other ways, too, that support advertising. Technological advances have improved the ability to embed ads creatively and to rotate and adjust ads within games. The advent of dynamic advertising delivery in game networks results in dramatic improvements in efficiency and effectiveness of game advertising. In the past, most advertising opportunities in games centered on static placements that were much like traditional billboard advertising. Delivering the ad in a game required hard programming of the ad into the game itself. Dynamic ads enable ads to be delivered electronically over time. Several ads can rotate within a game and across a portfolio of games, thereby delivering more ad impressions at a lower cost. Several networks already exist to provide dynamic advertising opportunities. Among the most powerful of these networks, Electronic Arts is partnering with IGA Worldwide to deliver advertising dynamically to Internet-connected console games.

"Advergaming" is another industry trend offering an effective utilization of game branding. Advergaming refers specifically to games that are developed by a brand with brand integration throughout the game's setting, story line, and characters. Joseph Jaffe explains the appeal of advergaming, noting that it can involve users, allowing them to interact with the brand while being entertained and engaged.[22] Jane Chen of Ya Ya Media, a video game developer, had this to say of advergaming's potential, "It is one of the few advertising mediums that effectively reaches target audiences in all day-parts—including hard-to-reach at-work hours.... The most effective advergames push deeper down the purchase funnel and can serve to qualify buyers and incentivize consumers to visit retail outlets or even purchase directly online. The natural interactivity of games provides the perfect stimulus and ongoing communication channel between brands and their customers."[23]

For both game advertising and advergaming, the game environment creates a higher impression value for the ad compared to that earned from traditional media placements. This is attributed to the frequency of exposure, the potential for interactivity with the brand's message, and the entertainment value of the platform. Millions of advertising impressions can be delivered in just a few weeks of game play at a cost as low as 25 cents per impression. That cost accounts for access to viewers as players are exposed to game ads. There is added value in the transference of meaning from game to brand and in the opportunity for players to feel engaged in a brand experience.

Games offer the benefit of accountability for advertisers, too. Game ad impressions are counted only when a gamer is actually there playing the game and viewing the ad. There is an industry push toward measurement with Nielsen Media Research offering a service for game advertisers. Called GamePlay Metrics, the service will provide independent verifications of demographic data for games as well as analysis on how video game play complements or detracts from the use of other media. In terms of the costs of using games as an advertising medium, cost is relatively low. Executions featuring static, in-game advertising can run into six figures, while dynamic options are available for as little as $10,000. There is little advertising clutter in games, particularly when compared to other media choices. The underutilization of game advertising is indicated by the average monthly household expenditure for game ads compared to television. Expenditures on game advertising amount to a paltry $.50 per household while broadcast television is $37.[24] Considering the audience size and time spent gaming, media spending is grossly underallocated.

There are downsides to placing adverts in and around games. One negative feature of in-game advertising is the market fragmentation. There are numerous games across multiple platforms and genres, and the audience is split among them. Another is scalability. Scalability refers to the ability of a system to adjust to increased demands given the system constraints. The issue of scalability has been a difficult one to overcome for many forms of online advertising with one notable exception. Search advertising with systems like those offered from Google and Yahoo! are highly scalable. They enable customized delivery of text ads based on targeting criteria with great efficiency and ease of operation. Game advertising, though, features product placements and in-game integrations, which require a long lead time and hard programming to incorporate individual ads into specific games. To make matters worse, there is the issue of inventory. Granted, there are numerous game titles and genres, but with the exception of dynamic ads inventory is fixed in supply. Only limited numbers of games are introduced each year. Consequently, publishers are constrained in regard to the number of campaigns possible on an annual basis.

In addition, research on the effectiveness of game advertising is mixed. Some studies show that players recall brands they saw in games and report that players' brand purchase behavior is influenced by in-game advertising.[25] A study of effects of in-game brand placements on memory found that in-game ads do influence memory.[26] But there are also as many studies that call into question the effectiveness of game advertising. One study found that participants in a first-person shooter game recalled their going past billboards in the game but had little memory of the specific brands or product categories promoted on the billboards.[27] Recall of brand names may be lower when gamers are highly involved, a conclusion that is counterintuitive, given the beliefs about the value of involvement in vehicles. Dan Grigorovici and Corina Constantin found that the higher a gamer's immersion in the game, the worse his or her recall of brands placed in the game.[28] This is problematic given that generally we would anticipate higher levels of involvement to reflect positively on brand recall. They also found that frequency of play had no influence on player ability to recall brands in the game. Brands might be limited in the types of genres selected. Racing and sports games are the two genres thought to be most appropriate to in-game brand placements.

Despite these constraints, game advertising is ripe with potential. There are far more advantages than disadvantages for branding with this medium.

- Games are a mainstream entertainment medium with strong reach across demographic groups.
- Games are sticky. Players tend to play frequently and for extended periods of time.
- Games are not subject to surfing, zipping, or muting (unlike in TV and other media).
- Players tend to be in a receptive mood when gaming.
- Advertising in games tends to result in more positive brand attitudes.
- Targeting is possible with demographic and behavioral information available about game audiences.
- The game environment is still relatively clutter free.
- There are opportunities for brand exclusivity, as well as for display advertising, product placements, and immersive branding.
- Game advertising can be easily integrated into a brand's integrated marketing communications campaign with opportunities for cross-promotion.
- Brands can benefit from association with the game, including meaning transference and character-induced internalization.
- Game advertising is relatively low in cost.

■ Types of Game-Based Advertising Opportunities

There are many opportunities for game advertising. First, advertising with games can be categorized as *around game* and *in game*. Second, in-game advertising can be further segmented into in-game *environment* advertising and in-game *immersive* advertising. These distinct segments of advertising opportunities result in numerous executions, including pre-roll, post-roll, and interlevel video ads, game Web site sponsorships, game tournament sponsorships, static in-game ads, dynamic in-game ads, game skinning, simple product placements, immersive product placements, and advergames.

Around-game advertising can include pre-roll, post-roll, and interlevel rich media advertising (video ads that run just before or after a game is played or between game levels), or sponsorship of game content Web sites (like Gamespot.com or Pogo) and gaming tournaments. In a survey by Macrovision, 83% of respondents said they would be willing to watch a thirty-second ad in order to be able to play an online video game for free.[29] Gamers are likely to visit game Web sites like Gamespot.com for the latest news in the gaming industry and reviews of games. These Web sites offer display advertising opportunities and enable brands to take advantage of contextual ad placements. Contextual advertising means placing advertising on a site in which the context of the ad matches that of the site. Contextual advertising enhances the likelihood that site visitors will notice the ad and elaborate on the brand's message. Display advertising on game-related Web sites offer a fairly large reach, short lead time, and targeting capabilities. The ads are limited in that they are simply online advertising as opposed to the immersive advertising featured in games and in other venues like ARGs.

A sponsorship of a game or game tournament gives the sponsoring brand 100% of the "share of voice" in and around the existing game. Share of voice refers to an organization's proportion of total promotional expenditures. Sponsoring brands earn brand exclusivity for the game during the sponsorship, with control over whether (and which) other brands have visibility. Sponsorships typically are sold at a fixed price, but other display advertising units are sold using traditional online pricing models, including CPM (cost per thousand impressions delivered), CPC (cost per click), and CPA (cost per acquired customer).

The NASCAR SimRacing Pedal to the Metal Challenge racing tournament, for instance, sponsored by Castrol GTX is a good example of leveraging an online game opportunity to create a branded sponsorship. The brand benefits from a sponsorship just as it would from any other event sponsorship. Those in the audience may feel a positive brand association because of the brand's support of something that is fun, enjoyable, and important to them. In addition, the sponsorship typically provides for several impressions of the brand's logo over the course of the sponsorship. Disadvantages are similar to those of off-line sponsorships. The reach is typically small per sponsorship and participants may not recognize the endorsement.

In-game environment advertising includes static ads, dynamic ads, skinning ads, and simple product placement. Static advertising has been used as a catchall term for all nondynamic advertising in games. Static ads include billboards, movie posters, store fronts, and other representations of branded products and logo-labeled areas. It includes logo placement within a game and "billboard" advertisements. Audio clips can also be broadcast within the game, including songs, public announcements, and radio ads when gamers are driving cars in a game. Static ads are essentially traditional display advertising within the game environment. These ads are hard-coded into the game and ensure that all players view the advertising. Static advertising does not enable tracking of ad viewing, and the advertising cannot be changed once the game is launched. Reach is limited to that of the game's distribution, and ad placements must be purchased and executed for each individual game title to be used in the campaign. Skinning ads refer to opportunities to brand aspects of the playing field.

Dynamic advertising is like dynamic billboards but within a game's environment. Different ads are rotated on the same fixed space within the game. This technique, managed by game networks, can be used for both online and console games when the gaming system is broadband connected. Ed Bartlett of *iMedia Connection* explains that dynamic advertising utilizes embedded software, a back-end infrastructure, and the Internet to update, change, and track the viewing of advertising placements in a game in real time.[30]

Dynamic advertising is valuable just for the high degree of control and real-time measurement it offers, but it also makes it possible to develop an ad network within game families. It makes it possible to aggregate numerous games, platforms, and genres into an ad network, thereby counteracting the fragmentation that exists in the market. By using an ad network approach, it also aids in achieving relatively high reach (the average percentage of people in a target audience exposed to a message). Buying ad space in games that sell dynamic advertising space requires a short lead time, and the messages can be easily and rapidly changed. This is the most intrusive form of advertising available in gaming and could garner negative associations from gamers.

The in-game ad networks offer advertising opportunities across multiple games and provide insertion technology to use dynamic advertising. In-game ad networks include Adscape, Double Fusion, Engage, Greystripe, IGA Worldwide, and Massive Inc. The networks contract with game publishers to place advertising in their games. By combining games from several publishers, networks create a large portfolio of in-game media opportunities for advertisers. The network will work with publishers to strategically embed advertising, sell the placement to advertisers, serve the ads into the games in the network, and manage the billing and accounting for the process.

Massive Inc. conducted a series of research tests to gauge the impact of dynamic in-game advertising. It found that in-game ads using dynamic advertising, brand familiarity, brand ratings, purchase consideration, ad recall, and ad rating increased significantly compared to a control group.[31] The study involving more than 600 gamers across North America comprised tests of several advertising categories, including automotive, consumer packaged goods, and fast food.

Product placements can be embedded at various levels in a game's framework. In-game environment product placements are simple placements. Cristel Russell describes two levels of simple placements: (1) screen placements and (2) script placements.[32] Screen placements refer to integrating the brand visually on the screen to enhance brand visibility and is perhaps the most common technique in game advertising. The brand is integrated into the visual context of the game much as it might be in a television program or movie. In Tiger Woods PGA Tour, for instance, Tiger is featured wearing his Nike brand clothing and using Nike golf equipment. Script placements refer to verbal mentions of the brand's name and attributes. Gamers note that product placements that are realistic enhance the game's realism, thereby making the game more enjoyable. In addition, the product placements can result in numerous advertising impressions. It does require lead time to ensure that the product placement can be embedded in a game, and it can be more expensive than other in-game options.

In-game immersive advertising opportunities include interactive product placements, branded in-game experiences, and sponsored extra levels. Simple product placements are common, but integration works best in games when product placements are interactive and immersive, meaning they enable a player to interact with the brand. Russell refers to this more immersive level of product placement as plot placement. Plot placements involve situations in which the brand is actually incorporated into the story itself in a substantive manner. They are more effective for generating positive brand attitudes, recall and recognition, and purchase intention in all uses of brand integration from television programming to movies to games.

Like static in-game advertising, product placements are hard-coded into the game and cannot be changed or tracked. It is also difficult to measure the return on investment with product placements. New technology will make it possible to combine the benefits of dynamic advertising and product placement and enable tracking and measurement. Sponsored extra levels are additional levels of the game, which can only be accessed with codes provided from the brand.

Adidas used several advertising opportunities to strategically leverage game advertising in the multiplayer online game Power Football. The Adidas brand placement operates at several layers in the game. Players can choose from several Adidas shoe models, creating a form of virtual sampling. Sampling, a common sales promotion technique, involves offering consumers a free trial of a product. Adidas accomplishes the goal of sampling within the game, by assigning game-play attributes based on the model of shoes. As players evaluate which shoe model they want, relevant product information is delivered within the game. Adidas also includes basic product placement, including a branded Adidas football, Adidas signage throughout the game's setting, and Adidas apparel worn by game characters. Sponsorship is utilized through the Adidas instant replay sponsorship. Adidas offers a brilliant example in that the brand was linked to the underlying story of the game itself, executed in multiple ways, all of which were meaningful and relevant for the audience and the story. Adidas went beyond the basics of game advertising to ensure the brand lived in the game space with the players.

In addition to the around- and in-game choices, brands can also develop and offer advergames. Advergaming is a technique for reaching gamers, but it varies from in-game advertising. With in-game advertising, the brand is embedding itself in a game. With advergaming, the brand is the context for the game itself. Advergaming involves creating an entirely new game that somehow relates to the brand. Advergames are almost exclusively distributed online because of the desire to have a cost-effective method of distributing the game to a large audience. They tend to be casual games, as opposed to core games. Orbitz successfully uses advergaming. Highly addictive and fun, its online golf game links players to the Orbitz Web site at the end of each game session. Even Lifetime television uses advergaming. Its new series of games, entitled Lifetime Presents, come embedded with advertising fit for the network's audience of middle-aged women, along with Lifetime TV promos. In one Lifetime Presents game called "Sally's Salon," players win by directing the lead character through the daily operation of a virtual beauty salon.

Advergames are brand experiences, and the popular ones have drawn a high level of reach. There are developmental costs to be considered, but advergames are sometimes "reskinned" versions of existing games. Casual games also tend to target a different demographic than real games.

For brands, this type of game advertising offers the advantage of complete control of the brand's message. The game is designed by the brand in keeping with the brand's positioning statement.

Lifesavers illustrated the value of advergaming with its Candystand.com Web site (which is now branded with the manufacturer's brand, Wrigley). Candystand was attributed with revitalizing the Lifesavers brand, resulting in a growth rate of 15% over two years. The Candystand site boasts more than 4 million unique visitors monthly who spend thirty minutes at the site on average each month. Why the popularity and site stickiness? Candystand offers a diverse mix of online casual games. It also encourages participation from real gamers with its special microsite for Nintendo Wii users. This section of Candystand offers online games, branded with Wrigley brands like Altoids, which Wii users can play with their Wii remotes.

Chrysler successfully used advergaming to reach women. Designed by Blitz Agency to function like an online personality quiz that asked, "What's your travel personality," the game collected user information and introduced players to Chrysler's line of cars. Although games were thought at the time to reach a young male demographic, Chrysler's foray into advergaming yielded an average player age of 45, 42% women.[33] It included a viral component and tracking of the viral e-mails sent revealed a 66% open rate, far higher than the industry average for permission e-mail marketing; 15% of the games players requested vehicle brochures, a significantly higher percentage than those requesting brochures from Chrysler's Web site.

Toyota is another brand working to create its own content for video games. Its Yaris is promoted in part through an Xbox game called Yaris offered free to all Xbox 360 console owners who can download the game from the Xbox Live Web site. Burger King has also used the Xbox platform for its own advergame. The Sneak King Xbox game was available at Burger King restaurants for $3.99 with the purchase of a BK value meal. Burger King reportedly sold 3.5 million games, resulting in an impression value of more than 1.4 billion thirty-second commercials.[34]

The key to success in the advergaming market is the quality of the game. Gamers tend to be thought of as people who eschew traditional advertising, but they will welcome a good game, whether or not it is made as an advergame. Advergames and display ads in and around games (especially static ads) account for most of the current advertising spending, but the benefits of dynamic ads will likely change the allocation of ad spending in the short term.[35] Dynamic in-game ad serving in PC, console, mobile, and casual games is expected to grow from 27% of the in-game market to 84% in 2012, or about $805 million in advertising expenditures.

■ The Playbook for Game Advertising

Games offer many advertising opportunities, both those that mimic the traditional real world of advertising media and those that offer characteristics of engagement common to virtual worlds and social networks. This chapter concludes with guidelines for maximizing the effectiveness of game advertising.

Fran Kennish sets out several guides for the game advertisers' playbook.[36]

- Don't assume video games are appropriate for any and every brand.
- Don't interrupt, delay, or alter game-play with ads in the game.
- Don't impose on a gamer's attention with communication that does not enhance the game.
- Don't assume that the brand's creative work used elsewhere will work in a video game environment.
- Don't think of advergames as an inexpensive way to target gamers.

John Broady, with CNET Networks Entertainment (which includes the Gamespot.com property), points out that while games are entertainment, gaming is quite different from other forms of entertainment like films and music.[37] Other entertainment sources tend to encourage passivity on the part of the viewer, but games are a task-oriented experience. Players consume games in order to challenge themselves and to compete with themselves and others. Brands marketing within the genre must ensure that the brand message is appropriate for the consumers' mind-set. The most important thing a marketer considering in-game advertising can do is to understand games. Play games and hire people who play games. The brand should enhance the game's experience, be relevant, serve as a conduit for gamer immersion into the game, and strengthen the game's sense of escapism.

To enhance the likelihood that the advertising will result in positive brand attitudes, consider ways for gamers to interact with the brand as a part of the game story. Follow the Adidas case study by finding experiences that involve the players and the brand. Build in surprises and positive reinforcement that links the brand to success in the game. This can be accomplished with the use of "Easter eggs." Easter eggs are hidden features buried in the game's code. Programmers use them to reward players, and they can be an exciting method of engaging gamers.

Marketers must consider the game's purpose and plot, genre and format, profile of its gamers, how, when, and where the game is played, culture of the game, as well as the brand's placement opportunities within the game. Ultimately, the best game ads will not feel like ads. They will not be perceived as advertising, but rather the brands will exist in and around the game as a prop, a tool, an aspect of the game's setting and environment, and perhaps even as a character. In games, ads should not feel like ads, but like an organic, natural extension of the game.

11 ▪ ▪ ▪

Social-Media Impact
Balancing Metrics and Insight for Advertising Success

Brands can benefit from advertising in social-media space. The approaches offer a means to engage consumers, enhance brand reputation and image, build positive brand attitudes, improve organic search rankings, and drive traffic to brand locations, both on- and off-line. The steps in any advertising campaign will begin with setting campaign objectives and end with assessing the effectiveness of the strategies and tactics to determine the degree of success in accomplishing the stated objectives and to inform the next campaign. The challenge is to develop a set of measures to assess success and plan for future strategies and tactics.

At this stage of development, social-media advertising lacks the standard metrics that have served as a primary advantage for online advertising. Online advertising as a form of direct-response advertising has measurability built into its very existence. Advertisers can measure reach (the number of people exposed to the message) and frequency (the average number of times someone is exposed), and analyze site stickiness (the ability of a site to draw repeat visits and to keep people on a site) and the relative pull of creative presentations (a comparison of the ability for different creative executions to generate response). They can also monitor clickthroughs (the number of people exposed who click on an online ad or link), sales conversions (the number of people who click-through who then purchase product), and viewthroughs (the number of people who are exposed and do not clickthrough but later visit the brand's Web site). These metrics are applicable to the use of display advertising in social spaces. If L'Oreal buys display ads on Facebook, all of these metrics are available to gauge effectiveness.

However, for the more innovative approaches available, metrics like number of unique visitors, page views, frequency of visits, average visit length, and clickthrough rates are either totally inappropriate or irrelevant, or simply fail to capture information about the objectives of a social-media advertising campaign. Our tendency is to count—count impressions, visitors, friends, posts, players. There is a place for numbers. For instance, knowing the number of community members involved in brand-related conversations can serve as an indicator of exposure, and the number of message threads and lines of text within a thread can serve as proxies of conversation depth. However, counting does not capture the essence of the interaction consumers had with the brand, the degree of engagement felt during and after the interaction, or the effects of the inter-action, exposure to brand messages, and brand engagement on measures like brand likability, brand image, brand awareness, brand loyalty, brand affiliation, congruency, and purchase intent. Jeep may have 8,500 MySpace friends, but the number does nothing to tell us how the friends feel about Jeep. An ARG may boast millions of players, but the sheer quantity of players does not reveal the success of the strategy. To measure outcomes of social advertising, organizations must balance quantitative metrics with qualitative insights.

■ The Measurement Process

The appropriate approaches to measurement will vary depending upon the campaign's objectives and the social-media strategies and tactics used. However, these are the basic steps any measurement program should include.

Step 1: Review the objectives set for the campaign.

Step 2: Map the components of the social-media strategy used in the campaign.

Step 3: Determine the criteria that will be used to assess the achievement of objectives, and the tools necessary to measure the criteria.

Step 4: Establish a baseline or benchmark with which one can compare accomplishments.

Step 5: Analyze the effectiveness of the campaign components given the outcomes measured and propose changes appropriate for moving forward.

Step 6: Keep measuring.

■ Reviewing Objectives

Step 1, reviewing the campaign objectives, assumes that the objectives were set prior to pursuing advertising opportunities in social media. Not all brands set formal objectives. Some are simply experimenting with social media, and for them the experience of executing a campaign using emerging platforms is sufficient. For most brands, though, failing to set clear objectives is a mistake. When it comes to assessing success, if there are no objectives, how do you know if where you ended up is where you wanted to be? The specific objectives identified can vary dramatically from brand to brand but usually encompass three overarching issues: (1) motivating some action like visits to a Web site or sales, (2) affecting brand knowledge and attitudes, and (3) accomplishing the first two with fewer resources than might be required with other advertising and promotional methods.

■ Mapping the Campaign

Step 2 calls for mapping all of the social-media aspects of the advertising campaign. This activity results in a visual representation of the tactics used and how they may interact. Mapping is a technique advocated by Chris Brogan on his blog (http://chrisbrogan.com). In a post entitled "Measuring Social Media Efforts," he explains that maps can be crude, simple drawings but even a rough sketch can be valuable as brands seek to measure accomplishments in the social-media space. A map would display the types of branded messages produced and distributed (e.g., written vehicles like blog posts and white papers, ads in the form of display ads or rich media video, and podcasts) and invitations for consumer engagement with the brand (e.g., games, consumer-generated advertising contests and promotions, and interactive brand experiences) as well as the online location for these materials. It should also include online locations where content relating to the brand may be distributed by others. For instance, are there viral videos on YouTube that highlight the brand? Are there product reviews on sites like Epinions.com? Are there MySpace pages with brand icons and information posted? Are there bloggers writing about the brand? Are members of del.icio.us tagging the brand's Web site, and are Digg members voting for branded content?

Once all the sources of brand information are identified, the map should sketch out the chain of touch points possible. A touch point is simply a contact point between the brand and the consumer. Mini Cooper "touches" a consumer when someone visits the dealer showroom, visits the Mini Web site or one of its microsites, receives brochures and other promotional material from the company, or brings a car in for service. These are all brand-controlled touch points, but many touch points that the brand does not control do exist, especially online. In addition to the consumer-generated content that relates to the brand, there may be conversational touch points going on. Are people reading the blog postings (or even responding to blog posts) that mention the brand? Are people watching videos posted on sites like YouTube? Are they voting for content on Digg? In other words, is the media (whether brand-generated or consumer-generated) being consumed by those it reaches and is it being "fortified" (as in CFM)? Ultimately, the map should show four levels of contact: (1) brand-generated content, (2) consumer-generated content, (3) consumer-fortified content, and (4) exposures to content consumers.

■ Choosing Criteria and Tools of Measurement

In step 3, the criteria for assessing effectiveness are determined, and the tools necessary for measurement are selected. The objectives and the map should direct the identification of criteria, as well as the best tools. For example, imagine that Secret deodorant seeks to develop brand awareness for two new products, Secret Clinical Strength deodorant and Secret Scent Expressions body spray. It also wants to drive traffic to the product Web sites and increase sales of these products. Lastly, it wants to reinforce Secret's image of celebrating women, their strength and their secrets. The brand enters the social-media space with an advertising campaign, which also includes traditional media components, called Because You're Hot. The campaign, by Leo Burnett Chicago, plays on the definition of "hot" to connect to the efficacy of the Secret brand benefit while recognizing characteristics that make a woman hot (being strong). The Secret Web site and two microsites, www.becauseyourehot.com and www.sparklebodyspray.com, would be sketched on a social-media map, along with other tactics like the Rihanna's Secret MySpace profile (which features Secret Body Spray as a sponsor). Visitors to the Scent Expressions microsite are encouraged to participate in a quiz to identify their ideal scent, and those visiting the Because You're Hot site can vote on what's hottest using Secret's Hot-o-Meter. Secret also runs a promotion in MTV's Virtual Laguna Beach, encouraging women to "share their secrets." Secret could expand the social-media aspects of the campaign by hosting a blog with contributions from a slate of strong female celebrities, having a virtual dance party with a Jennifer Lopez avatar (to tie in to the dance contest featured in the traditional media component of the campaign) in Second Life, and inviting women to develop videos that capture the essence of the slogan, Because You're Hot. These videos could then be hosted on a Secret channel on YouTube. These are some of the brand-generated messages and invitations for participation in the campaign. Consumers are generating content about Secret. Technorati lists blogs, posts, and videos that mention both products. YouTube also includes videos tagged with Secret deodorant and Secret Scent Expressions. Internet users have opportunities for exposure and can fortify the messages with comments and product reviews.

What criteria and tools then should Secret use to evaluate success of these techniques? Secret's objectives emphasized a desire to (1) build awareness of its new products, (2) drive visits to its Web sites, (3) drive sales, and (4) strengthen the Secret brand image. Objective 2 is easily addressed with traditional Web site metrics and measurement tools. The Secret sites can track hits, page views, and unique visitors; the sites enable registration, which can also be tracked. Organic search engine rankings can also be assessed for the brand name and its slogans. Secret is not performing well on organic search. The word *secret* generates a third-place spot for the Secret brand; the word *deodorant* places Secret in sixth place. Searches with the slogans "Because You're Hot" and "Share Your Secret" result in third-place listings.

Awareness can be suggested with the Web site traffic and traffic to other branded components. For instance, Rihanna's Secret MySpace profile boasts over 24,000 friends, some of whom have fortified the profile with comments. It can also be suggested with brand mentions in other online space. Secret might ask, "Is the brand being talked about? If so, how much, and where?" The criteria for answering these questions are straightforward. One simply needs to identify evidence of the brand in online conversations and publications, get a count of those occurrences, and note the source of the material. The tools necessary for this could include a virtual version of a clipping service to determine what is being said about the brand and the brand's competition online. This can be an in-house project, or outsourced to companies like CyberAlert, which can then monitor specific publications or the entire Internet for brand mentions.

Collecting brand mentions in house can be accomplished with tools like Google Alerts. These tools can provide a count of mentions, and the sources, but they should be combined with other tools to determine whether the communication was positive, negative, or neutral for the brand.

Next Secret might ask, "How many people are exposed to these third-party messages?" To assess the impact of these brand mentions across the Web, one can turn to companies that measure the size of a site's audience. Media Metrix, Nielsen Net/Ratings, and comScore offer measurement services that include hits, unique visitors, and page views for sites. It will need to consider all the locations of postings mentioning the brand and the audiences for each location.

Secret, in our example, also set out to strengthen its image. Its image can be influenced by what the target audience thinks and feels about the branding for the campaign. Are young women engaged with quick games like the Hot-o-Meter? Is the association strategy using Rihanna and Jennifer Lopez as celebrity endorsers effective? Do they feel that the Scent Expressions quiz and scent recommendations enable Secret as a brand to symbolize their own self images? The campaign itself will influence the brand's image. Secret may use primary research in the form of surveys and focus groups to answer these questions.

A key to social media is that the consumer-generated content and consumer-fortified content can also influence image. The viral nature of brand-relevant communication is why social media is both an opportunity and a threat for advertisers. To determine the relative influence and nature of that influence on a brand, one must consider the source of content, the relative authority of that source, and the content itself. Katie Delahaye Paine advocates a list of criteria for assessing the influence of blog postings about a brand.[1] It is easily applicable to all forms of social publicity, including mentions in news media (on- and off-line), online comments—whether a blog posting, responses to blog postings, or comments about videos—profiles, photos, message board postings, and online product reviews.

- Is the posting exclusively about the brand or is the brand simply mentioned in passing or along with other competing brands?
- What did the posting seek to accomplish? Did it intend to solve a problem, compare brands, or allow the author to rant or self-promote?
- How many times is the brand mentioned within each posting?
- Did the post include a recommendation about the brand like "do not buy this product"?

- Did the posting include any brand messages like the brand's slogan, mention of brand experiences, or benefits of using the brand?
- Does the post leave readers with a positive or negative impression of the brand?

Brands should gather the comments from all the touch points and social-media sources identified on its map. The comments can then be used as data for a content analysis that will reveal themes, concerns, and insights. Using codes, labels that are used to classify and assign meanings to pieces of information, analysts can use the comments to determine any themes that are reflected in the comments and what, if anything, the brand should do about what is being said. The coding categories used to classify the comments can include context codes to give information on the source of the comment, respondent perspective codes to capture the general viewpoint revealed in the comment, process codes to indicate when over the course of a campaign the comment occurred, relationship codes to indicate relevant alliances present within the social communities, event codes to refer to unique issues, and activity codes to identify comments that require some response by the brand.

Content analysis can be managed in house, jointly, by using a service to collect data and/or conduct the analysis, or be outsourced. Companies like BuzzLogic, Cymfony, Umbria, Narrative Network, and Nielsen BuzzMetrics promise to count and analyze conversations and comments in social-media space to provide insights that can then inform brand strategy. These services take the qualitative data and quantify it. BuzzLogic tracks conversations mentioning brands all over the Internet. It then develops conversation maps with indicators for those who are talking about the brand, whose opinions matter most, and the nature of the content. Oliver Ryan of *Fortune* magazine shares the story of a blogger who, frustrated with his Lenovo ThinkPad's failed hard drive, blasts a negative rant about the brand on his blog.[2] Within hours of the blog's posting, BuzzLogic notified Lenovo's vice president of global Web marketing, who promptly called the blogger with a promise to resolve the product defect. The blogger was so impressed by the company's response that he shared his pleasure on his blog and the story was then shared with other bloggers. The result was a widespread conversation benefiting the Lenovo brand that grew out of an initial negative post. BuzzLogic offers a range of services for its clients, including lists of the most influential bloggers and their profiles, social maps of the conversations taking place about the client brand, and ad targeting to enable brands to display ads in and around the spaces where relevant conversations are taking place.

The last objective in our Secret example was to drive sales of the two new products. It is more difficult to illustrate the effects of social-media advertising on sales, particularly for a packaged goods product like Secret, which does not sell to end users directly through its Web site. For brands with e-commerce sites, the branded social content will include links to the brand's retail site, and clickthrough and conversion rates can be assessed along with cost per acquisition. Even this does not capture the sales picture completely, for brands sold off- and online, and on multiple sites online. For example, what if the product in question was Rihanna's latest album, *Good Girl Gone Bad?* Sales could take place on multiple retail Web sites and at download sites like iTunes and in physical stores. It would be difficult to track sales conversions that originated with social media. Still, the concept of return on investment can be a useful metric.

Return on Investment

A common metric for gauging success is that of return on investment, or ROI. ROI is a measure of profitability. It captures how effective a company is at using capital to generate profits. Advertising ROI takes the ROI principle and uses it to assess how well an organization applied those financial resources deployed specifically for promotion to profit generation. Calculating ROI requires assigning a financial value to the resources used to execute a strategy, measuring outcomes financially, and calculating the ratio between inputs and outcomes. Return on investment answers the question, how much income was generated from investments in advertising? SMROI (social-media return on investment) seeks to answer the question, how much income was generated from investments in social advertising?

Social-media metrics gurus are working on the development of just such a measure. It is natural that the management would want to quantify the value of a corporate activity and use that value as justification for continuing and expanding the activity. The challenge when it comes to social media is the qualitative, viral, pervasive nature of the outcomes of social-media advertising. Investments in social-media advertising generate goodwill, brand engagement, and momentum, but how can one quantify the value of those outcomes?

A paper by Fraser Likely, David Rockland, and Mark Weiner on measuring the ROI of media relations publicity efforts provides a good road map for measuring SMROI.[3] They propose four approaches: (1) return on impressions model, (2) return on media impact model, (3) return on target influence model, and (4) return on earned media model, adapted here for social-media advertising. The return on impressions model demonstrates how many media impressions were generated by the social-media advertising tactics employed. An impression is simply an "opportunity to see" for the target audience. Online advertisers can buy impressions by paying to have a display ad rotated on a Web site. Social-media advertising provides impressions in a variety of other ways, though. The opportunity for exposure to the brand message might be delivered as part of a virtual-world event, on a social-networking profile site, with consumer-generated ads, product reviews, and so on. Impressions are valuable, according to this model, because we assume that impressions lead to changes in awareness, followed by changes in comprehension, then changes in attitude, and ultimately changes in behavior (sales). Using the percentage of people reached who ultimately purchase as a way to calculate sales value, we can then determine a return on impressions by taking the gross revenue estimated minus the cost of the social-media advertising program divided by the cost of the program. For example, if we estimate that Secret earns $500,000 in gross revenue due to its social advertising, at a cost of $100,000, the ROI for the campaign is 400%.

The return on media impact model attempts to track coverage across media and in different markets against sales over time. It requires advanced multiple regression analysis to analyze variables that may affect sales, including the mix of advertising and promotional tools used at each time and place. This approach offers the greatest potential for social-media advertisers because it can include lagged measurements that control for time order of events taking place online (for instance, the timing of an event in a social world, the point at which a profile was activated, the timing of a contest conclusion, and subsequent posting of consumer-generated ads). Return on social-media impact promises to determine how sales can be attributed to each element in a marketing mix and for tactics within the social-media advertising strategy. This is the most complex approach to measurement, requiring data to be compiled and analyzed by the market on a regular basis. Content generation and consumption is tracked and assigned algorithm scores to indicate weight of relative influence. Sales are also tracked at the same intervals, and then statistical analysis is used to determine how sales trends shifted according to the timing of the social-media advertising.

The return on target influence model relies upon survey data to assess the effectiveness of social-media advertising. Surveys assess whether participants were exposed to the social-media advertising tactics and what perceptions they formed as a result of exposure. The model then calls for calculating the change in the probability of purchase based on the exposure, using binary variable analysis.

The final approach is that of return on earned media model. AEV (advertising equivalency value) is a metric used primarily to equate (albeit crudely) publicity in news media outlets to its paid advertising equivalent. In other words, if a brand had paid for a mention in a specific space, what would it have cost? For social-media advertising, an AEV would attempt to equate source authority, source prominence, depth of brand mention, and recommendation with a paid advertising value. To calculate advertising equivalency, the cost to purchase a display ad on a site would be used to assign a dollar value to the impressions achieved socially. For example, if a display ad on Facebook costs $50,000 (CPM), we could assign an earned media value of $50,000 to a thousand page views of our brand profile on Facebook. The value can also be adjusted by the subjective importance of the earned media in question. For example, one might believe that profile visits are more valuable than a display ad rotation because it suggests that visitors sought out the brand interaction. The earned media value can be adjusted to account for variables like the popularity of the location, the relative influence of the source, and so on. The ROI calculation is then based on the difference between the AEV and the cost of the social-media advertising program divided by the cost of the program. For example, if the AEV for the Facebook profile is $50,000 but it cost $5,000 in time for its development and maintenance, the incremental gain is $45,000. The gain divided by the cost of the program expressed as a percentage reveals a ROI of 900%. This measure may be among the easiest to execute for those social-media spaces that also sell display advertising. However, it is not, truly, a return on investment measure so much as it is a measure of effective resource utilization.

Simple Ways to Start

Clearly, one can seek to measure effectiveness using a variety of criteria, approaches, and tools. Some advertisers, though, will want simple yet relevant metrics that are easier to assess than complex models of impact based on algorithm scores and advanced econometrics. Michael Brito highlights several engagement metrics in a blog posting on *Search Engine Journal*.[4]

- Content consumption: Who is interacting with and consuming the brand-generated and consumer-generated content?

- Content fortification: Who is fortifying content by continuing the conversation with response posts? How is the content fortified? What does the nature of the fortification say about the brand?

- Content sharing: Who is adding content to sites like del.icio.us, Reddit, and Stumbleupon? Who is recommending content at sites like Digg? At what rate are those exposed to the brand messages sharing the content with others using tools like "tell a friend"?

- Content loyalty: How many consumers have subscribed to branded content with RSS feeds or by registering for site access?

- Content conversations: Who is discussing the brand? Who is linking to brand Web sites? Technorati, a blog search engine, enables one to search for a domain to identify blogs that link there. For comments to brand content, what is the comment to post ratio?

- Content engagement: Who is friending the brand on social-networking profiles? Are friends sharing brand content like branded widgets? Are they sharing brand stories? Are consumers visiting brand experiences in virtual worlds? Are consumers contributing consumer-generated ads (whether organic or incented) to sites like YouTube? Brands should track views of profiles, number of friends, and the affect toward the brand reflected in the content shared.

In step 4, the brand establishes a baseline or benchmark with which one can compare accomplishments. In other words, knowing how many people friended Rihanna's Secret profile on MySpace does not really mean anything unless one has a point of comparison. If we note that other brand profiles typically have an average of 10,000 friends, the Secret profile seems successful. The average serves as a benchmark for gauging the success of the tactic. The point of comparison may be past attempts for the brand (like comparing the number of friends for Secret's last MySpace profile to the one used for the current campaign) or an industry benchmark or a benchmark from a specific competitor, when data are available for comparison purposes.

In step 5, the effectiveness of the campaign is determined based on the work conducted in steps 3 and 4, and changes for future strategies are proposed. This is a critical point. Without using the results of measurement as feedback for the future, the assessment is of limited value. Lastly, step 6 is a continuous process: keep measuring. Over time, brands will learn what works for them in the Web 2.0 world.

■ Detective Work and Other Sources of Online Insight

This final chapter focuses on measuring success of advertising online, and specifically with social media. But brands can use research techniques to do more than just measure success. Web 2.0 offers the opportunity to study social media in the context of social communities. Online research can take on many forms, mimicking various off-line versions. These forms include surveys, experiments, focus groups and interviews, and observations. The vast majority consists of Web-based surveys, but for advertisers using social media, two online research techniques hold great promise: online focus groups and netnography.

The role of market research is to provide decision makers with data relevant to marketing strategy. It provides a primary tool for exploring opportunities and markets, and testing ideas and concepts. When conducted online, discovery is fast and relatively inexpensive. Perhaps most important, online research studies consumers in the environment of interest. It is for this reason that social-media advertisers should consider complementing what they learn from their assessment programs and content analysis with primary research of consumers in an online space.

Online Focus Groups

Although online focus groups offer many of the same advantages as Web surveys (lower costs, speed, access to geographically dispersed participants and markets that are difficult to recruit), adoption of this approach has been far slower. In large part, this is due to the loss of information provided by nonverbal cues as well as other minor challenges. Focus groups are standard procedure for any study requiring a depth of inquiry into a topic. They are useful for generating ideas, screening new products, identifying underlying attitudes to product concepts and brands, discovering shopping intentions, evaluating creative concepts, and acquiring a depth of understanding about consumer behavior. Groups are flexible; they may disguise the study's purpose or not and vary in the extent to which they follow a structured guide. In addition, groups provide limited exposure to concepts that can protect information from exposure to competition.

Online focus groups offer the benefits of traditional focus groups as well as other benefits not commonly associated with in-person groups. One of their greatest advantages when conducted online is their appropriateness for dealing with sensitive topics. Further, there appears to be less inhibition and editing of thoughts among participants in online groups. Unrelated chatting and extensive input from one or a few participants is also less common. Prima facie, then, it might seem that online focus groups should be preferred by researchers as they resolve many of the problems associated with traditional groups. Unfortunately, online groups have their own set of challenges. Chief among these are the lack of nonverbal cues, the reliance upon typing to relay information, and the potential for technical difficulties in the focus group process. Still, given the advantages of online focus groups and the prevalence of focus groups for advertising research, we anticipate a growth in this application.

Groups can be conducted asynchronously using an online message board format or synchronously using a virtual facility and chat software. Respondents see all of the moderator's questions and the comments of other participants as they are submitted into the dialogue stream. Identities are protected by the use of pseudonyms. Clients observing the session can submit notes to the moderator, but respondents cannot see these entries.

The basic stages of the research process are similar for online groups as for those conducted off-line: setting objectives, recruiting and screening participants, developing discussion guides, moderating, and conducting data analysis. Most research companies offering online focus groups will provide turnkey solutions, including recruitment, screening, and facilities. Just as with off-line groups, recruitment may involve a variety of methods from using established lists, advertising for participants, or even telephone recruiting. The following guidelines are important considerations for managing the initial process:

- Develop screeners who can disqualify respondents without divulging the reasons for dismissal.
- Use blocks on e-mail addresses of disqualified potential respondents to discourage them from trying again.
- Provide invitations with passwords, instructions, dates, and times to those who are qualified for participation.
- Ask participants to visit the site in advance of the group to ensure that technology is compatible.
- Provide technical support contact information for all participants.

Just as in the case of off-line groups, the show rates for those recruited do vary from situation to situation; generally, it is wise to recruit 50%–100% more than what is desired in attendance. Although weather and traffic, two constant concerns for focus group participation off-line, are not concerns online, other factors remain, including lack of commitment on the part of those recruited, familiarity with the online venue, and other personal issues that can inhibit attendance. As recruits join the virtual room, rescreening should take place. During the rescreening, participant identities can be confirmed (to the extent possible), and if too many are available for participation, the moderator and client can select those who will remain.

The moderator and preparation of the guide is of utmost importance in an online venue. The questions must be prepared in advance and should even be preloaded for easy submission when needed. Because the moderator must read responses, assess how to reply, develop and administer probes, and determine when to administer the next question (and what that question should be), he or she should minimize the amount of typing necessary. For synchronous groups, the typical time span is ninety minutes with approximately forty to forty-five questions used during the discussion (question dialogues typically run about two minutes per question). Asynchronous groups vary depending on the number of days the group will last and the nature of the questions. Participants consider and respond to a new set of questions each morning. An advantage of asynchronous groups is that participants can spend more time responding to questions and reading comment threads than what is possible for participants in a synchronous group.

Although skeptics feel that much is lost in interpersonal interaction online, those skilled in online relationships will recognize that personalities and attitudes can easily be relayed online and relationships do develop among participants. Many who are willing to participate in online focus groups have previously participated in chat rooms and on message boards. Consequently, it is not difficult for participants to establish a rapport with one another. Moderators sometimes struggle to establish authority in online groups, and there are other drawbacks like the lack of security (particularly given the inability to confirm identities of participants), the minimal client involvement, and the inability to use tangible stimuli. Overall, though, online focus groups represent a temporary form of social community, and therefore offer an appropriate and powerful research tool for studying consumer reactions to social-media advertising.

Netnography

Robert Kozinets defines netnography as a "qualitative research methodology that adapts ethnographic research techniques to the study of cultures and communities that are emerging through computer-mediated communications."[5] The approach uses information available through online forums such as chat rooms, message boards, and social-networking groups to study the attitudes and behaviors of the market involved. It is an unobtrusive approach to research with a key benefit of observing what is likely to be credible information, unaffected by the research process. Many marketers already use a very informal and unsystematic form of netnography by simply exploring relevant online communities. However, to minimize the limitations of netnography, researchers should be careful in their evaluations, by employing triangulation to confirm findings whenever possible.

How can we use netnography? Kozinets recommends the following steps:[6]

- Identify online venues that could provide information related to the research questions.
- Select online communities that are focused on a particular topic or segment, have a high "traffic" of postings, have a relatively large number of active posters, and appear to have detailed posts.
- Learn about the group's culture, including its characteristics, behaviors, and language.
- Select material for analysis and classify material as social or informational and off-topic or on-topic.
- Categorize the types of participants involved in the discussions to be analyzed. There are four key categories of participants (this grouping is useful for reducing the data to be considered): (1) tourists, (2) minglers, (3) devotees, and (4) insiders. Tourists are casual visitors, while minglers are there for social needs. Devotees and insiders are the two groups with a strong interest in the topic, and it is their responses that should be the focus of analysis.
- Keep a journal of observations and reflections about the data collection and analysis process.
- Be straightforward with those in the online community about your purpose for participation by fully disclosing the researcher's presence in the community as well as his or her intent.
- Utilize "member checks," following content analysis of the discourse to ensure that members feel their attitudes and behaviors have been accurately interpreted.

Ultimately, online research is a valuable tool for advertisers operating in a virtual realm—not only because of clear efficiency advantages like cost, speed, and access but also because of the parallels in the online environment. When the insight from online primary research is combined with success metrics and content analysis, it provides a strong foundation to refine future strategies.

Epilogue

In a Web 2.0 world, advertising exists in an interactive environment characterized by user control, freedom, and dialogue. In this context, advertising means inviting the consumption of branded experience, ideas, and knowledge, engaging consumers, and inspiring interaction. It is no longer appropriate to serve up advertising as an interruption in the lives of consumers but, rather, to position brands as contributing members of vibrant, social communities.

Social brands contribute to communities by developing opportunities for interactivity, emphasizing the brand's relevance to individual members and the community at large, monitoring branded community assets (like profiles in social networks and facilities in virtual worlds) for needed maintenance, responding to feedback, providing new content over time, and always finding ways to show the community that the brand values the relationship. No matter the range of social-media outlets used in a social campaign, whether social news and bookmarking sites, virtual worlds, social networks, or blogs and wikis, brands must remember the community exists for the sake of community—not for the sake of branding.

People do not join a community to interact with a brand. They join to be a part of something. They join to make friends, share stories, have fun, publish creative work, have a voice, and to take part in the relational activities that make life interesting and enjoyable. They join for social support and to feel the comfort of contact. They join to get to know others and to let others know them. For a brand to succeed in a social community, the brand must be part of the community.

How can brands benefit from the social context of online communities? For brands to benefit from this phenomenon, they must *invite* consumer participation and encourage consumers to *engage*. Brand democratization is the invitation to consumers to participate in creating and then experiencing a brand's meaning, particularly within a social context. What happens when brands develop a reputation for embracing a social culture characterized by an appreciation for authenticity, transparency, participation, infectiousness, and advocacy? What happens when brands enter online social communities—social networks, virtual worlds, social news sites, community review sites, and communities of gamers—as contributing members, as sponsors, and as friends? Consumers embrace roles. They become content creators, storytellers, advocates, and communication vehicles. They seek out opportunities to immerse themselves in imaginary worlds, social fiction, and games, which are fortified, sponsored, and enhanced by brands. This is the promise of advertising in social media.

Glossary

Ad units:
A classification of standardized online ad types and sizes, defined by the Interactive Advertising Bureau.

Advergaming:
Games that are developed and distributed for the purposes of promoting a brand; branding is integrated throughout the game environment.

Advertising equivalency value (AEV):
A metric used to equate publicity in news media outlets to its paid advertising equivalent.

Advertising network:
A network representing advertising opportunities, which enable media buyers to reach a broader audience more efficiently using run-of-network buys.

Alternate reality game (ARG):
A cross-media game based on interactive fiction.

Avatar:
A graphic identity used to represent people in virtual worlds and social communities.

Banner blindness:
The tendency for Web site viewers to ignore display ads.

Beacon:
A line of code placed in an ad or on a Web page to track behavior, also the name of a Facebook service, which tracks and shares member behavior.

Behavioral targeting:
Delivering advertising with a high degree of relevance to those exposed, based on user behavior online.

Blog:
Short for Web log; an online commentary, which may take the role of diary or column.

Brand democratization:
The shared development and promotion of brand meaning by consumers and the brand's own architects.

Brand engagement:
The process or outcome of developing a meaningful, memorable, favorable relationship between a brand and its customers, particularly through interactive experiences.

Brand equity:
The financial value of a brand, developed as a result of high levels of brand awareness and strong, favorable, unique perceptions of the brand's image.

Brand terrorists:
People who seek to harm a brand by spreading negative information or by vandalizing branded areas in social communities.

Citizen advertising:
Content created by consumers using verbal and/or visual imagery to inform, persuade, or remind other consumers about a brand, resulting in an ad unit, also called V-CAMs (viewer-created ad messages).

Citizen endorsers:
Consumers who recommend products by submitting online product reviews.

Citizen marketing:
Marketing for a brand by customer enthusiasts who share information about the brand and generate media coverage.

Clickthrough:
The action of clicking on an online ad to reach the Web site promoted.

Clickthrough rate:
The response rate of an online ad, based on the percentage of those who were exposed to the ad who also clicked through.

Clutter:
The presence of too much advertising in a space.

Collective detective:
A term for the collaboration of a team of game players.

Compensated consumer-generated media (cCGM):
Consumer-generated content for which the brand has paid the consumer.

Consumer-fortified media (CFM):
Consumer-generated content that is created around the existence of some other content, such as responses to blog postings.

Consumer-generated media (CGM):
User-generated content that reflects first-person commentary about brand experiences.

Consumer-generated multimedia (CGM2):
A type of consumer-generated media that includes audio, video, and perhaps animation.

Consumer-solicited media (CSM):
A form of consumer-generated media to which consumers are invited to contribute content.

Contact comfort:
A motive for the development and maintenance of relationships online, especially in the context of social communities.

Contextual advertising:
Targeting of online advertising based on matching the content of the ad with the context of the Web site chosen to display the ad.

Conversion:
Response to an ad's call to action, especially in the form of purchase.

Conversion rate:
The percentage of people exposed to an ad who clickthrough and make a purchase.

Cost per acquisition (CPA):
The cost to acquire a customer, based on the total cost of advertising divided by the number of customers acquired, also referred to as cost per conversion, cost per inquiry, cost per lead, or cost per sale.

Cost per thousand (CPM):
The cost to reach 1,000 people; pricing is based on number of ad impressions served over a period of time.

Credlining:
A term that refers to the scorecards produced by consumers who analyze product information and post accurate information online for other consumers.

Crowdsourcing:
The use of the general public to accomplish professional work.

Curtain:
The invisible line separating the players from the puppet masters in an alternate reality game.

Digital dialogue:
A phrase used to denote the conversation that can exist between customers and brands using online media.

Dynamic advertising:
Ads displayed in video games, which are dynamically updated throughout a game network.

Friendvertising:
A branding and communication approach, which relies upon social networks to enable consumers to befriend brands and share brand information with other friends in their networks.

Grief:
A term that refers to attacks in virtual worlds, either on avatars or on branded facilities.

Gross rating point (GRP):
A measure of the weight of a brand's communication vehicles in the media market for a specific period of time.

Impression:
The opportunity to see an ad; an advertising exposure.

In World:
A term used to denote activity within a virtual world.

Incentivized consumer-generated media (iCGM):
Consumer-solicited media that is incented by the sponsoring brand.

Inventory:
The number of ad spaces available on a Web site or within a game.

Linkbaiting:
Packaging content to increase the likelihood that others will link to it.

Long tail effect:
The ability online to reach small, niche markets efficiently.

Lurkers:
People who follow the game but do not actively participate.

Mash-ups:
Content created using a mix of existing material.

Massively multiplayer online role-playing games (MMORPG):
Form of online game in which a large number of players interact with one another over time.

Meaning Transfer Model:
Consumers first assign meaning from the endorser to the brand. Then the meanings attributed to the endorser become associated with the brand in the consumer's mind.

Mechanistic consumer-generated advertising:
Consumer-generated advertising that is controlled to some extent by the rules, guidelines, and brand assets required by the brand's contest guidelines.

Media fragmentation:
The breaking up of large audiences into small fragments due to an increase in the media choices available.

Metaverse:
A three-dimensional online community, also known as a virtual world.

Microsite:
A separate Web site, distinct from a brand's primary site, with its own URL used as part of a promotional campaign.

Momentum effect:
The incremental gain in advertising effectiveness attributed to endorsements and pass-alongs by friends in a social community.

Netnography:
A qualitative research technique, which applies ethnographic research techniques to the study of online communities.

Network effect:
The increase in value that accrues to a social network as the size of the network community increases.

Newbie:
A person who is new to a social community.

Organic consumer-generated advertising:
Advertising developed by consumers without an incentive or invitation to do so from the brand.

Organic search listing:
Listings that occur naturally in response to a search; search engines do not sell the listing or listing rank.

Packaged consumer-generated advertising:
Consumer-generated advertising that is limited to specific brand assets such as brand-approved images and slogans.

Page view:
An instance in which a Web page is viewed by a visitor.

Pass-along rate:
The percentage of people who pass on a message or piece of content.

Position:
The relative perception a brand holds in the minds of the target market relative to the competition.

Post-roll advertising:
Video advertising shown at the end of content.

Pre-roll advertising:
Video advertising shown before a user is shown the content of interest.

Puppet master:
A person who plans, writes, and governs an alternate reality game.

Rabbit hole:
The first clue used to kick off an alternate reality game.

Reach:
The number of people exposed to an advertising message in a specific period of time.

Return on earned media model:
An approach to social-media return on investment that considers the value of the brand's exposure if the impressions were paid exposures rather than earned through social media.

Return on impressions model:
An approach to social-media return on investment that demonstrates how many media impressions were generated by the social-media advertising tactics employed.

Return on investment (ROI):
A measure of profitability.

Return on media impact model:
An approach to social-media return on investment that determines how sales can be attributed to each element in a social-media advertising strategy over time.

Return on target influence model:
An approach to social-media return on investment that relies upon survey data to assess the effectiveness of social-media advertising based on the extent to which the methods achieved changes in the desired consumer attitudes.

Rich media:
A type of advertising, which includes audio, video, and advanced graphics.

RSS feed:
A method of syndicating online content, enabling others to subscribe to receive the content automatically.

Rubbernecker:
A person who does not actively play in the game but may participate in forums about the game and contribute to the game's solution.

Search engine advertising:
The strategy of using search engine listing results as an advertising vehicle.

Search engine optimization (SEO):
The process of ensuring that a site is well positioned to achieve the best possible search listings, as part of a search engine advertising strategy.

Seed branding:
A technique for branding that involves building relationships between brands and consumers by "planting a seed" of interest in the minds of consumers. The "seed" is some form of interactive device such as a game that inspires consumers to cognate on the brand.

Shilling:
Distributing brand-generated content or incented content online while pretending the content is user generated.

Short:
A video that is longer than a commercial but shorter than a film.

Six degrees effect:
The notion that it is a small world, with everyone connected to everyone else within six contacts.

Social bookmarking:
The storing of URL bookmarks within a social community such that bookmarks can be tagged according to content and shared with others.

Social community:
A broad range of online groups, including forums, social networks, virtual worlds, bookmarking sites, and more.

Social fiction:
Another term for alternate reality games.

Social media:
The collection of social communities online, which enables members to create, share, cocreate, and fortify content, as well as interact as any community might.

Social-media impact (SMI):
A measure of the effectiveness achieved by a social-media advertising campaign.

Social-media marketing (SMM):
Broad category of online advertising that places promotional messages in the context of social communities.

Social-media optimization (SMO):
Optimizing a site so that it is more visible to social communities in order to increase links to a site.

Social-media return on investment (SMROI):
A measure of the revenue generated as a result of social-media advertising.

Social network:
Utility-based social communities, which enable members to build identity using profiles, communicate with other members, develop a network of friends, and participate in the community (e.g., www.myspace.com).

Social news:
News shared in social communities focused on content sharing and ranking (e.g., www.digg.com).

Steganography:
The tactic of hiding messages within another medium such that the message is undetectable for those who do not know to look for it.

Stickiness:
The ability of a Web site to keep a visitor at the site and to encourage a visitor to return to the site.

TINAG:
This acronym stands for a defining mantra of ARGS—This is not a game!

Trackback:
A method of tracking links back or references to a blog, also known as a linkback.

Trail:
A reference index of the game, including relevant sites, puzzles, in-game characters, and other information. Trails are useful for new players coming late into a game and to veteran players piecing together the narrative.

Transmedia storytelling:
A story that is told across multiple media platforms with each component valuable on its own and as a contribution to the story as a whole.

User-generated content:
Content created by an individual that (1) is made publicly available online, (2) reflects some creative effort on the part of the user, and (3) is created outside professional practice.

Viewthrough:
Visits to a target Web site at some point after exposure to the ad.

Virtual worlds:
Online, three-dimensional, economic social communities.

Vlobalization, Vlobe:
Phrases used to denote the universe of virtual worlds and the trend of brands participating in virtual worlds.

Widget:
A small program application that interacts with the Web browser to deliver content to the user.

Wiki:
A collaboratively edited Web page.

Notes

CHAPTER I

1. Internet World Stats, Usage and Population Statistics, February 10, 2008, www.internetworldstats.com.

2. Marketing Power, "Dictionary of Marketing Terms," American Marketing Association, http://www.marketingpower.com/mg-dictionary.php?SearchDefinitionsAlso=ON&SearchFor=nonprofit&Searched=1&Term_ID=.

3. Deloitte & Touche, "The State of the Media Democracy: Are You Ready for the Future of Media?" December 3, 2007, http://www.deloitte.com/dtt/article/0,1002,sid%253D2205%2526cid%253D156096,00.html.

4. Organization for Economic Cooperation and Development, "Participative Web: User-Created Content," April 12, 2007, http://www.oecd.org/dataoecd/57/14/38393115.pdf.

5. Jim Nail, "The 4 Types of Engagement," *iMedia Connection,* October 13, 2006, http://www.imediaconnection.com/content/11633.asp.

6. See Nail, "The 4 Types of Engagement."

7. Jimm Lasser, "Brand Democracy," Speak Up, May 9, 2006, http://www.underconsideration.com/speakup/archives/002682.html.

8. Rick Bruner, "The Decade in Online Advertising, 1994–2004," Double-Click, April 2005, http://www.executivesummary.com/archives/2005/04/the_decade_in_o.php, 3.

9. TNS Media Intelligence, "TNS Media Intelligence Forecasts 4.2% Increase in U.S. Advertising Spending for 2008," January 7, 2008, http://www.tns-mi.com/news/01072008.htm.

10. eMarketer, "US Advertising Spending," November 2007, http://images.emarketer.com/Reports/All/Emarketer_2000442.aspx?src=report_head_info_sitesearch.

11. eMarketer, "Strong Growth Still Predicted for Web Ads," January 24, 2008, http://images.emarketer.com/Article.aspx?id=1005850&src=article_head _sitesearch.

12. eMarketer, "Online Advertising Spending Growth to Level Off," February 26, 2007, http://www.emarketer.com/Article.aspx?id=1004600&src=article1 _newsltr.

13. Interactive Advertising Bureau, "Ad Unit Guidelines," http:// www.iab.net/iab_products_and_industry_services/1421/1443/1452.

14. Enid Burns, "Internet Users Plagued by Banner Blindness," *The ClickZ Network,* June 26, 2006, http://www.clickz.com/showPage.html?page=3616001.

15. Marketing Charts, "Online Ad Spending to Reach $42B by 2011," November 7, 2007, http://www.marketingcharts.com/television/online-ad -spending-to-reach-42b-by-2011-budget-shift-to-accelerate-2292/emarketer-us- online-advertising-spending-by-format-2006-2011jpg/.

16. J.L. Miller, "Internet Ad Future Is a Load of Bull," WebProNews, January 10, 2007, http://www.webpronews.com.

17. Ibid.

18. Bruner, "The Decade in Online Advertising, 1994–2004."

19. Pew Internet & American Life Project, "Tracking Study," Pew Research Center, December 2006, http://www.pewinternet.org/trends.asp.

20. Geoff Ramsey, "3 Hidden Trends in 2008," January 14, 2008, http:// www.emarketer.com/Article.aspx?id=1005817.

21. eMarketer, "Social Networking Demos Spread Out," March 13, 2007, http://www.emarketer.com/Article.aspx?id=1004674.

22. Chris Anderson, *The Long Tail* (New York: Hyperion, 2006).

23. Richard Fielding and Judy Bahary, "Are You Experienced? An Engagement-Based Planning Approach in Print," Worldwide Readership Research Symposium, 2005, http://www.readershipresearch.org/papers/ index.php?pclass%5B%5D=18&action=searchresults.

24. Big Research, "Simultaneous Media Usage Study," January 18, 2007, http://www.bigresearch.com/news/big011807.htm.

25. Magazine Publishers of America, "Engagement: Understanding Consumers' Relationships with Media," 2006, http://www.magazine.org/engagement.

26. Ibid.

27. Ibid.

28. Bruner, "The Decade in Online Advertising, 1994–2004," 19.

CHAPTER 2

1. Charlene Li, "Social Technographics," Forrester Research, April 19, 2007, http://www.forrester.com/Research/Document/Excerpt/0,7211,42057,00.html.

2. Joel Greenberg, "Coke Comes Clean about Second Life," Tuple vs. Kipple, August 27, 2007, http://blogs.electricsheepcompany.com/joel/index.php ?s=Coke.

3. Enid Burns, "Marketers Mulling ARF's 'Engagement' Definition," The Click Z Network, April 4, 2006, http://www.clickz.com/showPage.html?page =3595911.

4. Frank Rose, "How Madison Avenue is Wasting Millions on a Deserted Second Life," *Wired*, Issue 08-15 (July 24, 2007), http://www.wired.com/tech-biz/media/magazine/15-08/ff_sheep.

5. Greenberg, "Coke Comes Clean."

6. Ibid.

7. PR Newswire, "MTV Networks Virtual Laguna Beach Honored with Emmy Gold," January 8, 2008, http://www.reuters.com/article/pressRelease/idUS13404+09-Jan-2008+PRN20080109.

8. Greenberg, "Coke Comes Clean."

9. A. McConnon and J. Reena, "Beyond Second Life," *BusinessWeek*, June 11, 2007, http://www.businessweek.com/magazine/content/07_24/b4038417.htm.

10. Paul Gillin, "Spoils of Social Media Go to Those Who Wait," *B to B* 92, no. 17 (2007): 11.

CHAPTER 3

1. Pew Internet & American Life Project, "Tracking Survey," Pew Research Center, http://www.pewinternet.org/trends/Daily_Internet_Activities_8.28.07 .htm.

2. A. Lenhart and M. Madden, "Social Networking Websites and Teens: An Overview," Pew Internet & American Life Project, 2007, www.pewinternet.org.

3. Nielsen/NetRatings, "Social Networking Sites Grow 47 Percent," May 11, 2006, http://www.nielsen-netratings.com/pr/pr_060511.pdf.

4. Kristen Nicole, "comScore Report Shows Global Growth of Social Networks," comScore, July 31, 2007, http://mashable.com/2007/07/31/comscore -social-network-global-growth/.

5. eMarketer, "January 2008 Social Networking," Industry Stats and Data by eMarketer, www.emarketer.com.

6. Ibid.

7. Catherine Holahan, "Social Networking Goes Niche," *BusinessWeek*, March 14, 2007, http://www.businessweek.com/technology/content/mar2007/ tc20070314_884996.htm.

8. comScore, "More Than Half of MySpace Visitors Are Now Age 35 or Older," October 5, 2006, http://www.comscore.com/press/release.asp?press=1019.

9. Mark Snider, "iPods Knock Over Beer Mugs," *USA Today*, June 7, 2006, http://www.usatoday.com/tech/news/2006-06-07-ipod-tops-beer_x.htm.

10. Sid Yadav, "Facebook: The Complete Biography," Mashable.com, August 25, 2006, http://mashable.com/2006/08/25/facebook-profile/.

11. Fast Company, "Facebook by the Numbers," *Fast Company* 115, May 2007, 79, http://www.fastcompany.com/magazine/115/open_features-hacker-dropout -ceo-facebook-numbers.html.

12. Jay Meattle, "Top 50 Websites," Compete, October 30, 2007, http://blog.compete.com/2007/10/30/top-50-websites-domains-digg-youtube-flickr-facebook/.

13. David Hallerman, "YouTube's Audience—Not Who You Think," *iMedia Connection*, November 17, 2006, http://www.imediaconnection.com/content/12474.asp.

14. David Leonard, "Viral Ads: It's an Epidemic," *Fortune* 154, no. 7 (2006): 61.

15. Holahan, "Social Networking Goes Niche."

16. Joe Plummer and others, *The Online Advertising Playbook* (New Jersey: John Wiley & Sons, 2007).

17. Brad Stone, "MySpace to Discuss Latest Effort to Customize Ads for Members," *New York Times*, September 18, 2007, http://www.nytimes.com/2007/09/18/technology/18myspace.html.

18. Fox Interactive Media, *Never Ending Friending*, 2007, http://www.myspace.com/neverendingfriending.

19. Pete Snyder, "How Social Networks Are Courting Marketers," *iMedia Connection*, December 7, 2007, http://www.imediaconnection.com/content/17505.asp.

20. Malcolm Gladwell, *The Tipping Point* (New York: Back Bay Books, 2002).

21. Marian Salzman, Ira Matathia, and Ann O'Reilly, *Buzz: Harness the Power of Influence and Create Demand* (New Jersey: John Wiley, 2003).

22. Duncan Watts, *Six Degrees* (New York: W.W. Norton & Company, 2004).

23. Fox Interactive Media, *Never Ending Friending*.

24. Snyder, "How Social Networks Are Courting Marketers."

25. Abbey Klaassen, "Niche-Targeted Social Networks Find Audiences," *Advertising Age* 77, no. 45 (2006): 15.

26. Jack Loechner, "Brand Awareness Ads a Better Bet Than Trust on Social Media Sites," *MediaPost*, October 5, 2006, http://publications.mediapost.com/index.cfm?fuseaction=Articles.showArticle&art_aid+49102.

27. Nielsen/NetRatings, "User-Generated Content Drives Half of U.S. Top 10 Fastest Growing Web Brands According to Nielsen/NetRatings," August 10, 2006, http://www.netratings.com/pr/PR_060810.pdf.

28. Nina Lentini, "Who Is That Wearing That Milk Mustache?" *New York Times*, January 4, 2007, http://www.nytimes.com/2007/01/04/business/media/04adco.html?ref=media.

29. Andy Semowitz and Shannon Stairhime, "Chrysler, Coke: New Brand Buzz Leaders," *iMedia Connection*, February 8, 2007, http://www.imediaconnection.com/content/13526.asp.

30. T.L. Stanley, "Finding New Ways to Bring in the Benjamins," *Advertising Age* 77, no. 42 (October 16, 2006): 3–4.

31. E. Jensen, "'The L Word' Spins Off Its Chart," *New York Times*, December 18, 2006.

32. Witeck-Combs Communications and Harris Interactive, "Gays, Lesbians and Bisexuals Lead in Usage of Online Social Networks," Harris Interactive, January 2, 2007, http://www.harrisinteractive.com/news/allnewsbydate.asp ?NewsID=1136.

33. Brad Stone, "Social Networking's Next Phase," *New York Times*, March 3, 2007.

34. E. Steel, "Using Social Sites as Dialogue to Engage Consumers, Brands." *Wall Street Journal*, November 8, 2006, B2D.

35. Mark Drosos, "Branded Social Strategy: Easy as 3+3," *iMedia Connection*, January 17, 2008, http://www.imediaconnection.com/content/18009.asp.

CHAPTER 4

1. Nick Wilson, "The Problem with Virtual Worlds," Metaversed, October 23, 2007, http://metaversed.com/23-oct-2007/problem-virtual-words.

2. Matthew Schifrin, "Rocking the Virtual World," *Forbes*, December 24, 2007, http://www.forbes.com/claytonchristensen/forbes/2007/1224/103.html.

3. Janet Meiners, "Verizon's Web 2.0 Marketing Campaign," WebProNews, November 8, 2007, http://www.webpronews.com/blogtalk/2007/11/08/verizons-web-2-0-marketing-campaign.

4. Neil Stephenson, *Snow Crash* (New York: Bantam Spectra, 2000).

5. Robbie Cooper and Tracy Spaight, *Alter Egos: Avatars and their Creators* (London: Chris Boot, 2007).

6. Ketzel Levine, "Alter Egos in a Virtual World," *NPR*, January 10, 2008, http://www.npr.org/templates/story/story.php?storyId=12263532.

7. Shira Boss, "Even in a Virtual World, 'Stuff' Matters," *New York Times*, September 9, 2007, http://www.nytimes.com/2007/09/09/business/yourmoney/09second.html.

8. Robert Hof, "It's Not All Fun and Games," *BusinessWeek*, May 1, 2006, http://www.businessweek.com/magazine/content/06_18/b3982007.htm.

9. S. Tamer Cavusgil, "On the Internationalization Process of Firms," *European Research* 8, no. 6 (1980): 273–81.

10. Sun Microsystems, "Project Wonderland: Toolkit for Building 3D Virtual Worlds," https://lg3d-wonderland.dev.java.net/.

11. Combined Story, "The Virtual Brand Footprint," 2007, http://www .combinedstory.com/combinedstory_whitepaper.pdf.

12. Marketing Week, "Vodaphone's Second Life Interactive Island Opens," *Marketing Week*, February 1, 2007, 7.

13. "AvaStar Online Newspaper Launched in 'Second Life,'" *Telephone IP News* 18, no. 1 (2007).

14. Steve Rubel, "Micro Persuader," *Advertising Age* 77, no. 48 (2006): 20.

15. Joel Greenberg, "Coke Comes Clean about Second Life," Tuple vs. Kipple, August 24, 2007, http://blogs.electricsheepcompany.com/joel/?p=47.

16. Aili McConnon and Reena Jana, "Beyond Second Life," *BusinessWeek*, June 11, 2007, http://www.businessweek.com/magazine/content/07_24/b4038417.htm.

17. Mary Connelly, "Pontiac Seeks Real Sales from Make-Believe Internet World," *Automotive News* 81, no. 6228 (November 6, 2006): 17.

18. Ibid.

19. Jean Halliday, "Pontiac's Not Ready for Prime Time, by Choice," *Automotive News* 82, no. 6285 (December 10, 2007): 32B.

20. Combined Story, "The Virtual Brand Footprint."

21. Bob Tedeschi, "Awaiting Real Sales from Virtual Shoppers," *New York Times*, June 11, 2007, www.nytimes.com/2007/06/11/business/11ecom.html.

22. A. Sudhaman, "The Virtual World of Second Life," *Media*, November 3, 2006, 13.

23. Alex Veiga, "Virtual Designers Busy in Online Worlds," *International Business Times*, February 26, 2007, http://www.ibtimes.com/articles/20070226/second-life-designers.htm.

24. Daniel Terdiman, "There.com, MTV Launch Virtual Laguna Beach," CNET News.com, September 20, 2006, http://mp3.com.com/8301-10784_3-6117738-7.html.

25. Mark Wallace, "A Second Life for MTV," *Wired*, February 2007, no. 15.02, http://www.wired.com/wired/archive/15.02/mtv.html.

26. PR Newswire, "MTV Networks Virtual Laguna Beach."

27. Richard Siklos, "Not in the Real World Anymore," *New York Times*, September 18, 2006, www.nytimes.com/2006/09/18/business/media/18avatar.html? partner=rssnyt&emc=rss.

CHAPTER 5

1. Debra Aho Williamson, "Kids and Teens: Virtual Worlds Open New Universe," eMarketer, 2007, http://www.emarketer.com/Reports/All/Emarketer_2000437.aspx?src=report_head_info_reports.

2. Matthew Nelson, "Virtual Worlds Aren't Just for Reaching Adults Any More," The Click Z Network, July 5, 2007, http://www.clickz.com/showPage.html?page=3626340.

3. Williamson, "Kids and Teens."

4. Mark Glaser, "Virtual Worlds for Kids Entwined with Real World," Media Shift, June 11, 2007, http://www.pbs.org/mediashift/2007/06/your_take_roundupvirtual_world.html.

5. Nelson, "Virtual Worlds Aren't Just for Reaching Adults Any More."

6. Glaser, "Virtual Worlds for Kids."

7. Stephanie Olsen, "Kids' Virtual Worlds Poised for Growth Spurt," CNET News.com, September 24, 2007, http://www.news.com/8301-10784_3-9783551-7.html.

8. Kathryn Montgomery, *Generation Digital: Politics, Commerce, and Childhood in the Age of the Internet* (Cambridge, MA: MIT Press, 2007).

9. Rory Thompson, "Webkinz Slammed for Online Ads Aimed at Kids," *Brandweek*, December 13, 2007, http://www.technologymarketing.com/bw/news/tech/article_display.jsp?vnu_content_id=1003685136.

10. Brooks Barnes, "Web Playgrounds of the Very Young," *New York Times*, December 31, 2007, www.nytimes.com/2007/12/31/business/31virtual.html.

11. Robert Cialdini, *Influence: The Psychology of Persuasion* (New York: Quill, 1993).

12. Daniel McGinn, "Waving Bye to Webkinz?" *Newsweek* 150, no. 24 (December 10, 2007): 18.

13. Emily Bryson York, "The Hottest Thing in Kids Marketing? Imitating Webkinz," *Advertising Age* 78, no. 40 (October 8, 2007): 38.

14. Nelson, "Virtual Worlds Aren't Just for Reaching Adults Any More."

15. Williamson, "Kids and Teens."

16. Nelson, "Virtual Worlds Aren't Just for Reaching Adults Any More."

CHAPTER 6

1. Ed Keller and Jon Berry, *The Influentials* (New York: Free Press, 2003).

2. J.P. French, Jr., and B. Raven, "The Bases of Social Power," in *Group Dynamics*, ed. D. Cartwright and A. Zander (New York: Harper and Row, 1960), 607–23.

3. Andy Hagans, "Andy Hagans' Ultimate Guide to Linkbaiting and SMM!" Tropical SEO, February 4, 2007, http://tropicalseo.com/2007/andy-hagans-ultimate-guide-to-link-baiting-and-social-media-marketing/.

4. Rohit Bargava, "5 Rules of Social Media Optimization (SMO)," Influential Marketing Blog, August 10, 2006, http://rohitbhargava.typepad.com/weblog/2006/08/5_rules_of_soci.html.

CHAPTER 7

1. Gladwell, *The Tipping Point*.

2. Organization for Economic Cooperation and Development, "Participative Web: User-Created Content."

3. Deloitte & Touche, "The State of the Media Democracy."

4. Pete Blackshaw, "The Official CGM Glossary," *The ClickZ Network*, March 6, 2007, http://www.clickz.com/showPage.html?page=3625153.

5. Deloitte & Touche, "The State of the Media Democracy."

6. Abbey Klaassen, "Road to Digital Dialogue Filled with Potholes," *Advertising Age*, February 7, 2007, http://adage.com/abstract.php?article_id=114855.

7. American Marketing Association, "Consumers Like Companies That Let Them Create Ads, But Young Adults Still Not Buying It," December 1, 2006, www.marketingpower.com.

8. Louise Story, "Can a Sandwich Be Slandered?" *New York Times*, January 29, 2008, http://www.nytimes.com/2008/01/29/business/media/29adco.html.

CHAPTER 8

1. Arnold Brown, "The Consumer Is the Medium," *Futurist* 42, no. 1 (January 2008).

2. Watts, *Six Degrees.*

3. Louise Ainsworth, "Consumer Trust: Word of Mouth Rules," *Brand Strategy* 40 (November 5, 2007).

4. Eric Benderoff, "Stores Rave about Web Reviews: Online Analysis Provides Instant Feedback and Maybe New Customers," *Knight Ridder Tribune Business News,* October 25, 2006, 1.

5. Sam Decker, "Positives about Negative Product Reviews," *iMedia Connection,* January 29, 2007, http://www.imediaconnection.com/content/13386.asp.

6. Bryan Eisenberg, "How to Use Customer Reviews to Increase Conversion," *The ClickZ Network,* October 12, 2007, http://www.clickz.com/showPage.html?page=3627269.

7. Ibid.

8. Kelly Spors, "How Are We Doing? Small Companies Find It Pays to Ask Customers That Question," *Wall Street Journal,* November 13, 2006, R9.

9. Alex Burmaster, "Consumers Trust Others' Opinions More Than Ads," *New Media Age* 10 (December 6, 2007).

10. Todd Wasserman, "Online Reviews Get Kudos from Petco, Comp USA," *Brandweek,* March 13, 2006, 9.

11. Eisenberg, "How to Use Customer Reviews."

12. J.H. Huang and Y.F. Chen, "Herding in Online Product Choice," *Psychology & Marketing* 23, no. 5 (2006): 413–28.

13. Business Wire, "Leading Retail Analyst Shows Retailers Can Gain Market Share through Consumer-Generated Product Ratings and Reviews," August 15, 2006.

14. Bob Tedeschi, "Help for the Merchant in Navigating a Sea of Shopper Opinions," *New York Times,* September 4, 2006, www.nytimes.com/2006/09/04/technology/04ecom.html.

15. Business Wire, "Leading Retail Analyst Shows Retailers Can Gain Market Share."

16. Decker, "Positives about Negative Product Reviews."

17. Jason Anders, "Online: The Clout of the Online Critic," *Wall Street Journal,* June 2, 1999, B-1.

18. Brown, "The Consumer Is the Medium."

CHAPTER 9

1. Lewis Carroll, *Alice's Adventures in Wonderland* (London: McMillan & Company, 1865).

2. Unfiction, "Glossary," www.unfiction.com/glossary.

3. Jim Hanas, "Games People Play," *Creativity* 14, no. 1 (2006): 14.

4. Daniel Terdiman, "I Love Bees Game a Surprise Hit," *Wired*, October 18, 2004, http://www.wired.com/culture/lifestyle/news/2004/10/65365.

5. Henry Jenkins, *Convergence Culture* (New York: NYU Press, 2006).

6. Henry Jenkins, "How Transmedia Storytelling Begat Transmedia Planning," Confessions of an Aca-Fan, December 11, 2006, http://www.henryjenkins.org/2006/12/how_transmedia_storytelling_be_1.html.

7. Grant McCracken, "Transmedia: Branding's Next New Thing?" This Blog Sits at the Intersection of Anthropology and Economics. December 7, 2005, http://www.cultureby.com/trilogy/2005/12/transmedia_bran.html.

8. David Kiley, "Advertising Of, By, and For the People," *BusinessWeek Online*, July 25, 2005, http://www.businessweek.com/magazine/content/05_30/b3944097.htm.

9. Hanas, "Games People Play."

10. Kiley, "Advertising Of, By, and For the People."

11. A. Bourdeau, "Alternate Reality Games Suck Consumers into Your Brand's World," *Strategy*, February 2007, 32.

12. Paul Tyrrell, "Treasure Hunt Is the Clue to a New Marketing Tool," *Financial Times*, February 21, 2006, http://us.ft.com/ftgateway/superpage.ft?news_id=fto022120061405218098.

13. Teressa Iezzi, "Marketers Tapping into the Magic of an Alternate Reality," *Advertising Age* 76, no. 47 (November 21, 2005): 15.

14. Brand Strategy, "Case Study—Xbox: Cyberspace Invaders," *Brand Strategy*, December 5, 2005, 28–29.

15. Christy Dena, "ARG Stats," Universe Creator and Transmodiologist, http://www.christydena.com/online-essays/arg-stats/.

16. Ibid.

17. Jon Zahlaway, "Nine Inch Nails' 'Year Zero' Plot Hits the Web," *LiveDaily*, February 22, 2007, http://www.livedaily.com/news/11570.html?t=102.

18. Ibid.

19. Frank Rose, "Secret Websites, Coded Messages: The New World of Immersive Games," *Wired*, December 20, 2007, http://www.wired.com/entertainment/music/magazine/16-01/ff_args.

20. Muhammed Saleem, "Alternate Reality Games: What Makes or Breaks Them? *Read, Write, Web*, December 26, 2007, http://www.readwriteweb.com/archives/alternate_reality_games_viral_marketing.php.

CHAPTER 10

1. Interactive Advertising Bureau, Marketer & Agency Guide to Online Game Advertising, 2007, http://www.iab.net/iab_products_and_industry_services/1421/1488/1506.

2. David George-Cosh, "Multiple Platforms Are 'Holy Grail' of Gaming," *Financial Post*, January 21, 2008, http://www.financialpost.com/story.html?id=251854.

3. Paul Verna, "Video Game Advertising: Getting to the Next Level," eMarketer, 2007, http://www.emarketer.com/Reports/All/Emarketer_2000386.aspx?src =report_head_info_site earch.

4. Jack Loechner, "Advergaming," Research Brief, Center for Media Research, *Media Post,* October 24, 2007, http://blogs.mediapost.com/research _brief/?p=1550.

5. Louise Story, "Toyota's Latest Commercial Is Not on TV. Try the Xbox Console," *New York Times,* October 8, 2007, http://www.nytimes.com/2007/10/08/ business/media/08adcol.html?ex=1349755200&en=2f68967c646a8dbd&ei =5088&partner=rssnyt&emc=rss.

6. Julie Shumaker, "In-Game Branding: Get in While It's Hot," *iMedia Connection,* March 29, 2007, http://www.imediaconnection.com/content/14213.asp.

7. Interactive Advertising Bureau, *Game Advertising Platform Status Report,* October 2007, http://www.iab.net/iab_products_and_industry_services/1421/ 1488/1506.

8. James Belcher, "Your Mother Plays Video Games," *eMarketer,* September 29, 2006, http://www.emarketer.com/Article.aspx?id=1004176.

9. Interactive Advertising Bureau, Marketer & Agency Guide to Online Game Advertising.

10. Justin Ehly, "What Do Casual Games and Pharmaceuticals Have in Common?" *Media Post,* January 22, 2008, http://blogs.mediapost.com/video _insider/?p=147.

11. Interactive Advertising Bureau, Marketer & Agency Guide to Online Game Advertising.

12. Verna, "Video Game Advertising."

13. Loechner, "Advergaming."

14. Zachary Glass, "The Effectiveness of Product Placement in Video Games," *Journal of Interactive Advertising* 8, no. 1 (2007), http://jiad.org/vol8/ no1/glass/index.htm.

15. George-Cosh, "Multiple Platforms Are 'Holy Grail' of Gaming."

16. Josh Larson, "6 Steps to Market Your Brand in Games," *iMedia Connection.* September 6, 2006, http://www.imediaconnection.com/content/11086.asp.

17. Grant McCracken, "Who Is the Celebrity Endorser? Cultural Foundations of the Endorsement Process," *Journal of Consumer Research* 16, no. 3 (1989): 310–21.

18. Judith Garretson and Ronald W. Niedrich, "Spokes-Characters: Creating Character Trust and Positive Brand Attitudes," *Journal of Advertising* 33 (Summer 2004): 25–36.

19. Glass, "The Effectiveness of Product Placement in Video Games."

20. George-Cosh, "Multiple Platforms Are 'Holy Grail' of Gaming."

21. Jennifer Escalas, "Imagine Yourself in the Product: Mental Simulation, Narrative Transportation, and Persuasion," *Journal of Advertising* 33, no. 2 (2004): 37–48.

22. Joseph Jaffe, "Advergaming Equals Attention," *iMedia Connection,* May 5, 2003, http://www.imediaconnection.com/printpage/printpage.aspx?id=1060.

23. Dawn Anfuso, "Why You Need to Get in the Game," *iMedia Connection*, July 12, 2007, http://www.imediaconnection.com/content/15741.asp.

24. Yuanzhe Cai, "Electronic Gaming in the Digital Household: Game Advertising," Parks Associates Industry Report, June 2007, http://www.parksassociates.com/research/reports/tocs/2007/gaming-advertising.htm.

25. Michelle Nelson, "Recall of Brand Placements in Computer/Video Games," *Journal of Advertising Research* 42 (March/April 2002): 80–92.

26. Moonhee Yang and others, "The Effectiveness of In-Game Advertising," *Journal of Advertising* 25, no. 4 (Winter 2006): 143–52.

27. Isabella M. Chaney, Ku-Ho Lin, and James Chaney, "The Effect of Billboards within the Gaming Environment," *Journal of Interactive Advertising* 5, no. 1 (2004), http://www.jiad.org/vol5/no1/chaney/.

28. Dan Grigorovici and Corina Constantin, "Experiencing Interactive Advertising Beyond Rich Media: Impacts on AdType and Presence on Brand Effectiveness in 3D Gaming Immersive Virtual Environments," *Journal of Interactive Media* 5, no. 1 (2004): 31–53.

29. Gavin O'Malley, "Casual Games Are Red Hot: Lifetime Adds New Series," *Media Post*, July 23, 2007, http://publications.mediapost.com/index.cfm?fuseaction=Articles.showArticleHomePage&art_aid=64395.

30. Ed Bartlett, "Your Go-To Guide for In-Game Advertising," *iMedia Connection*, June 19, 2007, http://www.imediaconnection.com/content/15403.asp.

31. Loechner, "Advergaming."

32. Cristel Russel, "Toward a Framework of Product Placement," in *Advances in Consumer Research* 25, ed. J.W. Alba and J.W. Hutchinson (Association for Consumer Research, 1998).

33. Jaffe, "Advergaming Equals Attention."

34. Story, "Toyota's Latest Commercial Is Not on TV."

35. Zachary Rodgers, "Forecast: Game-Based Advertising to Hit $2 Billion by 2012," *The ClickZ Network*, June 29, 2007, http://www.clickz.com/showPage.html?page=3626301.

36. Fran Kennish, "In-Game Advertising Dos and Don'ts," *iMedia Connection*, March 3, 2006, http://www.imediaconnection.com/content/8489.asp.

37. Jodi Harris, "Get Serious about In-Game Marketing," *iMedia Connection*, May 22, 2007, http://www.imediaconnection.com/content/14973.asp.

CHAPTER II

1. Katie Delahaye Paine, "How to Measure Social Media Relations," Institute for Public Relations, April 2007, www.instituteforpr.org.

2. Oliver Ryan, "Policing the Online 'Buzz,'" CNNMoney.com, March 15, 2007, http://money.cnn.com/magazines/fortune/fortune_archive/2007/03/19/8402329/index.htm.

3. Fraser Likely, David Rockland, and Mark Weiner, "Perspectives on the ROI of Media Relations Publicity Efforts," Institute for Public Relations, May 2006, www .instituteforpr.org.

4. Michael Brito, "Measuring Social Media Marketing: It's Easier Than You Think," *Search Engine Journal,* June 30, 2007, http://www.searchenginejournal.com/ measuring-social-media-marketing-its-easier-than-you-think/5397/.

5. Robert Kozinets, "The Field Behind the Screen: Using Netnography for Marketing Research in Online Communities," *Journal of Marketing Research* 39, no. 1 (2002): 61–72.

6. Robert Kozinets, "E-Tribalized Marketing? The Strategic Implications of Virtual Communities of Consumption," *European Management Journal* 17, no. 3 (1999): 252–64.

Index

About the Author

TRACY L. TUTEN, Ph.D. is Associate Professor of Marketing at Long-wood University. She has authored more than one hundred journal articles, book chapters, and conference presentations; her research interests include Web-based survey methods, branding and identity, and online advertising. She serves on the editorial review board for the journals *Psychology & Marketing* and *Gender in Management* and serves on the academic advisory board for the Commercial Closet.